CARMEN McRAE

Miss Jazz

LESLIE GOURSE

BILLBOARD BOOKS
An imprint of Watson-Guptill Publications
New York

Senior Acquisitions Editor: Bob Nirkind
Editor: Audrey Walen
Production Manager: Ellen Greene
Cover design: Eric Baker
Interior design: Cheryl Viker

First published in 2001 by Billboard Books
An imprint of Watson-Guptill Publications
A division of BPI Communications, Inc.
770 Broadway, New York, NY 10003
www.watson-guptill.com

Library of Congress Cataloging-in-Publication Data
Gourse, Leslie
    Carmen McRae, Miss Jazz / Leslie Gourse.
       p. cm.
    Includes bibliographical references, discographies, and videography.
    ISBN 0-8230-7904-X
    1. McRae, Carmen. 2. Jazz singers—United States—Biography. I. Title.
ML420.M34185 G68 2001
781.5'9—dc21   2001025243

Manufactured in the United States

First printing, 2001

1 2 3 4 5 6 7 8 9 10 / 10 09 08 07 06 05 04 03 02 01

This book is dedicated to Ethel Gourse Herskovits.

Acknowledgements

The author wishes to acknowledge the help of the following people: First of all Carmen McRae, and Johnny Parker, W. Royal Stokes, Norval Perkins, Cecilia Perkins, Jack Rael, staffers at the Institute of Jazz Studies at Rutgers University, Larry Clothier, Marge Costa, Norman Simmons, Francois Vaz, Paulette Rubinstein, Mat Mathews, Dick Katz, Dave Usher, Billy Taylor, Marian McPartland, Devra Hall Levy, John Levy, George Avakian, Milt Gabler, Bill Simon, Herbie Mann, Cecilia McRae, Donna Perkins Potts, Ray Bryant, Aaron Bell, Walter Perkins, Bob Cranshaw, Nat Hentoff, Rhino Records and Videos, Gene Lees, Shirley Horn, Annie Ross, Bertha Hope, Red Holloway, John Collins, Marshall Otwell, Mark Pulice, Eric Gunnison, Scott Colley, Burrill Crohn, Denise Jannah, Gene DiNovi, Ray Ross, Mitchell Seidel, Frank Driggs, Eric Smith, Benny Golson, Jack McDuff, Art D'Lugoff, Sandy Jordan — and editors Bob Nirkind for his enthusiasm for the subject and Audrey Walen for her editing.

Contents

Introduction

Carmen McRae came of age during one of the most interesting, colorful periods of jazz's development. All periods of jazz during its first century had a certain vitality. But some were more alluring and dynamic than others. Carmen fell in love with jazz when bebop, the intriguing style first known as progressive jazz, was leaving behind the bouncing baby of the swing era with its familiar sounding harmonies and rhythms. Young musicians were embellishing the established music and developing a new, freewheeling, more expressive language with surprising rhythms, harmonies, and phrasing.

Carmen was influenced by the fine, older musicians she began meeting when, in her late teens, she hung out in the Harlem jazz circles of the late 1930s. She barely knew what she was doing there, but Carmen entertained dreams of a career in jazz. The music excited her. She pursued the struggle until she was thirty-four years old and nearly ready to give up, but in 1954, Carmen began to attract some well-deserved recognition.

Carmen learned some hard lessons during her slow rise to fame, which certainly molded both her character and her sound. Onstage her sound was intricate, subtle, and controlled. Offstage she became an increasingly mercurial diva with a legendary temper. She could fly into a rage if the hotel rooms where she stayed when traveling didn't have curtains thick enough to block out all the light and allow her to rest before performances. But despite this temper, her bebop vibe and outstanding abilities kept her steadily on course while she slowly crept toward fame.

Through the years, Carmen acquired credits, honors, and respect from her fellow instrumentalists and singers as well as from her audiences. Though she never won a Grammy Award, the consistent excellence of her work — her reputation as a perfectionistic interpreter of lyrics and a masterful improviser — elevated her to the ranks of that small, exclusive group regarded as the greatest jazz singers of all time, in the company of Ella Fitzgerald, Sarah Vaughan, and Anita O'Day. Carmen drew crowds to the clubs and jazz concerts where she headlined.

Carmen McRae sang before the public for the last time at the prestigious, glamorous Blue Note club in New York City from May 21 through 26, 1991. On the last night of the week's engagement, she climbed the stairs to her dressing room with great difficulty after the second set. No one in the audience realized how sick she felt or how arduously she fought for each breath. She herself didn't even realize how sick she was. She had talk-sung her way through that night with apparent ease. Her performance had the usual hallmarks of her mature style — the suspenseful use of space and emphases for her interpretations of lyrics, the uncanny pacing and rhythmic feeling, the unique reediness of her sound.

But before dawn, an ambulance was called to transport her from her hotel to Lenox Hill hospital on Manhattan's glamorous Upper East Side. After more than fifty years of struggle and acclaim, of professional battles and personal maelstroms, Carmen was tired.

Though she could have attempted rehabilitation exercises, she instead chose to retire. In her last days, Carmen McRae got along financially by the skin of her teeth, but the legacy of her music has the value of a diamond mine.

Chronology

APRIL 8, 1920: Carmen McRae, the only child of Oscar and Evadne McRae, is born at Harlem Hospital in New York City.

1920S TO 1930S: Carmen lives with her parents in the Bronx, then in 1934 the family moves to West 114th Street, and then to 880 St. Nicholas Avenue, in the prestigious Sugar Hill neighborhood in Harlem. At eight years old she begins to study classical piano, though Carmen prefers American popular music, and begins to sing popular songs for fun. Though Carmen has childhood asthma, it never grows severe, and eventually clears up.

1934 TO 1938: Carmen takes both academic and secretarial courses at the commercially oriented, all-girls' Julia Richman High School on Manhattan's Upper East Side. In general, Carmen is an average student. Her high school health report doesn't mention any respiratory problems. Carmen graduates in 1938.

1938 TO 1939: Attracted to jazz, Carmen meets jazz pianist Teddy Wilson's wife, composer and pianist Irene Kitchings. Irene introduces Carmen to many swing era jazz stars, including singer Billie Holiday. Carmen gives Billie a copy of one of her early jazz songs, "Dream of Life," which Billie records on January 20, 1939, on the Vocalian label; it is released at around the same time on the Brunswick label. Carmen becomes enamored of jazz and, though tentative because she's unsure of her chances of success, begins her lifelong commitment to playing and singing. Irene's and Billie's influence becomes so strong that Carmen eventually tells audiences: "If there had been no Billie and Irene, there would have been no me." On Marian McPartland's Peabody prize-winning "Piano Jazz" show in the 1980s, Carmen tells McPartland, "without (Irene), I wouldn't be sitting here now talking to you."

1940 TO 1943: Gregarious, slender, and girlish, Carmen becomes a fixture on the Harlem jazz scene, friendly with singer Sarah Vaughan and hundreds of other musicians and prominent figures in the African-American entertainment and sports worlds — Nat "King" Cole, Duke Ellington, Benny Carter, the Brown Sisters, who dance in Harlem clubs, Ben Webster, Joe Louis, Thelonious Monk, Dizzy Gillespie, and Kenny Clarke, to name only a few. Everybody knows Carmen. She hangs out at such central jazz-scene places as the Hotel Braddock Grill and Minton's Playhouse. Also during these years Carmen and Kenny Clarke, an adventurous drummer and founder of "the new thing" — progressive jazz and the bebop style of drumming — become involved.

1944: Carmen goes to Alabama and marries Kenny Clarke, who was drafted into service in 1943. She doesn't stay there with him for long. Carmen returns to New York, perhaps at Clarke's suggestion; she despises the confines of segregation in the South. Clarke soon goes AWOL for about four months, in order to play jazz. Perhaps Clarke's plan to leave the army and return to New York was the overriding reason for Carmen to leave Alabama.[1]

1943 TO 1946: Carmen goes to Washington, D.C. and takes a variety of jobs connected with the war effort. Soon bored with the routine and anxious to be playing music, she returns to New York City's music scene.

Carmen sings with Benny Carter's band in 1943, then with Count Basie's band. She plays piano with Mercer Ellington's band, and makes her first recording. Mercer's band tours in the U.S., but it doesn't last long, and breaks up while on the road.

Stranded out of town — no one now can remember where but it was either Chicago or Atlantic City — Carmen goes to work in the chorus at the Club Harlem on Kentucky Avenue in Atlantic City, a hub of the African-American entertainment world of the era.

(Author's Note: In some instances the chronology is approximate. It was largely based upon interviews with Carmen McRae, whose memory for dates may have been faulty. At the time of the interview she was already in her early seventies, and could not recall details such as the exact year she married Kenny Clarke, though she knew it was around 1943. Furthermore, she sometimes chose to alter dates; for example, by the time she was in her thirties, if not before, she was shaving two years off her age, claiming to have been born in 1922; much later in life, she would say she had been born in 1918. The actual date was 1920, according to official birth records in New York City. Most events did take place in approximately the years she recalled.)

1946: Kenny Clarke returns to New York. Clarke and Carmen live for a while in her family's house in Brooklyn. However, though back in New York, Clarke doesn't spend much time at home.

1947: In December, 1947, Clarke goes on tour in Europe with Dizzy Gillespie's band. When the tour ends in 1948, he stays in Paris for several extra months. He has become involved in an affair with a young singer, Annie Ross. Along with other wives of the returning musicians, Carmen goes to meet the ship, but Clarke isn't on it. Although the couple doesn't legally divorce at that time, the marriage is over. Their friendly feelings for each other survive, however, and they continue to play and record together on occasion through the years.

LATE 1940S TO EARLY 1950S: Carmen falls in love with Chicago-based mimic and comedian George Kirby, and moves to Chicago with him. When the relationship falls on hard times, she goes to work as a pianist and singer at the Archway Lounge, a favorite restaurant and watering hole among entertainers and gamblers. She also works in other Chicago clubs. After serving this apprenticeship in Chicago, teaching herself many tunes which she learns by ear from the radio, and honing her own specific style, she decides to return to New York. Her parents also encourage her to return, and Carmen goes home in 1952.

1952: Carmen works in an office by day, and performs at the Bandbox, a small club in Brooklyn, by night. Mat Mathews, the accordionist, is putting together a band. He hears Carmen perform and is bowled over. He asks her to front his band at Birdland and on tour.

1953: Clarinetist Tony Scott hires Carmen to be intermission pianist and singer at Minton's Playhouse, the club where bebop was developed in the 1940s. Tony Scott encourages Carmen to get up from the piano bench and stand up at the microphone to sing. She resists but finally takes his advice and finds that she attracts an even greater following.

Despite her local successes, Carmen is becoming frantic about her career prospects. She recognizes that she has made few inroads. The struggle has tired her out. Friends worry about her.

The recordings she has made in the early 1950s for the Stardust, Venus, and Bethlehem labels are well received and keep winning her fans. Carmen records for Bethlehem and Venus before Stardust, with which she had a contract, but the Stardust recordings are released first.

1955: Carmen signs a contract to record for the Decca label. According to Milt Gabler, an artists and repertoire man with Decca, he signs and records Carmen to the label after he hears her working with the Mat Mathews Quintet in a club in Philadelphia. Her first album on the Decca label is released in 1955 and gets sufficient distribution to bring her more national attention than even the Bethlehem records did. She also acquires the management of Associated Booking Corporation, owned by Joe Glaser, Louis Armstrong's manager. Under the auspices of A.B.C., Carmen is handled by Oscar Cohen. She begins to get prestigious bookings, and while on tour in Toronto, Canada, learns of her tie with Ella Fitzgerald for *Metronome* magazine's Singer of the Year award. Carmen is jubilant. She is also thrilled when *Down Beat* magazine votes her Best New Female Singer of the Year. She performs in an All-Star Jazz Concert on March 12, 1955, at Carnegie Hall. Carmen goes to Hollywood and sings with the Mat Mathews Quintet in the movie *The Square Jungle*.

1954 TO 1957: Carmen makes the rounds of prestigious clubs and concert halls and continues to record for Decca. In early spring, 1957, she headlines at Birdland, dubbed the "jazz corner of the world," the leading jazz club of the era. There she sings what was perhaps her biggest hit under her own leadership "Skyliner," from a 1956 recording on the Decca label, in her lusty, full-throated, powerful voice. The audience cheers. Already some of her voice's sweetness has begun to change, to lower and darken, with age, use, and from her addiction to cigarettes and liberal use of marijuana, though the change is still barely perceptible.

LATE 1950S: Carmen and Kenny Clarke are legally divorced. Touring with her own groups, one of her earliest including pianist Ray Bryant and bassist Ike Isaacs, Carmen continues to build her career. She and Isaacs have a good relationship, which leads to a love affair. They marry, and the relationship begins to go on a downswing. Various observers blame the difficulty on Isaacs's increasingly domineering attitude. Carmen, for her part, becomes more inclined toward asserting her independence, and is sometimes very difficult and feisty. Carmen makes a number of recordings on Decca, Kapp, Official, and Mercury that are influential on younger singers. She hires Dick Katz, Bill Rubinstein, Bob Cranshaw, and Walter Perkins to play in her group during these years.

1961: By 1961, Isaacs and Carmen separate and divorce. For the next few years, Carmen calls New York City home base, continuing to build her career and attract fans. She goes to England in 1961, where she scores a success in London, though not in other cities on the tour. She causes a fracas on British television by sharing her shocking, fiery opinions about commercialism in music: Carmen thinks that no one should sing a song just because it might become a financial success.

Carmen hires pianist Norman Simmons as her accompanist, though he is wary of working for her because of her reputation for being tough, outspoken, and highly opinionated. Simmons soon learns to love and respect his boss on a professional level; he observes that she simply doesn't let anyone "stomp around" in her life. At all costs she protects her career and artistry — and space and time. She takes charge, sometimes quite rudely, yet at the same time she nurtures young talents. Her efforts pay off with great reviews. Critics pay her homage, and by association her sidemen garner attention and hosannas as well.

In July 1961, Carmen appeared at Basin Street in New York with the Dave Brubeck Quartet. The song 'Take Five,' written by Paul Desmond, Brubeck's alto player, was included on the live recording released on the Columbia label. The album sold more than a million copies, and the song was Carmen's biggest hit.

Even so, she never has a million-selling record. Not even her big hit single, "Skyliner," wins a Grammy or sells a million copies. Carmen survives on the strength of her artistry and attraction for audiences. She eschews the usual round of publicity interviews, often avoiding the radio and television exposure that other stars accept as part of their *de rigueur* daily routine when they tour.

1967 TO 1968: Carmen moves from New York to Los Angeles to be close to her parents and other family members who had moved to a community near Los Angeles years earlier. From then on, California is home base. For a year, from 1967 to 1968, she has a live-in relationship with French guitarist François Vaz, who works in her group. Although they announce to audiences several times that they are married, they actually never wed. Carmen and Vaz split up in the fall of 1968.

1969 TO 1970: Norman Simmons leaves Carmen's group in 1969, Carmen leaves Associated Booking Corporation, and by 1970 Jack Rael is her manager. Among his other star clients are singer Patti Page and The Everly Brothers. A manager with vision for the overall career strategies of his clients, Rael manages Carmen, with few interruptions, until 1989.

Occasionally Carmen tries working with other managers. One is a well-known, highly respected jazz bassist, Ray Brown, Jr., who has little time to devote to Carmen's management, and limits himself to conducting her business affairs. Brown doesn't work for Carmen for very long. Kim Harstein also has a brief stint as Carmen's manager.

1970S: Honors accrue to Carmen. Since her success in 1955, she has been known as one of the greatest jazz singers of all time, alongside Ella Fitzgerald, Sarah Vaughan, and Anita O'Day. Carmen's history with record labels in this period is erratic. Many jazz artists find themselves without recording contracts while rock reigns supreme in the music world. Carmen works in large rooms in casinos in Las Vegas, though they are not her true milieu, as well as touring abroad. Like Sarah Vaughan and Ella Fitzgerald, Carmen belongs in top jazz clubs, festivals, and concert halls, but the economic conditions that exist for the top jazz artists in this era preclude her finding the appropriate regular exposure.

LATE 1970S TO 1980S: In the late 1970s and early 1980s, jazz undergoes a renaissance of popularity, and Carmen enjoys prestigious bookings in clubs, festivals, and concert halls. She makes a recording with bebop singer Betty Carter in 1987 for the Bet Car/Verve label, and begins recording for RCA Novus, where she does some important and ambitious work.

Marshall Otwell, Mark Pulice, and Jay Anderson frequently accompany her during the 1980s. Otwell leaves music altogether in 1986, and is replaced by Eric Gunnison. Scott Colley becomes Carmen's bassist from 1987 to 1987. By 1989, Carmen leaves the management of Jack Rael in favor of her good friend Larry Clothier. Clothier remains her manager for the rest of her life.

By now, Carmen has built a reputation for exuding charm, when she wants to, and acting as a role model for other singers. She has also become noted for being moody, testy, demanding, and even downright coarse and combative at times. People who knew her when she was young and friendly are surprised by how tough she has become.

Carmen has gained a reputation as being either bisexual or a lesbian. The issue of her sexuality is controversial. She confided in a friend that, as a teenager, she had her first sexual encounter with another woman with Billie Holiday. Carmen had other relationships and trysts with women, including with at least one other famous singer. Several friends and colleagues confirm that Carmen liked both men and women. A male friend recalls that she told him she much preferred relationships with men. Another male friend commented that, although she had lesbian friends, she was never a lesbian herself; he never saw her act demonstrative in public with another woman. However, she does sometimes behave in an insulting way toward men in public.

Carmen's relationships with women, whether friendships or sexual encounters, don't run smoothly. She privately insults Betty Carter's singing, and Carter repays her by showing up for one of Carmen's gigs at the glamorous Blue Note club in New York and not applauding or saying a word to her. Throughout her career, Carmen by turns charms and offends friends, some of them singers.

1988: Carmen records a complex, adventuresome tribute to Thelonious Monk.

1990: Sarah Vaughan dies. Carmen is very sad: She and Sarah, though both emotionally volatile divas, have probably never had a truly angry word pass between them. This may be overstating the case, but Carmen and Vaughan maintained a lifelong friendship over a forty-five year period. Vaughan, no slouch at tantrums and rudeness, simply sloughs off Carmen's temper, saying, "Oh, well, Carmen," to anyone who mentions Carmen's sharpness.

Other friends have objected strongly to Carmen's fierce feistiness, which thoroughly offsets her charm at times; some "best" friends have come and gone in her life. Singer Annie Ross, to whom Carmen has been, by turns, pleasant and very rude, spots Carmen sitting all alone with her head in her hands in her dressing room after a performance one night. Ross thinks to herself: How lonely and alone in the world Carmen seems. (It's possible that Carmen simply barred people from her dressing room that night, because ordinarily fans flocked to her for autographs and chances to meet her. But Carmen has grown to like to maintain a distance between herself and other people.)

1991: Carmen records a tribute to Sarah Vaughan. Carmen can bring audiences to tears with "Sarah," a song written for the album, which is Carmen's last.

Carmen performs in public for the last time from May 21st through the 26th at the Blue Note in New York. After the final performance, she is hospitalized for a few weeks before flying home to Los Angeles. Doctors tell her that if she undertakes an aggressive course of healthy living, she can regain her strength and go back onstage and continue her career. Suffering from respiratory problems, Carmen has spent most of her adult life smoking cigarettes and marijuana, as well as using other drugs such as cocaine, and now suffers from asthma, chronic bronchitis, and emphysema. Carmen doesn't make enough of an effort with rehabilitation exercises. She is never able to go back to work.

1993: Seated in a wheel chair, Carmen collects an award from the N.A.A.C.P.

Carmen rarely leaves her house. François Vaz, her former lover, telephones her on her birthday. She's delighted to hear from him. She often calls her former manager, Jack Rael, to ask him to do favors for her. People come to her house to help her, but sometimes she stays upstairs in her bedroom and refuses to see them.

January, 1994: Carmen receives a master's of jazz fellowship for lifetime achievement from the National Endowment for the Arts, but her manager and friend Larry Clothier has to accept the award on her behalf; Carmen is too ill to travel.

1994: Carmen's money and financial reserves nearly run out. She has become increasingly incapacitated. Her manager, Larry Clothier, who has become busy with his new star, trumpeter Roy Hargrove, has been worried for some time that Carmen's money wouldn't last as long as she lives. He learns that some people claiming to be her relatives — and heirs to her money — have come from Alaska and camped out in the hospital corridor when Carmen was hospitalized for a stroke in October in Los Angeles.

She falls into a coma and dies on November 10, 1994, at her home in Los Angeles at 2200 Summit Ridge Drive, her beloved hideaway with a well-tended garden where she has grown beautiful flowers and abundant marijuana, set far back from the road and overlooking a canyon. There's no money left for anyone to inherit.

Carmen leaves the legacy of her recordings. And she is quoted in newspaper obituaries as saying she wants to be remembered for one thing: her music.

Much of the information in this chronology comes from personal interviews with many people, including Mat Mathews, Paulette Girard, Dave Usher, Jack Rael, Larry Clothier, François Vaz, Dick Katz, Gene Lees, Annie Ross, Norman Simmons, Norval Perkins, Tony Scott, Milt Gabler, Bill Simon, George Avakian, Herbie Mann, and a Blue Note jazz club staffer.

[1] Hennessey, Mike, *Klook: The Story of Kenny Clarke* (London: Quartet Books, and Pittsburgh: University of Pittsburgh Press, 1990).

CHAPTER ONE

The Early Years

Oscar and Evadne McRae doted on their daughter, Carmen. Her Costa Rican father, Oscar, had already had children by three other women before Carmen's mother: his first wife was from Costa Rica; then he became involved with two women from Jamaica. A physical fitness buff who emigrated in 1915 to New York City, Oscar owned and operated a health club atop the McAlpin Hotel on West 33rd Street and Sixth Avenue. Carmen's mother, Evadne, a strait-laced Jamaican-born woman, arrived in New York in 1917; there are no records in the U.S. of her having had any marriages or children before her marriage to Oscar. Carmen, named for one of Oscar's relatives, was Oscar and Evadne's only child, born on April 8, 1920, in Harlem Hospital.

Oscar was a man of medium height, perhaps five foot nine. He played tennis and rode horses, as well as doing athletics and working out in the gym. Evadne was about the same height, a stately, brown-skinned woman with a strong West Indian accent. Though not athletic, Evadne was a trim woman, all the more surprising because of the rich, Caribbean food she liked to prepare. She liked oxtail, West Indian rice and peas, and seviche, fish marinated in vinegar and spices, sometimes cooked in an oven, and sometimes simply cured until it was cooked in its own juices. Carmen would always prefer these familiar dishes. She liked hot, spicy recipes and had a bottle of Jamaican hot sauce with her at all times when she went on the road later in life.

Both Oscar and Evadne were striving to improve their social standing and had high expectations for a good lifestyle for Carmen. Oscar supported his family well and worked hard at the McAlpin's health club. Evadne worked as a dressmaker. She was also very outspoken, and lent her efforts to improving and supporting women's rights in the workplace. Carmen was proud of her parents; she knew she could rely upon them to keep her safe, secure, and comfortable.

Carmen's early childhood was spent in the Bronx. She was raised a Catholic, but she stopped going to church when she grew up, and never joined another faith. Nevertheless, she believed in a Supreme Being. She felt that her life had been destined before she was born — that fate had a lot to do with her life. "If that is being religious," she said, "then I am." She was tantalized by the Baha'i faith, to which her good friend, Dizzy Gillespie, the trumpeter, introduced her when she was a grown woman, though she never embraced it. She explained that she was not an atheist, but unsure, saying about her faith, "I don't know."[1]

Most jazz musicians were deeply affected by the gospel and blues music they heard early in their lives. Many played instruments in churches, and the call and response form of gospel music and the blues became second nature. The music of the Baptist, Methodist, and Sanctified churches, which most African Americans knew so well, did not figure in her background or birthright. Carmen had to teach herself all the nuances of rhythm, harmony, and improvisation that other African-American children grew up with.

Carmen loved music, and learned many pop tunes from the radio. Her father was a very musical man, and several of her relatives had fine singing voices. Carmen believed she inherited her musical talent from her family.[2]

When she was about eight years old, Carmen began taking piano lessons, which she continued until the age of thirteen. Her parents hoped she would become a classical pianist, "But I'd keep sheet music for pop tunes in among the classical stuff on the piano," she said. "As soon as everyone was out of earshot, I let go with the pops."[3] Although Carmen never studied voice, she enjoyed singing for herself, and began teaching herself a few songs. By the time she was thirteen, Carmen had lost interest in studying the piano. "Between thirteen and sixteen, it was all dreams."[4]

Carmen's parents opposed her desire to have a show business career. They persuaded her to apply to the Julia Richman High School at 300 East 58th Street, then an all-girls public school concentrating on office skills and trades along with some academic courses. Students from all over New York City could apply to the school. By the time Carmen was enrolled at Julia Richman, when she was fourteen, in 1934, her family had moved to 724 West 114th Street in Harlem. While she was still studying, they moved again, to 880 St. Nicholas Avenue in the historic and prestigious Sugar Hill neighborhood, also in Harlem.

Carmen never liked secretarial work and never gave up her dreams for a life in music, but she acquitted herself fairly well in some courses; her marks occasionally ranged as high as 90 in health education, 98 in typing, and 80 in Oral English, and in the 80s in several other subjects. But the majority of her marks were in the 70s; some were considerably lower. Altogether she was an average student with an uneventful high school career — except for three days she spent as a truant in 1934, with no reason given on her school records. She graduated in 1938, pleasing her parents, both of whom had also graduated from high school.[5]

Just before Carmen finished her senior year, a momentous event occurred. She met Irene Kitchings, a Harlem neighbor, then known as Irene Wilson. Irene was recently separated from her husband, the pianist Teddy Wilson, who had recorded for Columbia, most notably with Billie Holiday, and played in Benny Goodman's small groups. The friendship between these two women was vital to them both. Carmen was supportive of the lovelorn woman grieving for her lost marriage, and Irene gave Carmen entree into the heady world of swing era jazz. Despite Irene's rift with Teddy Wilson at the time Carmen met her, Irene retained her friendships with the musicians she had met through him. She introduced Carmen to them — among them bandleader Count Basie, and tenor saxophonists Don Byas and Lester Young, and Nat "King" Cole, and Benny Carter, and Benny Goodman, and Duke Ellington — and even Teddy Wilson, "my idol as a pianist," Carmen would reminisce, "and Art Tatum — he admired my singing. More people did, too. I got into the crowd of people I had admired, such as Billie Holiday — Lady (Day) — and my very favorite singer," Carmen told Royal Stokes. "But after I met Billie Holiday, I wouldn't even open my mouth, if I could possibly help it."[6]

"(Irene) was a very, very unhappy woman," Carmen recalled, "at a very crucial point of her life. I think I helped save her life, because prior to my meeting her, she had tried to take her life. I have to preface it by saying that (Irene had an) aunt who helped her a lot and held her hand. 'Come on, Irene, life is too precious and beautiful,' and after she got through listening to her aunt and coming through, she wrote this tune called 'I'm Pulling Through.' The lyrics were about someone expressing her gratitude to another for helping her see how lovely life could be, and regaining hope. And the grateful one offered to do the same for her friend one day."[7]

It was during this period that Irene also wrote a song called "Some Other Spring," connected to her recovery after the end of her marriage. She introduced the song during an informal rehearsal, or jam session, in Harlem. Irene was an accomplished pianist and songwriter, though she suffered from discrimination against women in jazz, probably the most macho of all the arts at that time. But Irene knew many people in the jazz world who admired her talents and accepted her, to start with, on the basis of her relationship to Teddy Wilson. "I was around her," Carmen recalled, "and she would ask my opinion of certain things. And when she wrote these songs, (she) asked Arthur Herzog to write the lyrics. And Irene wanted Billie Holiday to record them. I would sing them for Billie, for Lady. And that's how Lady heard these songs."[8]

Another of Carmen's supporters was Art Tatum, the most respected jazz pianist of his time. He particularly encouraged Carmen about her singing. Despite the dim view her parents took of show business people, Carmen's mother used to allow her to go to after-hours clubs to listen to Tatum. "It was okay with her if I was with Art. Otherwise I couldn't do it on my own," Carmen reminisced to Royal Stokes for his radio show.[9]

Around the time of her high school graduation, Carmen wrote a song, "Dream of Life," one of the few songs she ever wrote, and gave it to Billie Holiday. Billie recorded it for the Vocalian/Okeh label on January 20, 1939, and it later came out on the Brunswick label. Carmen was really delighted and encouraged by Billie's attention. In those days, Carmen was caught up in hero worship of "Lady Day" with her high, soft, oddly-pitched voice, fluid, horn-like style, and whimsical improvisations. Carmen had frequently described Billie's singing as providing a guidepost and an oasis of beauty among all the possible ways one might try to sing. Though Carmen regarded herself as a piano player, and never studied voice, she still took great pleasure in singing. This was the overriding reason why Carmen was so smitten with Billie. Carmen's love for Billie was so great that they even had a love affair. If Billie had told her to do almost anything at all, Carmen would have done it, Carmen later said; that's how much she adored Billie. Carmen's only reservation was against heroin. Carmen would never have joined Billie in that habit.

In Carmen's large, extended family, Carmen particularly liked Norval Ellis Perkins, who was two years younger than her. His mother, Marie, had been married to Carmen's father. They had had a son, Roy (Carmen's half-brother). After they parted, Oscar went to Jamaica. Marie went first to New York City, where she married an American, Kendrick Perkins, and had five more children; Norval, Carlos, and three sisters, Floriencia, Ramona, and Hortensia. But of all of them it was Norval who became closest to Carmen. Norval recalled Carmen being a very attractive young woman - slender, about five foot five inches tall, with "a profile," he said, noting her sharp, striking, aquiline nose. Roy, the eldest of Marie's children, was half-brother to both Carmen and Norval. Carmen came to know the Perkins family through her aunt, Oscar's sister Inez, and through her half-brother, Roy. Norval recalled that, "the families were close and friendly." His mother remained close with Carmen's aunt Inez as well as with Carmen's mother and father.

Norval and Roy grew up in the same house in Philadelphia. After high school, Roy moved to his own pad in Harlem. When Norval finished high school, he also moved to Harlem and lived with his elder brother, Roy.

At the time the brothers were living together in Harlem, they were also spending a great deal of time hanging out with Carmen. All three of them loved jazz. Norval's introduction to jazz began when he was a boy in Philadelphia listening to Earl "Fatha" Hines, the pianist and bandleader broadcasting from the Grand Terrace Ballroom in Chicago. Norval recalled going with Carmen "to the Savoy Ballroom, and to a dance hall that I can't remember the name of — Teddy Wilson organized a big band in that place and opened it up." (The year was either

1939 or 1940.) "I don't know whether she introduced me to (tenor saxophonist) Lester Young or not. He was in the (Count) Basie band ... that was the beginning of the abstract way of playing jazz," Norval said. Tenor saxophonist Lester "Pres" Young had a small tone, a light sound, and a "cool" approach, without the warming element of vibrato. And he phrased his melodies with great fluidity in an irregular way. Though he was never a bebopper, the sensitivity of his style influenced the progressive musicians. Recording with Count Basie for the first time in 1936, Young played stunning solos on "Lady Be Good" and "Shoe Shine Boy." Younger saxophonists such as Dexter Gordon and Illinois Jacquet were inspired by the recordings, and many other saxophonists followed suit. "We really had great times up there, just going out." Norval also recalled a bar called The Fat Man on the Hill — Sugar Hill — that he and Carmen liked to visit, because it featured good music. Carmen did introduce Norval to alto saxophonist Charlie "Bird" Parker eventually. And Carmen's love for jazz reinforced Norval's.

Norval recalled that Carmen was thoroughly in the swim of Harlem's jazz world by the early 1940s, even if she wasn't working much or at all as a pianist herself. She occasionally worked as a secretary in offices by day, and also occasionally worked as a chorus-line dancer in Harlem nightspots. She continued to live with her parents, and they also handed her a little spending money — she didn't have to earn a living. This arrangement allowed Carmen to spend most of her time immersing herself in the musical riches of Harlem's jazz scene.

A girlfriend from St. Nicholas Avenue, Marge Costa, used to go to the clubs with Carmen, too. Even at that time, only in her early twenties, Carmen was an adventurous leader, a fearless risk taker. "I was afraid of the after-hours places in Harlem," Marge recalled. "I was afraid of raids. But Carmen said, 'C'mon.' And we went. We never got caught."

It was no secret that Carmen played the piano very well. She thought she might make a career for herself as a jazz pianist. But she found fewer opportunities open for women than for men. Still, she knew everyone on Harlem's jazz scene. And with her brilliant smile, bright eyes, and slender figure, she attracted attention and gained acceptance. She knew about music, too. She wasn't just a hanger-on.

Information and personal recollections for this chapter come from numerous personal interviews in 1999 and 2000 with Norval Perkins, Cecilia Perkins, Larry Clothier, Carmen's longtime friend Marge Costa, as well as from the Institute of Jazz Studies at Rutgers University, and an intimate male friend of Carmen's who requires that his identity be withheld regarding Carmen's affair with Billie Holiday.
[1] "Carmen McRae," from *Notes and Tones: Musician to Musician Interviews*, edited by Arthur Taylor (New York: Perigee Books, G.P. Putnam's Sons, 1977).

[2] Ibid.

[3] This came from a reminiscence to the *New York Sunday News* in 1962. The exact date of the article could not be verified prior to publication.

[4] "Since Minton's," an interview with Carmen McRae broadcast on July 19, 1978, WGTB-FM, Washington, D.C., with W. Royal Stokes, host.

[5] These details are to be found in Carmen McRae's academic record from Julia Richman High School.

[6] "Since Minton's," op. cit.

[7] McPartland, Marian, "Interview with Carmen McRae," *Piano Jazz* (National Public Radio, recorded 1982, released 1985).

[8] Ibid.

[9] "Since Minton's," op. cit.

CHAPTER TWO

Learning on the
Jazz Scene in Harlem

Carmen's discovery of the jazz scene in Harlem in the late 1930s and early 1940s coincided with the metamorphosis of swing into bebop. She listened very carefully while the music evolved, learning from the innovations just as they were being developed. The place where Carmen most often heard musicians experimenting with harmonies and rhythms and breathing life into the new music was Minton's Playhouse. And "the new thing," as the musicians first called bebop, became the focus of her life; bebop and the improvisations it guided her to create would influence Carmen's style most of all.

In 1939, Henry Minton, one of the first African-American delegates to the musician's union, a saxophonist himself, had a wonderful idea: He decided to refurbish a small, rundown room adjoining the Hotel Cecil at 210 West 118th Street in Harlem and open a jazz and dinner club. It was a good time for him to do so. In the 1920s and 1930s, Harlem had become a thriving arts community for African Americans, attracting musicians, writers, poets, and painters from all over the country. By day, musicians tended to travel in different circles from writers and other intellectuals. But at night, all creative people crossed paths in the clubs. Minton expected them all to show up and make his club a social priority.

He had good reason to hope that Minton's Playhouse would become a major attraction. Henry Minton was well-liked and respected in Harlem's creative community. He was an officer of the Rhythm Club, which functioned both as a meeting place and booking office for performers. Just like the Clef Club, its predecessor and counterpart for the West 52nd Street scene, the Rhythm Club regulated wage scales, gave artists a place to rehearse, and found gigs for them in Harlem clubs. Minton was also the first African-American delegate to the union, local 802 of the American Federation of Musicians. So he knew all about the personal, professional, and financial realities of jazz musicians. A gregarious man, he often made

17

loans of money to friends; a connoisseur of good food, he loved to cook and would often share meals with unemployed friends.

In 1939, swing music was still very popular. All the big bands passed through New York sooner or later to play in the clubs, theaters, and ballrooms. A riot in Harlem in 1935 had caused the fashionable, gangster-owned Cotton Club at 644 Lenox Avenue at West 142nd Street to lose its cachet. Whites no longer went there, and the club went out of business by February, 1936. But African Americans still went to Harlem's other clubs, cabarets, and after-hours joints to enjoy or play music and hobnob with friends.

Among the most popular spots was Clarke Monroe's Uptown House at 198 West 134th Street, which featured music after hours — after 4 A.M. Charlie "Bird" Parker played there. Musicians liked to jam after hours at Puss Johnson's club on West 138th Street, too. The Nest, a small place at 169 West 133rd Street, which had been popular even in the 1920s, was still thriving. Jock's Place, on Seventh Avenue at 137th Street, featured music. Small's Paradise at 2294 Seventh Avenue and West 135th Street enjoyed a long run as one of the most successful clubs in Harlem. And Fats Waller made Connie's Inn his second home.

At the ballrooms — the Savoy, Renaissance, and Golden Gate — the swingingest bands in the country competed fiercely with each other, "battling" in "cutting contests," musicians said, for the top ranking in each other's esteem. One of the most important bookings was the Apollo. The Apollo Theater, at 253 West 125th Street, was enjoying great popularity. It had exquisite chorus girls, including Dizzy Gillespie's wife Lorraine, as well as comedians, singers, actors — all kinds of entertainers — who played there day and night. Every week, it featured a different swing band led by such stars as Duke Ellington, Count Basie, Cab Calloway, Earl Hines, and Benny Carter. Singers Lena Horne and Ella Fitzgerald, comedians Moms Mabley and the team of Butterbeans and Susie, and dancers Buck and Bubbles and the Nicholas Brothers, to name only a few stars, headlined there. These were Carmen's haunts. Carmen knew them all and frequented them often, cultivating friends and occasionally sitting down to play the piano or sing a tune or two: People were aware that she had talent. Carmen was a great mixing spoon, an avid socializer in those days. She had so many friends and acquaintances that it was difficult to keep track of everyone she knew and everything she was doing. In the early 1940s, when Nat "King" Cole brought his trio and his first wife from California to New York City for the first time, Carmen had helped them find a place to stay in Harlem. Some people who never became well known outside of Harlem's entertainment circles formed friendships with Carmen in the 1940s — such as the Brown Sisters, a dance team who entertained locally and also toured, for example — and the relationships lasted all their lives.

At first few people from the Harlem scene went to Minton's. It featured familiar-sounding swing music played by a good band, but not a band with a national reputation. The tenor saxophonist who led it was a little-known disciple of Coleman Hawkins, the "King of the Tenor Saxophone," famed for his recording of "Body and Soul." People would have gone to Minton's to hear Hawkins himself, but not his imitators.

Searching for a way to give his club more appeal, Henry Minton asked his old friend, bandleader and saxophonist Teddy Hill, to manage the club and take charge of all aspects of the music.

Hill turned out to be the right man for the job. Eventually he would become even better known for his role as Minton's manager than for the leadership of his band. Hill's managerial abilities, his familiarity with the jazz world, and his sense of the pulse of Harlem's nightlife — expertise which he had developed as a bandleader — served Minton's Playhouse well.

Hill hired a revolutionary young drummer, Kenny Clarke, who had a modern conception of the proper role for a timekeeper. A few years earlier, Clarke had played drums in Hill's band, but Clarke's style had been too adventurous for swing, and Hill had replaced Clarke with a more traditional drummer. But Clarke's progressive style was just right for Minton's. Clarke kept time on the ride cymbal and used the high hat, snare drums, tom toms, and bass drum for cross rhythms and accents. He still played four beats to the bar on the bass drum, but he did it subtly, feathering the bass drum lightly, and used accents on the bass called "bombs," which could be played anywhere in a measure of music. All modern drummers soon followed Clarke's lead in "dropping bombs." Max Roach, for instance, learned from Clarke's style. Hill was also responsible for inventing Clarke's nicknames, "Klook" and "Klook-mop," in imitation of the sound of Clarke's accents on the bass drum at Minton's.

Kenny Clarke was born on January 9, 1914 in Pittsburgh, Pennsylvania. He began music lessons with his mother, a pianist, and played in local bands when he was eighteen. By the end of the 1930s, when he arrived in New York, he had acquired the solid experience of several years of playing in supper-club shows in the midwest.

Clarke was a sensitive, creative, and adventurous drummer, whose work served as a touchstone for all drummers involved in the bebop revolution and the styles that evolved from it. About ten years younger than Clarke, Max Roach listened to Clarke at Minton's Playhouse, where Max understood and picked up the polyrhythmic style from Clarke and embellished it further. Max's mature drumming style would be both intense and intimate; he could build a long, fiery, and fascinating drum solo; he could accompany the melody line with brilliance and smoothness.

In addition to Clarke, Hill hired journeyman trumpeter Joe Guy. Bassist Nick Finton came in for the rhythm section. Against Clarke's advice, Hill added pianist Thelonious Monk to the group. Monk had been a rhythm and blues, church-oriented player. He had even toured the country for a few years in a group fronted by an evangelistic faith healer. Clarke knew of Monk as a church player. But Monk had been writing his own unusual compositions and experimenting with harmonies, dissonance, and rhythms, and with spikey, hesitating phrasings since his teens. Long before he was hired to play at Minton's Playhouse, he had written "Round Midnight," one of the most famous songs to emerge from the jazz world.

Once Monk joined the group at Minton's, Clarke instantly recognized Monk's exciting progressive ideas. Monk and Clarke quickly became collaborators. They had a lot of admiration for each other, and worked together with enthusiasm. Together they introduced harmonic and rhythmic surprises, forging the new sound of jazz.

Henry Minton made his club stylish, creating an intimate space in the back of the long room near the bandstand, with an oak bar in the front. Miles Davis recalled in his autobiography: "It cost something like two dollars if you sat at one of the tables, which had white linen tablecloths on them and flowers in little glass vases. It was a nice place — much nicer than the clubs on West 52nd Street — and it held about a hundred or a hundred and twenty-five people."[1] Around the time that Hill stepped in as manager, Minton had been advertising: "Minton's Playhouse - De Luxe dinners at 60 cents, drinks 20 cents." Teddy Hill conceived of far greater attractions to draw crowds.

To ensure that Minton's Playhouse became irresistible as a social gathering place, Hill made a savvy arrangement with the Schiffman family, who owned the Apollo. The Schiffmans began paying for their entertainers to eat at Minton's on Monday nights. The Apollo entertainers had worked hard at the theater, playing about six shows a day from Tuesdays through Sundays, and the feast of Southern-style hash, grits, fried chicken, collard greens seasoned with ham, soft, fresh, hot biscuits, and free whiskey rewarded them — and also attracted other show people who had Monday nights off. All of them sat back and let themselves be entertained by Minton's house group. Other musicians started to show up with their "axes" — their instruments — both to sit in and dine contentedly.

Heeding Teddy Hill's advice, Minton permitted musicians to jam at the club. Ordinarily the musicians' local 802 of the A.F. of M. forbade jamming free of charge — musicians were fined for breaking that law. But Minton had enough influence to ignore it. No one would punish musicians for jamming in his little fiefdom. Musicians didn't like the no-jamming rule, anyway. Though it was a perfectly logical rule, because it stopped club owners from taking advantage of musicians, at the same time it prevented musicians from sitting in with the booked groups. And sitting in was the primary way for young musicians to learn and improve their playing. In those days, music schools for jazz musicians didn't exist.

A new spirit for playing music was in the air. The young musicians who came to Monday night sessions belonged to the generation of musicians getting their first opportunities to play in the established swing-era bands; among these young lions were the pivotal players trumpeter Dizzy Gillespie and alto saxophonist Charlie "Bird" Parker. Like all youngsters, they wanted to outdo their elders. And the jitters of the war years and the growing urge among African Americans to assert their rights inspired their daring music.

These musicians and others experimented with substitute and alternate chords and new harmonies, and they quickly changed the phrasing and complicated the rhythms of jazz. The important rhythmic emphasis or rhythmic unit, the quarter note in the swing era, changed to the eighth note for a more intense feeling during the bebop revolution. These inventive rebels also used altered chords with raised (sharped) or lowered (flatted) notes. The plaintive sound of the flatted fifth notes in all the scales became a hallmark of the new music. Altogether the musicians developed a more sophisticated, intense way of playing melody, harmony, and rhythm. Duke Ellington's innovative bassist Jimmy Blanton, the first modern soloist, sat in at Minton's.

"Minton's was a great place," said many musicians. People such as guitarist Eddie Condon, a bon vivant, noted wit, and a leader for the preservation of the New Orleans-rooted, Chicago style of jazz, criticized the beboppers, saying, "They flat their fifths. We drink ours." But the young lions persisted. In fact, they thumbed their noses at the old-timers, who were nicknamed "moldy figs." Minton's acquired a reputation for featuring the hippest sounds in the jazz world. Pianist Mary Lou Williams, whose apartment on Hamilton Terrace became a gathering place for jazz's young revolutionaries in the 1940s, called Minton's "the house that bop built." In truth, many Harlem clubs were nicer than the 52nd Street clubs, which were tiny places crammed into a few blocks that would one day become famous as Swing Street. Their lack of decor really showed up in the daytime, when the crowds were gone, and visitors could see only gloomy interiors illuminated by naked lightbulbs. In sharp contrast, Minton's had a touch of class.

Record producer George Avakian's strongest memory of Minton's came from a time shortly after his college graduation at age twenty-two from Yale University in June, 1941. He had already been going to Minton's occasionally. A friend of his had hired Kenny Clarke to do a Sunday afternoon concert in a bar/restaurant about 20 miles from New Haven, Connecticut. When it came time to pay the musicians, Avakian's friend was short $35. "Klook said he could wait," Avakian recalled. As a favor, Avakian volunteered to bring the money to Klook at Minton's.

Avakian drove down one late afternoon in his family's Dodge, which was packed to the roof with his own record collection and an Ansley-Dynaphone phonograph. "It cost a $100, a wonderful machine," he recalled. It was the first time he had driven to Minton's. He parked the car nearby and went inside to give Klook his money. "Kenny almost fainted. He said he never thought he would get it, and he told me to stay. We started talking. I stayed for two sets and never checked my car."

Destined to become a highly respected producer at Columbia, Avakian didn't remember much about the club's decorations. "All I gave a damn about was the music," he said. "It was a great deal more animated than anything else I was hearing in town. It was different from Nick's and Condon's and 52nd Street. Minton's was basically a black crowd, and the musicians there were more relaxed, exciting, and freer than in other places they played." He recalled the great guitarist, Charlie Christian, who played with Benny Goodman and jammed at Minton's, as "a shy, quiet guy and an exciting player who was different. He was playing an electric guitar."[2] Beginning in 1938, the electric guitar was another revolutionary element in jazz.

Hanging out at the clubs, Carmen and her friends could often be found at Minton's. By the early 1940s, Minton's and the other Harlem clubs had become Carmen's milieu and music school. She met Klook around 1940, through her friends Eddie West, a tap-dancer in a group called the Chocolateers, and his wife Pauline, who had gone to high school with Carmen. She would later say she found him very likeable. "And then I heard Kenny play," Carmen said, "and I couldn't believe it. I thought he was absolutely fantastic. We became very close and after a while he told me that he was in love with me and that one day we would get married. I told him he was crazy."[3]

However, Carmen did get to play piano. One night — perhaps it was on a Monday night, the night when everyone came for the free food and the jam session — Minton's needed a pianist in a hurry. Someone who had faith in her asked Carmen to play. This was quite an accomplishment. Ordinarily Minton's bandstand was an all-male preserve.

Carmen would see Klook most nights, either at his apartment, at Minton's, or at the Hotel Braddock Grill on 126th Street, where many musicians hung out. She was particularly attracted to the progressive style Klook and Monk were developing. And Klook definitely admired Carmen's piano playing, even if she would later reflect that he didn't encourage her. Klook certainly knew about the budding, forthright, opinionated expressions of her tastes in music in general — he and his colleagues were helping her form those tastes, while she was giving moral support, loyalty, admiration, and perhaps even some musical ideas to Kenny and his friends. After all, "I love to voice opinions," she would later say.[4]

Klook liked Carmen's pretty face with its chiselled features and remarkable eyes; they were by turns bright, soft, and somewhat questioning, even perplexed in expression, then spirited and analytical — and particularly bright deep pools when she smiled. Her eyebrows arched up over the bridge of her nose, curving in exactly the opposite direction from most other people's. Despite the questions that her eyes asked, Carmen was certain of one thing: She wanted to get away from the strictures of her family's house. Her father really didn't like her coming home late at night, but it was during the late-night hours that she heard the best music.

Sometimes, an exciting rehearsal would go on in the basement of the Braddock Grill, with musicians arriving after their jobs had ended. Or a band would come in from the road, and Carmen would bump into some of the older, swinging musicians as well as the struggling younger ones who hung around the clubs in the Braddock's neighborhood.

Among them were Cab Calloway, who had a band filled with talented players including bassist Milt Hinton, tenor saxophonist Ike Quebec, and trumpeter Doc Cheatham; they stopped at the Braddock when they played the Apollo. Earl "Fatha" Hines with his singer Billy Eckstine; bandleader Andy Kirk and his band, The Clouds of Joy; Duke Ellington and Count Basie and their bands all made regular stops at the Braddock. Carmen crossed paths with them all.

The great jazz vocalist, Sarah Vaughan, became the "girl singer" in Earl Hines's band in 1943 after she wowed audiences at one of the Apollo's amateur nights. Though four years younger than Carmen, Sarah had already far outstripped Carmen professionally. Carmen both envied and admired Sarah's gifts and accomplishments. For the rest of her life, Carmen would be mindful of Sarah's eminence and feel an urge to compete with Sarah. But Carmen's competitive spirit was always tempered by her real affection and respect for Sarah.

One day, Carmen was delighted when Sarah, seeing her at the Braddock Grill, said, "Hi, Carmen." Carmen was still completely unknown as a professional and had never met Sarah until that moment. Yet Sarah knew who Carmen was. The recognition made Carmen feel wonderful. The two young women became good friends and would hang out all night whenever they met in those days — and for the rest of their lives — "until seven, eight, nine in the morning, against the law, honey," Carmen would later reminisce.[5]

Years later, when the older big-band musicians waxed nostalgic about the good old days, they spoke of how cute and friendly Carmen and Sarah were: Slender and vivacious, full of moxie and dreams, hanging out at the Braddock.

Carmen learned a lot about music, stagecraft, timing, and all the little nuances that go into a polished performance from the musicians she was meeting. Pianist Mary Lou Williams, formerly part of Andy Kirk's band, The Clouds of Joy, encouraged Carmen as a pianist and offered advice. Carmen listened to the musicians talk and observed them on stages and bandstands. Later Carmen would recall how the experience of immersing herself in their artistry had educated her. "I was around these people. And so even though I wasn't aware of anything, some of it had to have rubbed off. Because I have reached back and didn't even know that I remembered it. And it helps me so very much."[6]

Carmen's reputation was growing in those days. Among the men who admired her was Joe Louis, the world heavyweight boxing champion, with whom she had a romantic relationship for a while. (Exactly when isn't certain, but she definitely had a liaison with him.)

Klook held on to his romantic notions about Carmen. When he was drafted for World War II in 1943, he did basic training in Alabama. He also discovered that wives qualified for a regular allowance, but he didn't have a wife yet. So he decided that Carmen should be his wife, thus qualifying for the money should he be sent overseas. He asked her to marry him.

In 1944, Carmen went to visit Klook at the U.S. Army training camp, Camp Seibert, in Alabama. She became the wife of Technical Sergeant Kenneth Clarke Spearman — Klook's real last name — in the nearby town of Gadsden, Alabama.

In one version of the story, Carmen couldn't stand the restrictions of segregation in the deep south. Chafing at the situation, she provoked Kenny into suggesting she go back north and wait for him there. In another version, Kenny couldn't stand the restrictions of life in the Army. Even though he played in a jazz group at the base, he missed the excitement of New York's music scene. Whichever is the case, Carmen returned to New York and Klook went AWOL for 107 days that year.[7] Supposedly he worked with trumpeter Cootie Williams's band and with singer Dinah Washington until the Army found him and stripped him of his rank. He was told he could either agree to go overseas, or he would find himself posted with his unit's band to Jackson, Mississippi. Kenny despised the racial situation in the United States. As Private Spearman, he was shipped to Europe at the end of September, 1944.[8]

Kenny landed in Liverpool in late September, 1944, and was stationed at Tetworth, the marshalling point from which American troops were flown to augment the Allied Forces in their post D-Day push through Western Europe.[9] Klook was eventually transferred to the 13th Special Service Unit near Rouen in Normandy, where he spent some time learning how to lay down smokescreens, and he also found time to form a choir in the Army and tour the active service units. In Rouen he met up with his old friend, Teddy Hill, from Minton's Playhouse.

Klook first toured with his choir in Germany, Belgium, and France. In Paris, he met many musicians and influential music-world figures, and he fell thoroughly in love with the slow-paced lifestyle as well as the relaxed racial attitude of Europeans. He expanded his circle of friends and acquaintances in Europe.

Meanwhile, Carmen went to work in Washington, D.C., where she had a series of jobs, one of which was in a defense plant, none of which she could clearly remember years later. The highlight had been the lunch hours which she whiled away by "getting high" with friends, she recalled. She knew she was supposed to be helping out with the war effort, but eventually she couldn't muzzle her ambition any longer and went back to New York City to do what she felt she was supposed to be doing: Playing music.

Carmen sang with Benny Carter's band in 1944, and afterward with Count Basie's band for a while. She even played piano with a band led by Duke Ellington's son, Mercer. Mercer, who was playing trumpet at that time, was expected to be a talented musician because he was Duke's son, but he needed time to develop. When he picked up the trumpet, after trying a variety of instruments, he sounded so awful that people in his band just looked at each other, Carmen recalled. In any case, in 1946 she made her first recording, a tune called "Pass Me By," with his band.

Carmen's distant relation, Norval Perkins, kept a copy of Carmen's record for a long time, but the recording, a 78 rpm (revolutions per minute) with a black label with silver lettering in the middle, wasn't widely distributed. The band itself doesn't appear to have lasted very long. One version of Carmen's stint with the band says that it broke up in Chicago. Another story says it folded in Atlantic City.

Carmen went to take a job as a chorus girl in the Club Harlem on Kentucky Avenue, the hub of the African-American entertainment world in Atlantic City, a twenty-four hour town. After the girls finished working for the night, they got together with a bottle of whiskey, which the club owner gave them. And Carmen played piano, sang a few ballads, always her favorite songs, "torch songs," she called them, for the other girls. "And I talked about the man I love and he's funny that way," Carmen reminisced poetically about the tone of the nights and the songs she sang, as she and the girls hung out, gossiping and laughing. But gregarious as she might have been, Carmen was dreaming intensely of a more illustrious career in show business. And time was passing her by.

Klook was shipped back to Fort Dix in New Jersey for demobilization in 1946. In April, he immediately headed for New York — and Carmen. They were in love, and they stayed together for nearly three years. At least for part of that time, they lived in the McRae family house at 1466 Dean Street in Brooklyn. This was an ironic arrangement for Carmen, since later in her life she would say to a writer that she had married Klook strictly to get out of the house, and she hadn't ever really loved him. Carmen's attitudes about her youthful marriage to Klook had changed radically by the time she was in her seventies, in the early 1990s.

Whatever the true story of their love affair, Carmen would tell the tale that her parents had objected to her marrying Klook. They hadn't even met him, she said, though Carmen had known him for years in Harlem. Most likely, though, her parents must have met Klook, even if they didn't know each other well.

In any case, her parents had objected to the match, asking her, "Why do you have to get married, Carmen? We don't know anything about this guy." Carmen responded by telling them, "Well, I'm the one who is going to be living with him." Whatever their reservations, they loved Kenny very much when they met him.

"I was impressed with his charming, dignified manner from the first time I saw him," Carmen said. "He always talked softly and made sense. And I never saw him really mad — not about anything. He could get his point across without raising his voice — and he would never say anything bad about anybody. He was a very sweet, gentle man."

In the early days, Carmen could seem like a simple housewife. One day, Dave Usher and Ray Glassman, in partnership in the 1940s with a record label named

Emanon, set out in a snowstorm to see Klook at Carmen's house. Klook was planning to tour Europe with Dizzy Gillespie's big bebop band, and he wanted Dave and Ray to hear a song he had written, "Algerian Criticism," that the band would play. At the house, Klook introduced Carmen as his wife, Carmen Clarke. She was wearing a plain dress with an apron, and played the song on the upright piano in the dining room for the men. Usher had no idea that Carmen sang. He recalls that she mentioned that she had to look for a job as a secretary. He remembered, too, that the couple had two Doberman Pinschers, who had a bone on a wooden platform under the dining table; they gnawed on the bone until they made a hole in the wood. "I was scared of those dogs," Usher recalled.

Carmen couldn't recall any major fights with Klook, but he was simply never around. He went his own way. She did ask him to try to help her get a job singing with Dizzy's band, so that they could tour Europe together, but Klook absolutely refused. "When Kenny was with Dizzy and they needed a singer, I really wanted to try for the job," Carmen said. "But I guess Kenny didn't want me around because it would have restricted his freedom. That turned me off — it was what made me want to get away from him. I thought, 'Either he thinks I can't sing or he doesn't want me — or both.'"[10] Marooned in a marriage with an absentee husband, Carmen realized she would have to build her own, independent life.

In December, 1947, Klook set out for Europe with Dizzy Gillespie's big bebop band including the great Cuban conguero, Chano Pozo. In retrospect, Klook would say that he had wanted to avoid that tour. He said that he "really wanted to stay home and spend some time with Carmen." However, Klook toured several countries with Dizzy, ending with a great success at a concert at Salle Pleyel in Paris.

When it came time for the band to return to the U.S., Klook didn't get on the ship with the other musicians. He stayed in Paris with a young singer, Annie Ross. Carmen went with the other band members' wives to meet the boat — and Klook didn't get off. Norval Perkins recalled that incident clearly. That's when the marriage was truly over, Norval said. His affair, which produced a son with Annie Ross, didn't last a long time. Klook came back to New York a few months later — in August, 1948. Klook and Carmen remained friends, and Klook rented an apartment on his own — in Brooklyn, to be near Carmen.

---

[1] Davis, Miles with Quincy Troupe, *Miles: The Autobiography* (New York: Simon & Schuster, 1989).

[2] Interview with George Avakian by Leslie Gourse, 2000.

[3] Hennessey, Mike, *Klook: The Story of Kenny Clarke* (London: Quartet Books Limited, 1990, and Pittsburgh: University of Pittsburgh Press, 1990).

[4] "Carmen McRae," from *Notes and Tones: Musician to Musician Interviews*, edited by Arthur Taylor (New York: Perigee Books, G.P. Putnam's Sons, 1977).

[5] Interview with Carmen McRae by Leslie Gourse, 1990.

[6] McPartland, Marian, "Interview with Carmen McRae," *Piano Jazz* (National Public Radio, recorded 1982, released 1985).

[7] Ibid. (There's no mention in *Klook* of the possibility he might have been jailed for going AWOL. That omission was extremely strange.)

[8] Hennessey, op. cit.

[9] Ibid.

[10] Ibid.

CHAPTER THREE

From the Chicago Clubs to the Jazz Critics' Polls

C armen met a Chicagoan, George Kirby, a comedian and mimic, in New York following the breakup of her marriage to Klook. Kirby worked in New York for a while in 1948, and planned to go back to Chicago. He wanted to marry Carmen and take her home with him.

Carmen wasn't eager to take a chance right away on another committed relationship — not a marriage anyway. She also didn't want George to go home without her. So she discussed her quandary with her mother Evadne, confiding that she wanted to live with George for a while and see how the relationship worked out. Her proper mother shocked her by saying, "I don't blame you a bit, child." Carmen decided to go with Kirby to Chicago. Some people recall she had taken him seriously enough to call herself Carmen Kirby for a while, though she was still actually Kenny Clarke's legal wife.

In Chicago, Carmen suffered through all the drudgery of housework without any of the fun of playing music or singing in public. "I couldn't cook shit," Carmen recalled. "My mother did all the cooking. And George loved to eat. So I used to cook and cook and throw shit out and start again. This went on for a while. Then George, who didn't want me to work, wouldn't send the money to pay for the rent. I wasn't used to that. My father had bought a brownstone in Brooklyn so we would have a decent place to live. And I never had to pay rent before in my life."[1]

George didn't bother to pay any of their bills. The pressure of poverty and George's cavalier attitude toward the bills drove Carmen to seek help and refuge with a girlfriend, Lulu. George may have already begun to use heroin at that time. He would later serve a long prison term (about 20 years) in Lexington, Kentucky, for his drug involvement, interrupting his promising career. (This did not happen until Carmen had left his life and gone on to make her own way in the world.

Though George got over his addiction, he stayed in jail so long that he never recovered his professional momentum, though he was a great mimic.)

Lulu and Carmen had worked together in the chorus line at Club Harlem in Atlantic City. Lulu immediately came up with a solution to Carmen's situation: Carmen could take a job at the Archway Lounge, owned by a South Side nightlife figure, "Killer" Johnson, where Lulu was working as a waitress. Carmen was unsure if she was ready for a club gig and said to her girlfriend, "WHAT? I know eight songs!"

Lulu said, "That eight will do."

So they went to the Archway, a charming-looking little restaurant and club with good food. The place attracted a well-to-do crowd, including gamblers when they were winning or looking for a profitable game to get into. A few years later, Sarah Vaughan would meet her second husband, a gambler, who wreaked havoc with her income, in the Archway.

Chicago was also a town with many good places to hear jazz, the blues, and popular music, and to see dancers and comedians. Though Chicago had lost its cachet as the most important jazz and blues center after the Depression, and New York had become pre-eminent, talented African Americans and whites still often gravitated to Chicago before they moved on to New York or Los Angeles. Chicago remained an important stop on the itineraries of musicians on tours throughout the twentieth century.

Since Carmen had no money to join the musician's union, Killer Johnson, who took an instant liking to the pretty woman's appearance and talent, put up the money for her. He also gave Carmen money to rent a piano, so she could practice new tunes, many of which she learned from the radio. The job was supposed to last a short time, perhaps two weeks. Carmen said to herself, "Great. At least I'll get money to go back to Brooklyn."

But instead the gig lasted much longer, perhaps four months — different stories mention different amounts of time. And Carmen herself, talking about the gig in later life, couldn't remember how long she worked at the Archway. She stayed on in town for years, perhaps for as long as three-and-a-half years, she said, but she wasn't absolutely sure. What is definite, she said, was that "I went through all kinds of stuff, and I learned how to play. Sarah Vaughan used to come there. She and I always used to hang out when we saw each other."[2]

Carmen was into "wild stuff" in those days. She already regularly smoked marijuana, and, like Sarah, Carmen was attracted to the wild lifestyle. She never used any illegal drug to the extent that it ruled her and threatened to destroy her, but she did say: "You've got to use something to be in this business. It's very hard to get by without drinking or smoking or whatever people feel they physically need to make it.... You can come from a completely normal family and have had a very normal and beautiful childhood, and when you get into this business, it's like something else. I think it's foolish for someone to try to destroy himself, but I do believe some sort of stimulant must be used by those who feel they need it in order to survive.... I can't say it's wrong."[3] However, throughout her life, Carmen battled her addiction to cigarettes, and they would take their toll on her health and her voice.

While in Chicago, Carmen worked very hard at learning to sing and play, broadening her repertoire and improving her technique. She learned to play in two keys; when she had begun at the Archway, she could only play in one key to accompany herself. And she stopped calling herself Carmen Clarke and Carmen Kirby and used her own name, Carmen McRae. She baptized herself and really launched her professional career during her Chicago sojourn.

The pianist Billy Taylor, who had first met Carmen in New York City when she was unhappily married to Kenny Clarke, happened to cross paths with Carmen one night in a mutual friend's apartment in Chicago. Billy was delighted to find out that Carmen was "just really happy," he said, at last working all the time as a singer.

Another night, when Duke Ellington was performing in Chicago, he went to a Chicago club where Carmen was working as an intermission pianist for the singing team of Jackie and Roy. As Carmen told this story years later to Marian McPartland on *Piano Jazz* for National Public Radio, Carmen asked Duke if he would play something for her. "I wanted to show him off. He got up and played a few things. I asked him to play his song 'I Never Felt This Way Before,' and he said, 'How does it go?' Well, I said, 'Get down off of that stand, I'll play it for you.'" Carmen said. "And I'll do it for you now," she said to McPartland. Carmen crooned the romantic ballad. She had a percussive way of playing at times, and she hit some unusual notes, too, as she often did while performing. Carmen continued by saying to Marian about her unrehearsed rendition of Duke's song, "What am I doing?" She laughed, and she scatted a little: "I never felt this way before I never felt this way ay ay ay I never felt this way ay ay ay ay ay, I never felt this way sho oee uh." To Marian she said, "You would ask me to do that."

Marian said, "Oh, such a nice percussive touch. It's really knocking me out."

"Oh, thank you, it's very kind," Carmen said.

Marian then announced she would create an impromptu musical portrait of Carmen — an impressionistic feat Marian often did for her guests. Marian played something lyrical, then made it turn percussive, darker, and louder; then she waxed lyrical again, then percussive. That surprising juxtaposition of the lyrical and the percussive brilliantly analyzed Carmen's personality. The portrait ended dreamily, trailing off.

Carmen, very impressed with Marian's interpretation, said, "Marian, is that me? That's marvelous.... I'm very flattered, and I cannot thank you enough, and you make me feel very, very good...."[4] Perhaps she had already been playing that way in her Chicago days. And she liked the complications, conflict, and colors in the musical portrait.

"People (in Chicago) kept telling me to record," she later said. "I thought, well, I should go home. Even if I don't record, it's nice to know I've been in Chicago this long and made a living from playing and singing. I can do that at home. New York is the best place to do that." Her parents had wanted her to return anyway that year, 1952. "So I went home."[5]

Carmen's arduous, convoluted career climb continued. She had long watched her younger friend Sarah Vaughan acquiring the trappings of success. In the early and mid-1940s, Sarah had already done stints with important bands — Earl Hines's swing era band, then Billy Eckstine's, the first big bebop band. In addition to touring in the country with her own group beginning in the late 1940s, Sarah had also starred at important jazz rooms in New York City — Cafe Society Downtown, an integrated club and important showcase for African-American entertainers, in Greenwich Village, and in the little, wall-to-wall clubs on 52nd Street, to become known as Swing Street, and in the most important jazz club in the world at that time, Birdland. Sarah's first husband, George Treadwell, had thrown a birthday party for Sarah at Birdland, and *Ebony* magazine had photographed the celebration. Sarah had also enjoyed having recording contracts beginning in the mid-1940s. Treadwell had done a fine job of managing his gifted wife at that time, and he would continue well into the 1950s, shepherding her from the Mainstream to Columbia to Mercury labels. Carmen had none of that boost or luck. She was struggling all that time on her own, without a mentor or manager, and sometimes without even a gig, never mind a prestigious one, in the offing. In 1952, she had still made exactly one recording — the 1946 recording of "Pass Me By" with the Mercer Ellington band.

Immediately after Carmen came home from Chicago and moved back in with her parents, she took a job doing clerical work in an office by day, and a gig singing and playing piano in a little Brooklyn club called the Bandbox at night. The money for the job was not very grand — probably much less than the $65 a week that some musicians remembered earning for steady gigs at Minton's Playhouse in the same era. Klook found Carmen a bassist to work with her. But that man, Jimmy Woode, who would become well-known as a veteran of the Duke Ellington band, spent only a week with Carmen at the Bandbox; he took a cab to and from Manhattan and never got paid, he said. Carmen, who would always be known for paying all her debts and salaries to sidemen, may not have received any pay herself at the Bandbox, or perhaps it was just too small for her to share. She continued there as a solo act.

Carmen was in truth barely holding her own in the jazz world in 1952 and 1953. She was already thirty-three years old. She kept reflecting on how, for years, she had struggled along with low-paying jobs in New York, Atlantic City, and

Chicago, all the while honing her style, developing distinctive tastes for her repertoire, and becoming thoroughly polished. Carmen was also growing increasingly distraught about her future prospects. She had many important friends among jazz musicians — not only Kenny Clarke, but also Louis Armstrong, Nat "King" Cole, Thelonious Monk, Dizzy Gillespie, and Charlie "Bird" Parker and others. Even so, with only the most tenuous entree as a performer on the fringes of the jazz world, she had little practical reason to feel confident about her future. Carmen would later reflect that she had become "burnt out" in those days. Her friends worried about her.

Cecilia, Carmen's niece by her half-brother, Roy, recalled going to the McRae house in Brooklyn for dinner on Sundays — "the usual full-fledged dinner," Cecilia said about the West Indian tradition of Sunday meals. "I remember peas and rice, and ice cream after dinner, and the travel on the subways. And they had a female cousin who lived with them, probably Evadne's cousin, with a heavy accent," Cecilia recalled. "The kitchen was downstairs, perhaps in the basement, with grey and salmon-colored decorations, a huge kitchen fixed up very well, with a dining area on the same level. On the ground floor was a living room with an upright piano in it, and a bedroom. Upstairs were more bedrooms."

Cecilia saw Carmen at the Dean Street house only a few times. Though Carmen lived there, she was seldom at home. When she was home, she usually sat at the piano and sang. In Cecilia's memory, Carmen was "just starting out, mainly playing the piano, and singing on the side."

One night, when Carmen was struggling to find work in New York, a similarly struggling trumpeter named Johnny Parker was visiting a friend of Carmen's, Joan Shaw, a singer. Shaw's apartment on West 45th Street was next door to Snooky's, a bar and jazz club, and trumpeter Howard McGhee lived near. Many musicians used to stay in the little hotels on the street, getting by on very little money. Carmen called and talked about her stressful life for a while to Shaw. Shaw finally passed the phone to Parker, who had never met Carmen, though he had heard her sing and thought she was very good. He was sensitive to her situation; he shared it. Carmen told him about her career problems.

"Do you think I'll ever make it?" she asked.

Parker had his own career worries and was still chasing success. He had sat in with Billie Holiday at Snooky's. He had subbed in Duke Ellington's band. He had even hired tenor saxophonist Sonny Rollins and Thelonious Monk for a litle gig for $12 apiece in a club in Queens a few years earlier. Parker had once even tended foul-smelling elephants in a circus. He often didn't know where his next hotdog was coming from. But he said reassuringly to Carmen, "Sure you will, you'll be all right."

The conversation would stay in his mind for the rest of his life, especially because, soon after that talk, Carmen McRae began rising out of the rank and file of struggling musicians. Her first big boost came about through a fluke.

A Dutch accordionist, Mat Mathews, was looking for a singer for his little group. In 1952, he had arrived in the United States with his American wife, Paulette Rubinstein, an actress and songwriter, after having worked in North Africa for the American armed forces. In those days, he needed a sponsor to help him emigrate to the United States; Mathews found one among the American soldiers he had entertained in Tripoli. Not only did the soldiers like his music, but his troubles during the war years impressed them. He had worked for the Resistance in Holland, and when the Nazis discovered his activities, they picked him up and imprisoned him for a year and a half in a military police jail. Amazed that he had survived the torture of that period of his life, he suffered from terrifying dreams about it and often woke up in a panic for the rest of his life.

When they arrived in the U.S., Mat Mathews and Paulette Girard, an adaptation of her mother's maiden name, went to live in Brooklyn in her family's apartment. There, as Paulette recalled, Mathews felt timid about trying to form a group with American jazz musicians. He said that he played an unpopular instrument, the accordion, and that real jazz musicians would laugh at him. And he didn't think he played it well enough anyway. Paulette knew he was silly to doubt himself. He had an uncanny talent with the accordion.

Mathews applied for a musician's union card, which took six months to come through. During that time, he wasn't supposed to work steadily, only single-night jobs. Mathews knew Klook from Europe and they renewed their acquaintanceship in New York. Mathews also hung out in Birdland, then the pre-eminent jazz club in the world, where he met many other American musicians.

By the time Mathews's union card came through, he had formed a quintet with Klook, the bassist Percy Heath, guitarist Benny Weeks, and flutist and saxophonist Herbie Mann. But they needed a singer. Joe Glaser, Louis Armstrong's manager and head of Associated Booking Corporation, who booked Mathews's group for Birdland, sent Mathews to this little club, the Bandbox, in Brooklyn, to hear a singer with a dazzling range similar to the Peruvian Yma Sumac's.

Mathews was fairly impressed with the Bandbox, a decent-sized room which had a couple of bars and a dance floor. He liked the club more than he did the singer with the grand range. Then another singer came out: Carmen.

"She had split teeth, a gap beween her front teeth, and she was in her thirties or forties," Mathews remembered. "She sat down at the piano and played and sang, 'You're My Thrill.' And I fell on my ass. I said 'Holy shit, what is this?' and I went over to her. I asked her to join my little band as a soloist."[6]

Carmen said yes.

Mathews told Paulette about this "terrific" singer at the club. A good songwriter herself, Paulette went to hear her. She was also impressed. Carmen could still only play piano in two keys, and she had to sing her songs in one or the other. But, Paulette recalled, "She sounded only like herself, with an original, new sound."

Paulette told Mathews, "I'll bet she'll be very well-known. She'll make it."

Carmen went to work with Mathews's quintet at Birdland, but the owners didn't like her singing. "'What is this?' I asked the owners," Mathews said. "One day you are going to find out this is one of the best vocalists in the world bar none."

"She could hear a song and sing it right away. She was unbelievably musical. And she had very good musicians behind her," he said.

So Carmen McRae's painful odyssey was not quite over, even though she was making progress. Flutist and saxophonist Herbie Mann recalled that Mathews took the group on the road, playing in Buffalo, and at the Rouge Lounge in Detroit, Michigan, at the Blue Note in Chicago, and at the Blue Note in Philadelphia, among many clubs in other cities. One time in a Southern city, Mathews drank out of a fountain marked "Colored" instead of the fountain marked "Whites." A local got upset with him; Mathews was shocked and retorted that the water was the same color from both fountains. As a European, he had never had any experience with that kind of prejudice. Segregation puzzled and distressed him terribly.

In Detroit at the Rouge Lounge, Dave Usher, the record producer and a very close, lifelong friend of the trumpeter Dizzy Gillespie, heard Carmen singing with Mathews's group. Two friends had insisted Usher go with them to hear her; they thought she was great. Word of mouth was spreading, building a reputation for Carmen; this was always the way she would attract audiences and turn them into devoted fans. Usher loved her voice. He remembers that he saw her dressed up in an evening gown, with her hair upswept. (Dizzy became a devotee of Carmen's, too, and he and Usher shared their admiration for the polished, passionate singer.) Afterward, Usher's friends introduced him to her. He didn't recognize her at first, but she said, "Dave Usher, you know me!" Then he realized Carmen McRae was the woman he had known as Carmen Clarke, Klook's wife, who had played the piano for him back in Brooklyn in 1947.

Mat Mathews recalled that Charlie "Bird" Parker, a good friend of Carmen's from the days when she was totally unknown to the general public, was playing in Detroit at the Statler Hotel. Bird was supposed to play until 4 A.M., and Carmen and the Mathews Quintet finished their gig at 2 A.M., after which they would go to listen to Bird, the primary creator of bebop, every night. Bird was playing with a house rhythm section, but he wanted to play with Mathews's rhythm section, which included Klook and other "real heavyweights," Mathews said. So one night Bird arrived to play with Carmen and the Mathews Quintet, instead of going to his own gig at the Statler.

The group completed its tour and landed back in New York, home base. Mathews wanted to record with Carmen. As he recalled, he and Paulette took Carmen to a lyricist named Chuck Darwin, a Canadian with whom Paulette was collaborating as a songwriter. Darwin took Carmen to the Bethlehem label. They recorded in a studio on Broadway and 52nd Street, near the popular club, Basin Street, with Herbie Mann, Mundell Lowe, Wendell Marshall, and Klook. Yet another version of Carmen's first recordings comes from Herbie Mann. Fresh out of the Army in 1952 and looking for work, Mann, a tenor saxophone player, had a friend who played drums in a club next door to the Bandbox. The drummer knew that Mat Mathews was looking for the flutist, Sam Most, to record with Carmen. So the drummer told Mathews that Most was out of town and suggested he should use Mann instead.

The drummer then called Mann and asked: "Do you play jazz flute?"

Mann answered, "Now I do."

Mann owned a flute, because his teacher had told him that, to earn a living in the studios, he had to play all the woodwinds. So Mann had acquired the flute and used it to play the mambos and chachas popular in the early 1950s.

Prompted by this conversation, Mann called Mathews and said: "Of course I play jazz flute. But my flute's being repaired." At that time, Mann didn't play his flute often.

Mann learned the music on his tenor and clarinet, then tried to learn how to play it on the flute. He used both the tenor and the flute for the recordings on Venus, which came out later on the Bethlehem label ten-inch. Guitarist Mundell Lowe also played in the quintet accompanying Carmen. (Another guitarist, Benny Weeks, would tour with the group eventually.) Mathews recalls the Bethlehem recordings preceded Carmen's recordings for Stardust. And that's the reason that Len Frank never objected to Carmen's releases on the Bethlehem label; they were recorded first but released after she signed a contract with Frank's label, Stardust. Darwin may also have recorded Carmen for another little label, Venus Records.

It is unclear precisely which labels released and recorded these songs first. One of the early recordings was "If I'm Lucky," for which Paulette wrote the music and Darwin the lyrics. Carmen also sang "A Foggy Day" and "Tip Toe Gently," a composition by Paulette, this one done in collaboration with her husband Mathews. Some people remember these being among Carmen's Venus Records recordings, although Mathews remembers "A Foggy Day" as a Stardust label recording. Stardust was a little label being set up by Len "Zeke" Frank, a wealthy businessman.

Len Frank became very interested in Carmen as soon as he heard her sing. Carmen really helped him start his label in 1953. According to American critic James Goodrich, Carmen had cut "Tip Toe Gently" for the Bethlehem label, not Stardust.[7] It may be that Carmen recorded a version for Stardust, too. What is clear is that there is some confusion about Carmen's early recording career. The official discographies did try to straighten out which songs she did when and for what labels.

According to Bill Simon, a well-known journalist and saxophonist, Chuck Darwin recorded Carmen on Bethlehem, and the recordings she had done for Venus and Stardust, which had come out as single records, were released on a ten-inch long-playing record by Bethlehem in 1954. One of the songs on that LP was called "Misery," which clarinetist Tony Scott originally wrote for Billie Holiday. Billie didn't record it, however, and so Scott gave it to Carmen; he had heard Carmen sing at Minton's. When Billie learned that Tony had given the song away, Billie screamed, "You gave my song to that bitch!" But it wasn't really a problem, for all of them were friends. That was simply the way Billie talked. Simon recalled hearing Billie sing the song at one of the clubs on 52nd Street in 1954 or 1955.

Mathews recalled taking Carmen's recordings to disk jockey Jazzbo Collins in 1953, who played them for a half-hour straight on the radio. "She got all kinds of phone calls and then she got a contract at Basin Street," Mathews said. "But 'A Foggy Day' really made it. That sent her off in 1953." Whatever the actual sequence, the variety of memories lends an air of mystery to Carmen's earliest recording ventures. They were neither greatly chronicled, nor heralded, nor pub-licized, though they were significant within the jazz world.

Carmen later recollected some of the circumstances of her early days as a recording artist. Len Frank was a millionaire businessman, she said, who dabbled in recording. Mathews wanted Carmen to record with his group, and Len Frank became smitten with her singing from the moment he first heard her. He told her she was the singer he had been looking for all his life, the person who could inspire him to start his own record label at last.

"I thought he was crazy," Carmen recalled. But she was thrilled to help start his little label. "And we made records upon records upon records," she said. What happened to them, if they were so numerous, is unknown. These recordings were made approximately between 1953 and 1954, though exact dates are unclear.

It was to *Down Beat* magazine a few years later that she would confide she had been feeling "burnt out" when she first returned to New York. Len Frank's atten-tion came at the right moment. But after she started recording for Frank, she became fraught with angst for another reason. Frank didn't like her professional image and tried to give her the Pygmalion treatment. "It was terrible," she told *Down Beat.* "He was completely remaking me into something I wasn't. I just couldn't take it anymore."[8]

Bill Simon recalled that Len Frank signed Carmen to some kind of "crazy" contract and tried to control every aspect of her life. Simon thought Frank treated Carmen with condescension. He told her how to dress and whom to socialize with. "She bristled," recalled Simon. "It was not a happy relationship."

Simon was friendly with bandleader Larry Elgart and knew that Elgart got an orchestra together. Charlie Albertine, who invented the Elgart band's sound, wrote the string arrangements for a recording session with Carmen for the Stardust label. Larry Elgart played an alto sax solo for the session, too. By the time the musicians did the last recording, Carmen was tired from the long day's work; furthermore, Len Frank, unable to achieve a good balance for the last song, "Along About This Time Last Year" written by Bill Simon, may not have done an adequate job of recording it. Len Frank was angry and frustrated after the long day of work; that track never came out. In any case, the bright singer nearing middle age hadn't had to tolerate the usurpation of her autonomy by Len Frank at Stardust for long. She went on tour with the Mathews Quintet soon after, and was in continuous demand from 1954 on for nightclub engagements. With the Mathews Quintet, she toured the East and Midwest for a year and a half, until 1955. Then she traveled with other groups. Stardust eventually went out of business. Nonetheless, her relationship with Len Frank had given her yet another lesson in the value of maintaining independence of thought and not letting anyone tell her what to do. She would become virtually a fanatic about that as time went on.

Carmen's first records with Stardust, Bethlehem, and Venus reached a limited number of people. But they were important people in jazz circles and in Jazzbo Collins's radio audience. In those days, she was singing with a soft voice and a straightforward sound, clearly under the influence of Billie Holiday's phrasing, timing, and storytelling talents, yet with her own fresh voice, true intonation, and artful improvisatory instincts for her choices of notes. Her style was also informed by her knowledge of the piano that she studied as a pre-teen, she would later tell Marian McPartland on McPartland's show, *Piano Jazz*.

In 1982, McPartland would ask Carmen, "Did you always do that? Were you always able to improvise? It's like a horn within the song."

Carmen would answer, "It comes from playing an instrument. You just automatically do that, if you sing, I think — automatically improvise when you sing."[9]

Carmen used plenty of subtle vibrato in the 1950s, when she still had a youthful sound; her voice was high and feminine, and her lines stretched out like colorful streams of candy ribbon. Her sound would darken and flatten out as she grew older. Carmen herself would always think that her voice was at its best for her early recordings — or so she said late in her life.[10]

The lightly distributed first recordings helped her land a regular job as an intermission pianist and singer at Minton's Playhouse in 1953. She had definitely intrigued the leader of the house band, clarinetist Tony Scott, who knew who Carmen was and how well she could sing and play. Scott recalled that Klook had introduced Carmen and Scott, probably as early as the 1940s.

Joan Shaw, Carmen's friend, was singing at Minton's Playhouse in 1953, with Tony Scott's band which consisted of pianist Dick Katz, bassist Milt Hinton, and drummer Osie Johnson.

Shaw decided to go to England, where she changed her name to Salena Jones, combining the first names of Sally Blair and Lena Horne, two of her favorite singers. Carmen took over the job as intermission pianist and singer at Minton's. For a while Carmen and Joan may even have worked at Minton's at the same time. When Joan left for England, Tony wanted Carmen to sing regularly with his band.

An emotional, driving musician and a gregarious man, Scott insisted that Carmen get off the piano bench and stand up to sing at the microphone. She was terrified at the thought. It meant she would have to depend upon the musicians behind her to play the right things at the right moment to support and enhance her. The best singers always know what they want for accompaniment. Carmen was used to supplying exactly the right notes for herself at the piano.

At first she said no to Scott, but he insisted: "You have to do it."

Scott nagged and cajoled Carmen until she tried it reluctantly — and found her true vocation. Standing at the microphone with nothing familiar to do with her hands challenged her. "I knew just what to do vocally ... [but] I didn't know what to do with my hands. I wanted to cut them off," she later explained to Marian McPartland on *Piano Jazz*.

Carmen began to get a following who went to hear her sing with Scott's band. Harry Belafonte arrived several times a week for them. Sugar Ray Robinson, the boxer, became a fan. "Carmen was sensational," recalled Bill Simon. Mat Mathews remembered that Ella Fitzgerald and Sarah Vaughan went to hear Carmen sing at some of her gigs. They admired and supported her. Carmen and Scott would always remember how they had conferred about her standing up; how he had virtually forced her to position herself in a way to become a star.

Pianist Dick Katz, just starting his career in New York, recalled his days of playing in Tony Scott's house band at Minton's in 1953 and 1954. For this he at first earned about $65 a week. They worked Mondays through Saturdays, from 10 P.M. to 4 A.M., except on fight nights. "We would have been killed if we started playing before the fights were over on TV," Katz recollected. Other sidemen who passed through the house band after Milt Hinton and Osie Johnson left were bassist Earl May and drummer Philly Joe Jones. Johnny Mandell, also just beginning his career as an arranger and musician, went to Minton's in February, 1953, recorded the house group without Carmen in it, and sold the recording to Bob Thiele, who put it out as a ten-inch LP, *Music After Midnight*, on the Brunswick label.

Carmen always did one tune accompanying herself at the piano; otherwise she stood up at the microphone, which was set on the floor in front of the bandstand, bassist Earl May remembered. Other performers were a female shake dancer and the tap dancer Baby Lawrence; most musicians regarded him as the best of all the tap dancers. One night the tap dancers — Teddy Hale, Baby

Lawrence, and Bill Bailey, singer Pearl Bailey's brother, who later became a minister — dueled. The duel was talked about for months before it took place. Katz admired how well Osie Johnson, for one, could play for dancers. Hale did many types of acrobatics, but Baby Lawrence performed completely with his feet. They called him "Bird on his feet," referring to Charlie "Bird" Parker. And Lawrence won the duel.[11]

Another night, at a jam session, Katz was bumped off the piano bench by Bud Powell. "It was an honor to be bumped by Powell," Katz said. "He was out of his mind, but he sat down and played countless choruses of 'I Got Rhythm' or 'Crazy Rhythm' — something like that — and almost never played the bridge. He was a demon. He was gone."[12]

On Monday nights, Katz didn't play as much as he usually did, because so many pianists showed up to jam. Horn players came in droves, too. Jimmy Heath recalled a tenor saxophonist who often arrived to jam but couldn't play very well. The other horn players nicknamed him "the demon," with the opposite implication from Katz's sobriquet for Bud Powell. Every time "the demon" stood up to play, the other horn players jumped up to play, too, and prevented him from playing. Eddie "Lockjaw" Davis, Dizzy Gillespie, trumpeter Harry "Sweets" Edison, and others blocked him. But "the demon" kept coming.

Most of all, the musicians remembered the ineffable spirit of the club and the great pleasure and pride they felt about playing at Minton's — the cradle of the progressive jazz revolution. The bar had rose-colored lights shining down on the bottles and the drinkers; the back room housed the bandstand positioned against the rear wall.

A Harlem artist had painted a mural behind the bandstand in 1947 or 1948. Richard Ellison, famous for his book, *The Invisible Man*, described the mural in his article. "Minton's":

"Above the bandstand there later appeared a mural depicting a group of jazz men holding a jazz session in a narrow Harlem bedroom. While an exhausted girl with shapely legs sleeps on her stomach in a big brass bed, the musicians bend to their music in a quiet concatenation of unheard sound: A trumpeter, a guitarist, a clarinetist, a drummer; their only audience a small, cockeared dog. The clarinetist is white. The guitarist strums with an enigmatic smile. The trumpet is muted. The barefooted drummer, beating a folded newspaper with whiskbrooms in lieu of a drum, stirs the eye's ear like a blast of brasses in a midnight street. A bottle of port rests on a dresser, but it, like the girl, is ignored. The artist, Charles Graham, adds mystery to, as well as illumination within, the scene by having them play by the light of a kerosene lamp. The painting, executed in a harsh documentary style reminiscent of W.P.A. art, conveys a feeling of musical effort caught in timeless and unrhetorical suspension, the sad remoteness of a scene observed through a wall of crystal."[13]

That mural, supposedly depicting guitarist Charlie Christian, a major attraction at the club in the early 1940s, and the white clarinetist Tony Scott, who played at Minton's even before he led the house band in the early 1950s, would remain intact on that rear wall long after Minton's closed, and for the rest of the century. When jazz was declared a national treasure, and the Cecil Hotel, including Minton's, an historic landmark on September 18, 1985, the mural was included in that proclamation. It seemed as if the mural would be assured of a future as long as Minton's would stand. But by the 1990s, long after Minton's closed, plans to renovate the building had to be scrapped, because the building was too unstable; it couldn't be renovated, and the future for the mural seems shaky, too.

Katz recalled that Carmen could sing in any key. She was slender — "a beautiful woman just to look at," he said. "She had a nice smile." He also noticed that she already had a terrific temper. "And she never apologized. Sometimes at Minton's she would complain about anything, some technical thing, the wrong chord. We were all young, and we were learning. There were a lot of personal dynamics. But I cherish the memories."

After Carmen's recordings for the Stardust label came out, her recordings of 1954 for Bethlehem were released: Bethlehem was a separate company from Decca. Carmen was not yet signed to Decca.

Paulette Girard found Carmen a gig at a small club in the West 40s and an accompanist, Don Abney. Abney accompanied Carmen off and on in the 1950s. (The first mention of Carmen recording with Don Abney as her accompanist was in 1958 for Decca, and she recorded and toured with Ray Bryant as her accompanist before then, but this doesn't mean she wasn't working with Don Abney in live performances in the early and mid-1950s.) At the time Paulette was promoting Carmen, she was also auditioning for a play called *The Seven Year Itch*. When Paulette was called to appear in the New York company of the play, with Tom Ewell and Vanessa Brown, she couldn't have been happier, yet she still hung out with Carmen. Once, in an after-hours club, they were talking together in a group, and Carmen said that some unpleasantness going on in someone's life had its basis in racial prejudice. Paulette was unwilling to accept that such a thing could be so, and she said, "Bullshit, that shouldn't make any difference." Carmen looked askance at Paulette and said, "Where have you been?" Carmen told Paulette she wasn't as aware as she should have been.

Paulette went on with her career as an actress and songwriter. After *The Seven Year Itch* she would appear in *The Boyfriend*, and she would drift away from songwriting, primarily because she was never able to collect royalties for her songs. She also became disenchanted about writing liner notes for albums, because she got very little pay for her work.

After *The Boyfriend* closed, Paulette found herself in dire need of money. In the days when she had been helping Carmen, Paulette had never taken any money from Carmen. During a lunch they had together, when Paulette was broke,

Carmen handed Paulette a $100 bill. That was a lot of money in those days. Carmen said, "Don't worry, everything will be okay. I don't want this back until you've paid off every debt you ever had. Keep this money until you're in the clear totally." Paulette was very touched by Carmen's kindness.

Years later, Paulette discovered that someone else may have taken all the royalties for her songs and not told her that they were due her. It was the sort of fiasco that many people in music, including Carmen in various ways, had to suffer through at times.

One of the branch people working for Decca Records in Philadelphia told Milt Gabler, in charge of pop artists and repertoire for Decca Records in New York, to go to listen to Carmen performing with the Mathews Quintet in a club in Philadelphia. On this tour, the band stopped at the Streamliner in Chicago, again at the Rouge Lounge in Detroit, the Tia Juana in Baltimore, and the Showboat in Philadelphia. "She's wonderful," the branch man reported to Gabler.

Gabler recalled years later, "I went to hear her, and I signed her to record for Decca. She was a natural follow-up to Billie Holiday and Ella Fitzgerald. And then after that, Joe Glaser, who had the agency, Associated Booking Corporation, took her on. And Oscar Cohen at that agency became her manager. Carmen was an intelligent gal, with a great sounding voice, and I signed her to have that quality. She had a beautiful voice and the feeling for jazz and show tunes and stuff like that. She was nice looking; she was easy enough to work with. I never had any problem with her or any of the acts I recorded from Bing Crosby on down to Sammy Davis, Jr., and Roy Eldridge."[14]

Paulette Girard recalled that she took Carmen to Bob Thiele, then at Coral Records, a subsidiary of Decca Records. Although it may be possible that Thiele had also called Gabler's attention to Carmen, Gabler didn't recall it that way. Decca also owned Brunswick, which had been acquired from Columbia, but Brunswick was eventually sold to someone else. Around the time that Brunswick was sold, Decca started the Coral label. Bob Thiele offered Carmen a contract at Coral.

They did make an album called *Carmen McRae: Here To Stay* on the Coral label, or MCA Coral, including the songs "Love Is Here To Stay," "How Many Stars Have to Shine?" "Sometimes I'm Happy," "I Can't Get Started," "Just One Of Those Things," "My One and Only Love," "I'll Remember April," "You Took Advantage of Me," "Until The Real Thing Comes Along," and "A Room With a View." However, Dennis Brown's discography, but not Lord's, mentions the Coral recording date for Carmen as 1955. There's no year mentioned on the extant album cover. A friend of Dizzy Gillespie, Dave Usher, agrees with Mat Mathews that Carmen had her first hit with the song "A Foggy Day," which he believed he heard on the Coral Label, although the MCA Coral release doesn't list it; instead, the discographers say it came out earlier on the Venus label. Mat Mathews recalled it from even before then, probably as a Stardust recording.

Decca used its own small studio at 50 West 57th Street, then the World Broadcasting Studio at 711 Fifth Avenue, and then the Pythian Temple on 70th Street, an old ballroom with very good acoustics, excellent for recording Carmen singing with an orchestra. She was far from her days as a solo act. Decca gave her the full production treatment with strings. Her career had become a heady affair, and she loved it. Gabler produced all her recordings for both Decca and MCA, which bought Decca. (At that time, MCA was not a recording label, but an agency.) Gabler recalled that he was inspired by Joe Glaser's bookings of Carmen. "I wanted someone with that much voice and talent to be with us," he said.

There was a hitch about her recording for Decca at first. Len Frank of Stardust objected to her doing so, and he held a contract on her. Len Frank would eventually become angry with her when she decided to sign a contract with Decca. And, Bill Simon theorized, Frank may have hidden or destroyed some of her Stardust recordings. But she did sing such songs as "In Love In Vain," "Autumn Nocturne," "A Foggy Day," and "Wanting You" for Stardust, and they survived. Bill Simon recalled that the recordings, such as "In Love In Vain," for Stardust had been wonderful. When Stardust had a conflict about Carmen going to record for Decca, Decca finally extricated her from the Stardust contract, whose terms, Simon recalled, had been unfair to her. Once she left Stardust's contract behind, Frank, who owned the record company, the pressing plant, and the recording studio, withdrew Carmen's records from the market and never did anything commercial with them.

Among her first Decca releases were her 1954 recording of "If I'm Lucky," coupled with "Ooh! What'cha Doin' To Me," "Keep Me in Mind," and "They All Laughed." In 1955, she made a highly publicized recording with Sammy Davis, Jr. and the Jack Pleis Orchestra, pairing "A Fine Romance" with "I Go For You." "Both sides come as listenable, humorous music and are excellent exhibits of two great talents at work together," wrote James Goodrich.[15]

Sammy Davis, Jr. said he thought Carmen was a "fantastic" singer and predicted: "If good singing comes back, Carmen has got to be the biggest star that ever happened." Ella Fitzgerald heard Carmen's recordings and said, "She just kills me. She sings with so much heat, so much feeling. She's my girl." And Carol Channing, a Broadway musical comedy star in *Gentlemen Prefer Blondes,* went backstage to see Carmen in a club one night, probably Basin Street in New York City, and told her: "You've got a haunt in your voice. You'll go far." Nobody asked where the haunting sound had come from. Nobody delved very far into her memories of the years of personal and private uncertainties, when she had accepted minuscule fees in exchange for the largesse of her artistry.

With the Mat Mathews Quintet, including Klook, on *Here To Stay,* produced on the Coral label in 1955, Carmen proved herself a thorough-going child of bebop. And on the album *By Special Request* recorded in 1955, also with the Mat

Mathews Quintet, she was finally headed toward the mainstream clubs whose sophisticated audiences had money and influence. Carmen was always mistress of the arts of tasteful, intelligent, meaningful phrasing, storytelling, and improvisation. She sang Charlie Parker's "Yardbird Suite" on *By Special Request* along with an Ellington-Strayhorn tune, "Something To Live For," with Strayhorn at the piano, and the Mathews Quintet. Strayhorn happened to be in the studio when she was recording his tune; he wound up on the album by a mere fluke — he simply asked if he could sit in. The pairing was brilliant. On another song, Dick Katz played piano; on "Suppertime" Carmen accompanied herself. These early recordings strongly suggest the way Carmen must have sounded at Minton's and before that, at the Bandbox, and probably in Chicago, too. Though her voice and style would mature and gain in sophistication, drama, grittiness, and bite as the years went by, her interpretation of "Sometimes I'm Happy, Sometimes I'm Blue," on *By Special Request*, was as alluring as any song she would ever do.

In 1954, Carmen was voted Best New Female Singer of the year in *Down Beat* magazine's annual critics poll. Then *Metronome* magazine gave her the Singer of the Year Award in a tie with Ella Fitzgerald — "one of the biggest thrills," Carmen would comment years later.[16] She never forgot the victory. When she learned about it, as she was performing in Toronto, she finally realized that she had arrived. If any singer realized how much harder a woman had to work than a man did, and how tenaciously she must swim against the tide, it was Carmen, on her own, years before any women's liberation movement existed to offer her moral support or encouragement. She didn't begin as a tough person, "but she learned how to be tough," Herbie Mann would reflect about her metamorphosis from a basically sweet woman into a very tough one, "because a woman has to be twice as tough as a man in the business, because it's tough."

Critics never lingered on the twists and turns Carmen went through for survival. When she recorded a single for Decca in 1955 pairing "Come On, Come In" and "The Next Time It Happens," a Rodgers and Hammerstein ballad, James Goodrich simply wrote about her *fait accompli* — the successful face she presented to the world: "She swings on just about everything and is never dull."

By 1954, Carmen was known nationally as a celebrated, stand-up singer. She appeared on the most popular television shows of the era, Ed Sullivan's *The Toast of the Town* on CBS TV, and Steve Allen's *Tonight Show* on NBC TV, and with Teddy Wilson on the CBS radio show, *On a Sunday Afternoon*.

After she began to appear in such nationally known clubs as Basin Street in New York, a leading jazz critic, Leonard Feather, wrote that Carmen soon found herself in a position of prestige comparable to that enjoyed a decade earlier by Sarah Vaughan. Feather did not mention that Carmen would never forget how much harder and longer she had struggled than any other highly lauded woman singer/pianist of her era. Like most critics, he simply basked in the reflected glory of her stardom. Critics said her vocal inflections and improvisations on melodies were exciting; they called her the freshest talent they had heard since Sarah Vaughan.

Sarah also was an accomplished pianist. Some predicted that Carmen would eventually become more lionized for her piano playing. "That will be real cool, man, real cool," she said. But she intended to strive for a lasting place as a "cool" singer, she said. *Hue* magazine in January, 1955, hailed her as the newest "cool" singer in the bebop generation.

On March 12, 1955, Carmen was featured in a Carnegie Hall All-Star Jazz Concert. She was in elite company, with such people as baritone saxophonist Gerry Mulligan, by then a star for his cool jazz group started in California, and others featured on the bill. She performed "Yardbird Suite" written by Charlie "Bird" Parker, who had been so pivotal in the creation of bebop, while he lay dying across town in the Stanhope Hotel. Out of affection for Bird and respect for bebop, she later included the song on *By Special Request* recorded in June, 1955. It was that sort of anecdote that intrigued critics and their readers, while the story of Carmen's lonely climb held less allure for them, even though the journey would always remain a powerful element in her mind.

Climaxing a series of successes, Carmen left for Hollywood to sing with Mat Mathews's group in a Tony Curtis movie, *The Square Jungle*, 1955, at Universal International Studios. The composer, Henry Mancini, called Mathews in New York and asked him, "Can you play hot?" Mathews said yes, so when Mathews was called to Hollywood he took Carmen with him. The group for the movie included Johnny Miller, the bassist in the Nat "King" Cole trio, and Irving Ashby, the guitarist who followed Oscar Moore into the Cole trio; both of them had left Cole by the 1950s. Others in *The Square Jungle* were Paul Kelly and Ernest Borgnine. Carmen and Mathews stayed in Hollywood only briefly, and then went back on the road.

For Mathews, the traveling became burdensome. "I got fed up with the traveling and the jazz joints," he would recall, "only black joints. I was the only one who was white, and my band was black. We didn't make any money really." On the bright side, he became friendly with great musicians — Dizzy, Monk, bassist Oscar Pettiford, everybody on the scene in those days. "Yeah, those were the days, we didn't think they'd ever end. I was young. Carmen was fun. We laughed a lot."

Jack O'Brien, a columnist for the New York newspaper, the *Journal-American*, was so impressed by her, he wrote in his column that he had called Joe Glaser, Carmen's booker, to urge him to take Carmen on as a client. This tale is apocryphal, since it was Mat Mathews who had earlier taken Carmen to Joe Glaser after hearing her sing in the Bandbox in Brooklyn in 1952. But O'Brien's tale — a press agent's dream — was the one that circulated at the time. Even if he wasn't responsible for obtaining Carmen's booking agent for her, O'Brien must have discussed his admiration for Carmen with Glaser. And with his column, O'Brien certainly both called the public's attention to her and underscored it.

According to O'Brien's tale, Carmen went to Glaser's office and sat in the waiting room, planning to ask him to take her on, while Glaser was on the phone in his office, culling through all his connections by telephone, trying to find her in the big city. He wanted to bring her in for an audition. When he finally discovered Carmen sitting right in his office, she auditioned for him. Because she was so nervous, she sang very badly. He was pretty puzzled about what all the fuss was over Carmen McRae.

After a little pause, Carmen began singing again, and this time she convinced Glaser she was the singer he had been hearing about. Oscar Cohen of Associated Booking Corporation immediately took on the assignment of booking her. He later confirmed that O'Brien's version of Carmen's meeting with the men at A.B.C. wasn't true. Carmen would never have wandered into Glaser's office on her own. She wasn't that naive and knew she needed an introduction. And if she hadn't been nervous in front of Duke Ellington, she certainly wouldn't have quaked or quavered for Joe Glaser.

However, O'Brien's column was good publicity. Carmen's income had risen from less than $100 a week to about $1,000 a week for night club engagements in 1955. For a national tour that year in November, she earned $2,500 a week, traveling in the company of the Dave Brubeck Quartet, the Gerry Mulligan Sextet, and the Australian Jazz Quartet. She appeared on Steve Allen's *Tonight* show seven times. Her annual income that year was $50,000, and the prediction was that she would earn $150,000 from all sources in 1956.

Ebony magazine called her "the fastest rising and easily most promising female popular singer in America ... a chunky, casual, delightfully untemperamental woman...." Only the accolade of "untemperamental" was patently ridiculous. It was true, however, that she had come from "practically nowhere" to "challenge the leadership of Sarah Vaughan and Ella Fitzgerald."[17]

Carmen began hobnobbing with opera stars and CBS executives, with whom she was photographed for newspapers and magazines. The photographs show her face aglow with serenity and triumph in the rarefied atmosphere of stardom.

But Carmen had climbed alone and arduously for so long that the delayed stardom had served several practical purposes — to give her perspective on how tough life could be, how chancy, chaotic, and demanding show business was, and how much authority she wanted over her own life and career. It would be a point of pride with her forever that she would emphasize good songs with lyrics which she could handle in a way that communicated her understanding of life's experiences. She did not let stardom turn everything upside down for her.

Ebony suggested that Carmen's allegiance to the hip sound of bebop had slowed her rise. Friends and colleagues would always think Carmen remained mindful of her struggles during the years when Sarah and Ella had reigned as jazz singing stars, and Carmen could only look up from her tenuous position in nowhere.

Carmen never liked singing any old popular song that was handed to her. Eventually she would insist on making her own choices about her material. But since she didn't suddenly, or ever, come up with a million-selling hit, Carmen had to keep convincing people to be her fans day by day, gig by gig. Once they heard her sing they became loyal fans, ready to be charmed by anything she sang. They trusted her to be impeccable and exciting.

In 1955, Carmen told James Goodrich, the American critic for *Storyville* magazine in Britain, "My style hasn't changed because I can't sing any other way than how I feel. As for now, I intend to keep on singing the way I feel. And though I'll do some pops in appearances and on records, I'll sing only the current ones if I think they're good."[18]

Carmen was very well schooled in the chord changes, Goodrich noticed. "Sure I sing changes and always have," she told him. "But I stick pretty close to the melody so that if someone walked into a room halfway through a performance, he'd know what the tune was." Goodrich also mentioned that Carmen had her own ideas about how far afield a singer should go in phrasing a melody. "Certainly you bring your own ideas to a song when you interpret. But it's only fair to the composer to have his ideas heard, too. After all, the reason you choose to sing a tune is because you think it's pretty. At least, that should be the reason."

Carmen was in continuous demand from 1954 on for nightclub engagements. With Mathews, she toured the East and Midwest for a year and a half. Then she traveled with other groups.

Associated Booking Corporation put out a publicity package on Carmen, including the comment by Carol Channing that Carmen had a "haunt" in her voice. Proving how firmly she had arrived, Carmen was given the traditional "Blindfold Test" by Leonard Feather in his column for *Metronome* magazine that presented records to famous musicians and asked them to identify who was playing and rate their performances; eventually the column moved over to *Down Beat*. The column ran on May 18, 1955, and showed how acute Carmen's hearing was and how wide-ranging her knowledge of the contemporary music scene.

For one arrangement played by Stan Kenton's band, she said: "The arrangement is such a hollering and screaming thing that it doesn't move me at all.... I like to listen to more subdued things." For Peggy Lee's recording of "How Bitter, My Sweet," on the Decca label, Carmen praised Lee — "the most wonderful Peggy Lee." She awarded it four stars "because it's Peggy." She recognized Al Hibbler on a Decca recording of "Daybreak" and said he was one of her favorite male singers; the recording was so soulful that she gave it five stars. She caught

Paul Desmond playing a little flat, or so she said, on "Soon" released by Fantasy. She mistook Betty St. Claire for Annie Ross and praised Annie's song "Twisted" but didn't like this recording of "Out Of Nowhere" and gave it only two stars. It's interesting that Carmen liked Annie's singing at all and mentioned it for the "Blindfold Test," because it was Annie Ross who had a son by her affair with Klook in Paris in 1948, just as his marriage to Carmen was ending. But Carmen seemed to bear Annie no ill will. Carmen and Annie met previously in New York, when Annie first arrived in 1952, and the women had cordial relations. If Carmen had any feelings of anger toward Annie, she didn't reveal them at this time. And Annie admired Carmen's singing, which Klook had introduced her to. Carmen accurately identified Mahalia Jackson singing "Walk All Over God's Heaven" on a Columbia release and criticized it only for the accompaniment, which made the spiritual sound like a rhythm and blues song. That assessment was quite accurate; Carmen's ears and taste didn't fail her. Critics would often offer the same criticism about Mahalia's commercial recordings for Columbia. Carmen knew King Pleasure was singing "I'm Gone" on a Prestige release, and Louis Armstrong was paired with Gary Crosby on "Struttin' With Some Barbecue" on Decca. "Ha! Ha!" she laughed. "That's a cute record." She thought Armstrong sounded like his "old self," meaning that he didn't sound purposefully commercial, and that Crosby did a fine job: She gave the record four stars.

Carmen didn't like Jaye P. Morgan's version of "Softly, Softly" at all and said she would give it four stars if it was supposed to be a commercial record, but since it wasn't, and she didn't like the song, she was giving it no stars. "I don't know what's happening with that one," she said in her no-frills, decisive way. She also gave no stars to a recording of "Ooky Ook," a song on Mercury by Lola Dee. She couldn't understand the lyrics on this rhythm and blues record, and "I just have no feeling for it whatever," she summed up bluntly.

Never one to mince words, Carmen would become increasingly blunt in the future, often unconcerned about whose feelings she hurt. There were times when she would give minus-stars in later blindfold tests about songs she heard, some of them performed by her famous friends. They were often aghast. But she didn't pause to reflect upon her effect. Ms. McRae was developing into a mercurial woman, by turns a charmer and a terror.

Much of the information in this chapter comes from personal interviews with Billy Taylor, Norval Perkins, Milt Gabler, Dick Katz, Bill Simon, Herbie Mann, Mat Mathews, Cecilia McRae, and Johnny Parker.
[1] From an interview with Carmen McRae by Leslie Gourse in 1993.
[2] From an interview with Carmen McRae by Leslie Gourse in 1990.
[3] "Carmen McRae," from *Notes and Tones: Musician to Musician Interviews,* edited by Arthur Taylor (New York: Perigee Books, G.P. Putnam's Sons, 1977).

[4] McPartland, Marian, "Interview with Carmen McRae," *Piano Jazz* (National Public Radio, recorded 1982, released 1985).

[5] From an interview with Carmen McRae by Leslie Gourse in 1993.

[6] From an interview with Mat Mathews by Leslie Gourse in 2000.

[7] Goodrich, James, "On the Records," *Storyville* (1955).

[8] McRae, Carmen, *Down Beat* (*c.* May 18, 1955).

[9] McPartland, op. cit.

[10] From an interview with Carmen McRae by Leslie Gourse in 1993.

[11] From an interview with Dick Katz by Leslie Gourse in 1993.

[12] Ibid.

[13] Ellison, Ralph , "The Birth of Bebop," *Esquire* (1952), reprinted in *Esquire* (January, 1959), reprinted in a similar form as "Minton's," in the anthology *Reading Jazz*, edited by Robert Gottlieb (New York: Pantheon Books, 1996).

[14] From an interview with Milt Gabler by Leslie Gourse in 2000.

[15] Goodrich, op. cit.

[16] From an interview with Carmen McRae by Leslie Gourse in 1993.

[17] From an article in *Ebony* (February, 1956). The author was unspecified.

CHAPTER FOUR

Touring

By 1956, booked by Oscar Cohen at A.B.C., Carmen was leading her own groups on the road. Pianist Ray Bryant joined her group in Philadelphia for an engagement at the Blue Note, the city's leading jazz club. The group's bassist was Ike Isaacs, a tall, handsome man from Akron, Ohio, with whom Carmen was enjoying a love affair. "The ladies loved him," Bryant noticed. Ike was as much in love with Carmen as she was with him. They were personally and musically compatible, Bryant observed. During these years, Carmen's career was becoming firmly established, and she began to feel the demands and responsibilities of leadership and stardom more than ever. On the road, she had to maintain discipline, keep all kinds of people from trying to take advantage of her, and uphold her standards for the quality of her music and performances.

The good reviews that she received for her Decca albums, such as *Torchy!*, recorded in 1955, prompted audiences to turn out for her live performances. Though Carmen herself felt she sounded best in clubs, reviewers didn't necessarily agree with her; they praised the flow of her lines, her time, her clear enunciation, and her understanding of lyrics as recorded on her records. The eminent critic Leonard Feather extolled her "voice that is at once gentle and authoritative, sweet and self-confident, tender and firm."[1] Other reviewers didn't think her voice had exceptional quality, but with her taste and musicianship she had honed it into an instrument with a warm tone. That was the dominant impression of her quality at that time.

Carmen's group, with Bryant and Isaacs, left Philadelphia to go to Milwaukee, then to the Newport Jazz Festival in Rhode Island, and on to Cleveland's Cotton Club, and clubs in Pittsburgh and Kansas City, for week-long stays in some places, longer gigs in others. In those days, the long gig was the norm.

In October, 1956, Carmen settled into Mister Kelly's in Chicago for a four-week engagement. A critic for the *Saturday Review* wrote a review that hinted at Carmen's moodiness and sensitivity to her surroundings. He found her first set in the club "tinged with frigidity, uncomfortable restraint, uneasiness, and even appreciable straining for crucial intervals," he wrote. He knew she had already gone on record as saying she preferred small clubs, because, she said: "There's a chance for coldness in big places." It wasn't the size of Mister Kelly's, "a reasonably tight little island," as the critic wrote, that was to blame. It was simply Carmen's uneasiness in her manner for the opening set of her opening night, but she included some fine songs from her current Decca LPs — "I'm Putting All My Eggs in One Basket," "My Foolish Heart," "Nowhere," "My Future Just Passed," and "Just One of Those Things." "That was the *cool* set," the reviewer wrote.[2]

Once she warmed up, Carmen charged through an exciting version of "A Foggy Day," declaiming the lyrics with her arrestingly eccentric phrasing, to wrest every drop of meaning from the song. She swung "Blue Moon," and communicated the heartache of "Good Morning, Heartache," italicizing that key word with her emphasis of its separate syllables. By the time she reached "They All Laughed," Carmen was operating at the zenith of her storytelling abilities. When she took over the piano bench to accompany herself in a solo performance of "Stardust," the reviewer noted: "Her honest, unadorned approach ... made the tune more lustrous reality than legend. Her forceful piano (for she had a percussive push in her style) helped make 'Lush Life' impressive." She closed the set with an exhilarating interpretation of "Exactly Like You." And "After an obviously chilly beginning, Carmen relaxed and realized that home is where the feeling is," the reviewer summed up.

Ray Bryant made some historic recordings with Carmen, among them her hit recording of "Skyliner," played by every jazz and pop disk jockey in the country, and the first recording of "Guess Who I Saw Today?," which became even more famous when Nancy Wilson recorded it in May, 1961, but always remained emblematic of Carmen's charisma as a storyteller. She sang it throughout her career for audiences that always cheered her. Her strong voice soared and thrilled her fans.

By the time Carmen got to Birdland, "the jazz corner of the world," for her first booking there in the spring of 1957, her fans packed the tables and the peanut gallery to hear her sing "Skyliner" in person. The audience cheered her performance, though her voice had begun to lower and darken with age, use, and the consequences of smoking. This gig at Birdland was a great accomplishment. It signalled that Carmen had arrived at the top of her profession.

Carmen, Bryant, and Isaacs also played the Town Tavern, a leading jazz club in Toronto, and several other rooms there, before traveling south to Dallas, Texas in 1957. There, Ray Bryant recalled, they were booked to play in a big supper club, but they weren't allowed to mix with the white customers. Furthermore, when they walked down the street, they saw water fountains marked "Whites Only." That was Ray's first experience of what he called "that kind of shit." Coming from Philadelphia, a northern city where there were no such signs, Ray would always recall, "That's enough to upset you." Carmen had seen those racist signs before, when she had gone south to marry Klook and later when she had toured with Mat Mathews, so she wasn't as shocked as Bryant was.

Bryant played for Carmen from 1956 to 1958. During that time, she and Ike Isaacs got married, with Bryant serving as their best man. He couldn't remember exactly where the ceremony took place, but Marge Costa, Carmen's long-time friend from their teenage years in Harlem, thought the couple chose Carmen's family's house in Brooklyn for a small ceremony. Afterward they held a reception in Greenwich Village at Cafe Society Downtown in Sheridan Square, the first racially integrated club in downtown Manhattan. Carmen and Ike invited many musicians as well as their friends outside of the music world to the party.

Donna Perkins, Norval's daughter, remembered Ike Isaacs very well. Donna, who was born in 1945, described him as "sharp, a tall and slender man with deep set eyes and heavy, high eyebrows and a little goatee. He had Harry Belafonte's coloring and intensity, and he wore beautiful clothes, with a lot of style."

Ike endeared himself to Donna. Once, when he and Carmen stayed at the Perkins's house just before Christmas, they asked Donna what gift she wanted. She told them she wanted a bicycle. So they bought her a beautiful, metallic blue bike with a white leather seat and hand brakes. The gift was really Ike's idea. He was always thoughtful. The bike was very modern; it might have been a Schwinn, or some other name brand. "It was like getting a car," Donna recalled. Her parents didn't like the idea of their twelve or thirteen year-old daughter, with her hair in long pigtails, riding a two-wheeled bike around town. "My folks thought it was too dangerous, and they weren't happy in the beginning. But they got over it," she said.

In those days, when Carmen went to Washington to play either in the clubs or occasional concerts at the Carter Baron Amphitheater, she always stayed with the Perkins family. "It seemed like she was a frequent visitor when I was growing up," said Donna, who enjoyed Carmen's visits enormously. Donna had been nurtured with jazz by her father, and that exposure heightened her love of the music and her appreciation of Carmen as a glamorous celebrity aunt. "(Norval) had jazz playing in the house from early morning until everyone went to sleep at night," Donna recalled. "Listening to jazz was like his life. That wasn't all he was doing, but he always had it on.

"As soon as Carmen came to town, the whole rhythm of everything in the house changed," Donna continued. "It wasn't always a happy situation for my mom. Things turned upside down. My mom wanted her house perfect, she didn't want the routine interrupted, and she wanted everything right.... I loved it because I was excited, but there would be discord. Mom would be fussing about buying the groceries, things being wrong, whatever we weren't doing to her liking. Then Carmen came in like a diva, wanting everything her way. Her group came in and rehearsed in the living room. We lived in a small, semi-detached duplex, and the music would fill the whole place — the bass, drums, and piano, and Carmen singing. The whole neighborhood could hear the music. That was exciting. I'd go outside and tell my friends what was going on inside.

"There was a lot of girl stuff with Carmen, mommy, and me. Carmen had lizard shoes and bags that matched; they came from Beverly Hills. Really beautiful stuff. 'Oh, you want that, you can have that,' she said to me as I watched her get dressed. So I had a turquoise lizard and leather bag. I guess I loved blue all my life. The bag part was lizard and dyed turquoise, and the matching flap was of patent leather. You weren't going to see another bag like that. She wore fabulous outfits. Seamstresses made everything. She had big diamond rings and manicured nails. I loved to watch her put on her makeup, her eyelashes, and fix her hair."

Donna remembers Carmen eating Mrs. Perkins's collard greens, rabe, and watercress. "My mother likes to fix that," Donna said. "My mother's a good cook, and all the musicians knew that. When they came, my mother cooked pigs feet, collard greens, lasagna, eggplant parmigiani, and chicken burgundy. She had a big range, and she would cook for big groups of people. Dinners were serious.

"Carmen would feed her little doggy, Pepe, eggs for breakfast. I think she loved dogs a lot. It freaked my mother out that Carmen used one of her little plates for the dog. We had country breakfasts, with bacon, home fries, biscuits that came in a tube; you banged them and cooked them up. My mother also made drop biscuits. She spooned them out; she used to whip up that dough herself. Breakfast was a big deal on the weekends, and when Carmen was there we had to add a few things. Before we left the house to go to whatever concert, there was that anxiety and stress about meals. Even if Carmen wasn't staying with us, there was a meal prepared for her to come by for. That was what she wanted — a home cooked meal. She ate in hotels all the time."

Ike and Carmen had been traveling together happily for at least a year by the time they made their love official. But soon after the wedding the couple was fighting. Norval thought Ike tended to try to dominate Carmen, and she rebelled forcefully against his attempts; she became outspoken and even insulting to Ike. Marge Costa thought Carmen's marriage to Ike might survive, but she soon realized that even though the couple traveled on the road together, they didn't have the time to establish the intimacy a couple needs to nurture their love. "It wasn't a secure thing," Marge recollected. "And with Carmen's disposition and talent, I didn't think she was capable of loving. Also, the business being so tough on women on the road — that was part of the trouble. It was not an easy life. And it wasn't particularly easy for Carmen." Carmen was the group leader and Ike's boss as well as his wife; their dual roles created a perfect breeding ground for combat.

Furthermore, Marge thought that Carmen was an underrated talent, not getting the recognition she deserved. "She might have made more money if she had sung rock 'n roll. But she would not do it, and that was that," said Marge. Carmen, however, didn't seem to underrate her own choices, talent, or her standards. She had absolute confidence in herself and chose all her own musicians and material. Her perfectionistic streak and the pressures of her lifestyle fed the fire of her quarrels with Ike. Her career and her high ideals about what she should sing and how she should sound came first.

When Ray Bryant left Carmen's group in 1958, Carmen hired pianist Don Abney again. In 1958 he recorded several albums with her including *Birds of a Feather* for the Decca label, and one of romantic ballads with the Frank Hunter Orchestra on the Kapp label, which included the bassist Joe Benjamin. In 1959 bassist Aaron Bell went on the road with Carmen and Abney for a two-month tour, about a year before Bell went on to play with Duke Ellington's band. Exactly why Ike didn't play in the group all the time isn't clear, but the couple no longer had smooth sailing in their relationship.

Pianist Dick Katz went on the road with Carmen as an accompanist in 1959. He was flattered that she asked him to travel with her. Ike was still playing in her group during that tour. Dick heard Carmen say "some pretty caustic things" to Ike during the few months Dick worked with her. "But so what?" Dick said. "There aren't any people who don't talk caustically to each other at some time, unless they're Mother Teresa."

Katz, too, had some problems with Carmen during the tour. She picked on him, and they argued about the treatment she accorded him. "I was responsible for beating off the tempos," he recalled, "and most of the time there was no problem. But sometimes she would stop the group and beat off the tempo herself. I didn't like it." Katz told her he couldn't read her mind and suggested that if she decided to change the previously agreed-upon tempo once she got onstage, she should subtly snap her fingers to signal him. "But she did it her way. I had unlimited respect for her gifts, but you couldn't get close to her," he said.

Katz had loved Carmen's first husband, Klook, who was a tough but playful character. Katz couldn't imagine Klook taking any abuse from Carmen — or from anyone for that matter. Katz recalled that in 1955, when he had played with the Mat Mathews Quintet, Carmen and Klook had acted in a very friendly way toward each other, though they had already been separated for a long time.

Katz thought Carmen was an exceptionally beautiful woman. Yet "she was acting very masculine by 1959, driving the car, and cursing like a man. On the way back from our tour in Canada, we played in a place in Connecticut, a road-house that had jazz. I remember that after the gig we waited around for the longest time to leave. It seemed like she was never coming out. She was in there with the owner. I went in to see what was wrong. She was almost in tears. The owner was giving her a hard time about the money. He was merciless. She was really, really upset. That's the kind of stuff that musicians and singers had to go through in those days," Dick reminisced. He felt that incidents of that sort changed Carmen's personality and forged her increasingly flinty character.

An accompanist named Bill Rubinstein went to work for Carmen in 1959, succeeding Katz in the piano chair, and traveled with her on her first trip to England, to play at the Flamingo Club in London. A well-known jazz critic, Bob Dawbarn, writing for the *Melody Maker*, a leading British music magazine, gave her a lukewarm greeting, saying he was "unconvinced by Miss McRae's talents during her season at the Flamingo (in 1959)."[3] She was not the only American artist to meet with disinterest on her first venture into England. Nat "King" Cole had suffered grievous slights; the critics in London hadn't liked him at all.

Carmen made a number of recordings on the Decca label between 1955 and 1959. These were the glory years of her voice, when it was nubile, maleable, and musical. She performed with her own accompanists and studio orchestras. She favored American standards such as "Star Eyes," "Blue Moon," "Until the Real Thing Comes Along," "My Romance," "Angel Eyes" and countless other favorites with the public. She peppered her repertoire with a few novelty tunes, and the gospel hymn "His Eye Is on the Sparrow," and even such sophisticated and relatively exotic songs as Noel Coward's "If Love Were All" and "World Weary," and other songs that jazz singers didn't usually consider including in their repertoires.

Carmen was always searching for interesting material. Her fresh contralto had, at times, the airiness of a soprano; she could hit the high notes in the song "Flamingo" with ease. She already knew everything about exploring harmonies; the last words "heartache" on "Good Morning, Heartache" conveyed the dissonance of bone-chilling heartache. She was savvy, impeccable, and innovative, singing "frigid-aire" as two separate words for "frigidaire" in "I'm Through with Love." By this time she had adapted some of Billie's vocal quality and emphases for her own uses. She also began to suggest the eccentricity of singing words as if she were italicizing them. She would later use that trick constantly, in part because it was so attention getting, and it helped her underscore her meaning and feelings and tell her stories; it also diverted audiences from noticing her decreasing respiratory powers. But in the late 1950s, each of her interpretations had its own specific qualities — the triumph of her brash sound and the improvisational ideas on "East of the Sun, West of the Moon," and "Guess Who I Saw Today?" and the pleasantry of her own romantic tune, "Dream of Life," though that song didn't have the panache and clarity of her version of "Something to Live For."

Perspicacious young singers began to pay attention to Carmen's live performances and recordings as master classes. Among the younger singers who came to regard her as "the professor" were Carol Sloan, Annie Ross, and Helen Merrill. Generations of singers to come would learn by ear from Carmen's recordings. If they were lucky enough to meet her, they sometimes got brilliant advice about singing from her, and they would be extremely grateful to her for her insights. Eventually some of them visited her at her house and learned their lessons in quiet surroundings. With them she could be patient and supportive.

In 1959, the same year that Rubinstein joined her group, Carmen hired a young bassist, Bob Cranshaw, and drummer Walter Perkins. Before joining her group, Cranshaw had seen Carmen in performance at a club in Chicago. Carmen had also heard him play in Chicago; he may even have sat in with her once or twice a couple of years earlier, and she had wanted him to join her group. But he was still in college, even though he was already working professionally on the side as a bassist, so he didn't accept her invitation. But in 1959, Cranshaw and Perkins arrived in New York from Chicago with Perkins's group, MJT plus 3 — Modern Jazz Two plus 3 more instruments, altogether a rhythm section and two saxophones. They played for a couple of months at the Five Spot, the famous club on the east side of Greenwich Village where pianist Thelonious Monk, saxophonist Ornette Coleman, and others on the cutting edge of the jazz world attracted followings. When the MJT Plus 3 found itself out of work, its musicians simply hung around in New York to see if they wanted to stay. Carmen offered Cranshaw the job as her bassist again. This time he took it. He would stay with her for about four years.

Cranshaw knew that onstage and offstage Carmen could be extremely critical of her musicians, embarrassing them, even humiliating them at times. "I knew Carmen could be rough," Cranshaw recalled, "and I went to her immediately and told her: 'you hired me, and you can fire me. I want to do the best job I can. If I'm not doing what you need, get someone who can.'" Cranshaw felt that he put his terms to her in a very nice but clear way. "I wasn't buying anything rough on the stand. I was going to treat her like a lady, and I was a man. I let her know at the beginning of the relationship that I was going to demand respect and give her respect."

Cranshaw had already observed Carmen working with Ike Isaacs onstage. "She and Ike fought like cats and dogs. That's why I made my statement to Carmen early. I would go to the wall for her, but I wasn't going to let her go wild. Other than that, Carmen was a joy to work for. I had some wonderful times, and when the (music) was happening, and the band was cooking as it did most of the time, she was pretty happy with the trio. We locked in well and enjoyed doing it. We weren't trying to be the stars. She had the stage, and we were trying to cook behind her."

She and Walter Perkins (the drummer) had a different relationship, Cranshaw recalled. "They were swearing at each other," and then "they would end up laughing and hugging. But I didn't want that for myself. Carmen and I never got into hassles. She understood that she was never coming on the stage and making me look bad. Carmen could wipe you out."

Cranshaw had seen Carmen humiliate piano players before he played for her. She did not suddenly become a bastion of civility just because Cranshaw demanded she consider his feelings and image. "There were times when the group would play something, and she stopped the music because I wasn't in the right tempo. But she never addressed anything to me," Cranshaw remembered.

"Bill Rubinstein was an excellent piano player. He and Carmen had words onstage. But he was kind of like the bandleader, and so he took more of the brunt of what was happening. She would hold him responsible." (The piano player is always the group leader behind the singer, and all the other musicians take their cues from the pianist.)

The group worked in many clubs, with Cranshaw acting as the road manager. Serving his own interests as well as Carmen's, he became a stickler for keeping track of where and when they were going to work, because he had a wife and three kids at home. "I didn't have any time to dilly dally," he said, "and if she weren't working enough, I would have to take other jobs." So he kept in touch with Carmen's booker, Oscar Cohen, at A.B.C. — "and kept it straight."

Between 1958 and 1960, Carmen's recordings were cut for several labels other than Decca — Kapp, Official, and even one album for Mercury, with which her buddy Sarah Vaughan had a contract. And an especially praised album, *Carmen McRae Sings Lover Man and Other Billie Holiday Classics*, arranged by pianist Norman Simmons, would come along in 1961 — Carmen's first record for Columbia — to crown all of Carmen's earlier albums. Throughout the 1960s, working with Simmons as her accompanist, Carmen would achieve a high styled maturity as an artist and establish her reputation as a great interpreter of lyrics, imbuing them with a depth of feeling and understanding.

In 1960, when Carmen went to London a second time, Bob Dawbarn of the *Melody Maker* changed his tune and accorded her praise for her vocal range, enunciation, intonation, and innovative phrasing. However, the advance ticket sales for her shows out of town were so disappointing — she still wasn't well enough known there — that a few of her engagements were cancelled. She didn't tour outside the city alone but was added to a touring show called "Jazz From Britain," including four locally known British groups. The audiences that did show up were enthusiastic. Nonetheless many seats remained empty in such places as The Savoy Cinema, Hayes, Middlesex.[4]

In London, Carmen appeared on a television show as a panelist and aired her views about pop singers who sang any piece of musical dross just for the sake of pursuing the goal of a hit recording. She was so outspoken, opinionated, and adamant that she caused a ruckus on the show, whereas the other panelists remained sedate and mild.

By 1961, Bill Rubinstein left Carmen's group, and she traveled to England a third time. On this tour she was accompanied by Don Abney, who had played with her in 1958. They recorded for the British label, Ember, live at the Flamingo Club. Carmen was always singing beautiful old, tried and true ballads, such as

"Angel Eyes," "My Romance," and "The Thrill Is Gone." On the English recording with Abney, they played "Body and Soul," first made famous by Carmen's friend, tenor saxophonist Coleman Hawkins, in a classic recording in the late 1930s. She also mixed in some of Billie Holiday's repertoire with her own. "Lover Man" also showed up on the English recording.

Wherever the group went in the U.S., Carmen flew, taking her little pet dog, Pepe, with her, while the men drove in a car. They played in so many clubs that the names became a blur to them. But Cranshaw remembered one funny incident in Ohio. Carmen had some marijuana as usual, and a girl working with her, traveling on the road as a valet, dresser, and all-purpose maid, gave Cranshaw, then barely out of his teens, a joint to smoke. "I was so high that I couldn't read the music. I was in a panic at that point. I hadn't done that much smoking. I was sailing. I was out there. I didn't know where I was and wasn't sure of what I was doing. I started to get paranoid. I was in such a panic that I was getting ready to lay my bass down and walk off the stage. I knew I would get fired. I told myself: You big dummy, you'll be fired. And so I stayed. During intermission I went and drank coffee and tried to calm down. Carmen just laughed."

If club owners wanted anything special from Carmen — perhaps a particular song — they approached Cranshaw to request it, "because she could lay people out and not mince words," Cranshaw recalled. "I can't repeat the words. She would say anything. She was a hard lady." Cranshaw theorized that hard women such as Carmen became that way as a result of having to survive in a predominantly male world. For Carmen, Ella Fitzgerald, and Sarah Vaughan, the music world was a rough place. Carmen seemed to be like Billie Holiday, who could fight hard and rough. And the only way to fight and win was to do it that way. "But down deep down Carmen was really a lovely lady and a pussy cat," Cranshaw said. "She had this front to keep people off of her. I assume that was the case, because when she was nice, she was just lovely. And you would wonder why she took on the other persona. Why was that? But I figure that, in the case of Ike Isaacs, their being together all the time must have led to fights. And they were closed off from each other. I wasn't going to let that happen to me."

Audiences seemed unaware of Carmen's temperament, which was usually kept under wraps behind the scenes, except for the times when she reprimanded musicians onstage. Her fans were more engaged by what she looked and sounded like.

Morris Duff, a music writer for the *Toronto Daily Star*, interviewed Carmen when she was performing at the Colonial Tavern. He asked her if a female jazz singer had to have sex appeal in addition to a good voice and artistic command. "A girl must develop sex appeal regardless of whether she is singing or just sitting," Carmen replied. "There's no doubt that the public likes something good to look at." But Carmen didn't think sex appeal had much to do with fame and fortune. She said the public wouldn't admire Ella Fitzgerald, for example, if she lost a lot of weight and her voice at the same time. It was her voice that audiences loved.

Carmen herself had gained some weight by 1960, and she was on a diet, not even taking a drink in the bars where she worked. She simply thought she would "feel better and live longer if she weighed less," she said. But Duff thought she was very attractive. He liked the way she held out her arms to embrace air or grip the microphone in the Colonial Tavern. "Along with her eyes and her eyebrows, which slink up and down, these are often almost as expressive as her voice," he wrote.[5]

Carmen did give hints of her highly opinionated personality to the press, telling Jon Ruddy of *The Telegram* in Toronto for his column "See-Hear" for December 8, 1960, "I hate (television.)"[6] She liked to go onstage and do her songs, not rehearse them ad infinitum as she had to do for television. She disliked Ed Sullivan's show the most, because she was required to go through so many rehearsals for it. "Don't even mention it," she said about an upcoming appearance on the Sullivan show. She did television shows only because she had to, she said. They afforded performers the best exposure, and most of them suffered the hardships of television gladly, without voicing complaints: But not Carmen.

Walter Perkins, then about twenty-eight years old, thought Carmen, though a beautiful person to work with, could be "real mean" sometimes. But he learned a good lesson from her. One day, when they were playing a festival, the drummer in the group preceding Carmen's left his drumset on the stage. Perkins asked if he could use the drums. The drummer said "yes," relieving Perkins of the responsibility of putting his own drumset in place. But when he went onstage to play, the previous drummer's equipment was missing. That drummer may have needed it for something else. Carmen scolded Perkins. "And she was right," he said. "'Have your stuff up there. I hired you.' She was correct. I was quicksilver to get my drums up on that stage. Ever since then I have taken my own drums on stages. When you're young, you learn a whole lot of things." In general, he said. "It was fun working with her, an honor to do things with her."

Much of the information in this chapter comes from interviews with Donna Perkins Potts, Marge Costa, Ray Bryant, Aaron Bell, Walter Perkins, Bob Cranshaw, and Dick Katz.

[1] Source unknown, but probably *Down Beat* magazine (July 25, 1956).
   That critic quoted Leonard Feather, from an unspecified or undocumented publication or conversation.
[2] Gold, Don, *Saturday Review* (October 31, 1956).
[3] Dawbarn, Bob, *Melody Maker* (1959).
[4] Dawbarn, Bob, "Carmen's OK," *Melody Maker* (1960).
[5] Duff, Morris, *Toronto Daily Star* (February 28, 1959).
[6] Ruddy, Jon, "See-Hear" column, *The Telegram* (December 8, 1960).

Kenny Clarke in the late 1950s.

A glamorous publicity image of Carmen McRae. Photo: James Kriegsman.

Mat Mathews and his accordion, circa 1957.

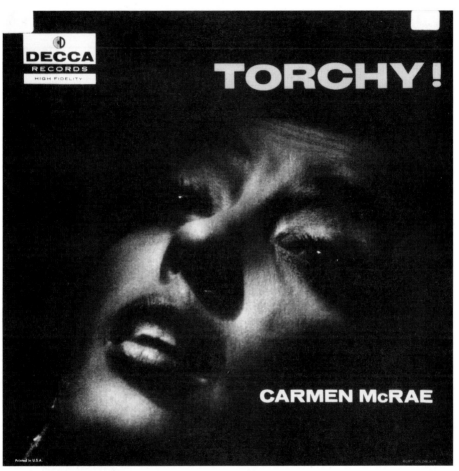

Torchy! *One of Carmen's popular albums on the Decca label 1955.*

A casual shot of Carmen.

After Glow *featuring Carmen, Ike Issacs on bass,
Specs Wright on drums, Ray Bryant on piano, 1957.*

Carmen for Cool Ones *with the Fred Katz orchestra.*
Note the glamorous image of this rising star. December, 1957.

Note the stylish makeup and hair.

This was a popular album on the Kapp label.

At the Newport Jazz Festival in July, 1961.
Photo: Raymond Ross.

1961 publicity photo of Gene Wright on bass, Dave Brubeck, and Carmen.

Carmen recording in the 1960s.

A mature Carmen.

Onstage in Japan.

The Years with Accompanist Norman Simmons

Norman Simmons became a dominant feature in Carmen's group from 1961 until 1969. Simmons was one of the most sensitive accompanists any singer could have. Though she didn't realize it until more than twenty years later, when Carmen was thrilled to find out how perceptive he had always been about her, throughout the 1960s Simmons functioned as a kind of musical Tiresias, an all-hearing, all-seeing, all-knowing eye; he understood his boss to an exquisite degree.

Simmons, nine years younger than Carmen, was recruited for the accompanist's job by the drummer Bob Cranshaw. Simmons was wary of the upcoming task. At the same time as he was approached by Cranshaw, Simmons had also received a call from Eddie "Lockjaw" Davis and Johnny Griffin, two tenor saxophonists co-leading a group then at the Apollo, and he set off to see if they were going to offer him a job. But when he got there, they told him they were calling on behalf of Carmen, who wanted to hire him. They had nothing but encouragement for him about the job with Carmen. Another pianist, Nat Pierce, also advised him to take it, saying that Simmons had an uncanny ability to get along with singers.

"I wanted to play for her," Simmons recalled, "but she had a fearful reputation. 'Jaws' was my mentor. He always called me 'son.'" Simmons paid attention when Jaws said, "You and Carmen will be perfect together." Jaws, with his vision for Simmons, helped boost the young Chicagoan's morale for the task.

Cranshaw spent time helping Simmons learn the book — Carmen's repertoire and arrangements. "I stayed up for nights doing that," Cranshaw recalled. "I took Norman through everything. He was very surprised that I was patient, and he was appreciative. But I didn't want Carmen to go off on my friend."

Simmons's first run-in with Carmen turned out to be amusing. They went to play in Hartford, Connecticut. Under his tuxedo, Simmons wore garters to hold his stockings up. Everyone could see the garters, because he was sitting high up on a stage. Carmen noticed the garters, suddenly pointed down at his foot, and asked loudly enough for everyone to hear, "What's that on your leg?" His garter had dropped down. Rather an introspective, quiet, proud man, he was very embarrassed. But he could see the humor in his situation, and at least the audience's peek at his garter had nothing to do with the quality of his playing.

Soon after Simmons joined her group, Carmen signed with Columbia Records. For her first recording, the Artists and Repertoire man told her she could do anything she wanted. So she decided on a tribute to Billie Holiday and told Simmons she wanted several songs loosely arranged. He wrote a few charts for her. When she looked at them, she was so pleased, she told him, "Do the whole thing."

Carmen's confidence inspired him, and he did the best writing he had done to date. In the group were himself, Cranshaw, Perkins, and tenor saxophonist Eddie "Lockjaw" Davis, cornetist and trumpeter Nat Adderley, and guitarist Mundell Lowe. When Simmons arranged the song, "Lover Man," for the album, *Carmen McRae Sings Lover Man And Other Billie Holiday Classics* (1961), he believed that Carmen could see that he was truly attuned to her emotional approach to interpretations of songs. He didn't just write some charts; they were uniquely tailored to Carmen. She paid such attention to every detail that, for the word "sparkle," she sang the first syllable on a low note and finished the word with a sparkling high note. Simmons understood her instinctively; he could predict how she would phrase and emphasize lyrics. The record went smoothly, and he would always be proud of it. Critics praised it, regarding it as a classic from the moment it was released. One of Carmen's best recordings, it would be released several times under different titles as years went by.

The album included the song "Strange Fruit," about the tragedy of lynchings and bodies swinging from the trees. Almost nobody but Billie had ever recorded it, and radio stations were loath to let their disk jockeys broadcast it. Carmen interpreted it in a spellbinding, quiet way, underscoring the drama and horror. The song had its genesis at Cafe Society, where the owner Barney Josephson had taken the material from left-leaning songwriters and presented it to Billie Holiday; although she had been reluctant to sing it at first, she finally decided to go ahead, saying she was after all "a race woman."

Cranshaw and Simmons loved the album. "It was a good album, one of her better ones." Simmons was grateful to Carmen for giving him the leeway to do such creative work. Cranshaw also recalled that she wanted Miles Davis to play on the album, because Miles was signed with Columbia. It would help publicize her Columbia record to have such an illustrious star as Miles on it. She telephoned

Miles in front of Cranshaw and invited him to play on the recording. Miles told her, "Carmen, it should just be you and a harp." When he said that, "she called him every kind of motherfucker," Cranshaw recalled. "She laid him out. He was being facetious, and she took it seriously. I know he wished he hadn't said that because she laid him out."

Around this time, Ralph J. Gleason, a syndicated jazz columnist for the *Times Mirror* in Los Angeles, wrote an article, "Carmen McRae Joins the Elite," saying: "Recently it was my great luck to hear Carmen McRae for the first time in several years. Since I last heard this gifted singer she has moved out into the rare category of the tragedienne in song.... It's a rare talent Miss McRae has and one that makes her performances events not to be missed. Singers like this do not appear every day. It's more like once in a generation."[1] Gleason, one of the most respected jazz critics, became an unwavering and especially sensitive supporter of Carmen's career.

Carmen never gave Simmons directions about how he should write for her, nor did she tell him much about the way he should play. Understanding each other instinctively as well as they did, they didn't have to discuss such matters much. Their strong friendship and ease of communication was based on their love for the music and their understanding of each other's gifts. Carmen never gave him a hard time onstage or off. Though she occasionally criticized and guided him, he never got upset. Their relationship was in many ways a collaboration.

Simmons knew that other musicians had suffered under the onus of Carmen's criticism when they didn't live up to her standards. That was why he had been so fearful of going to work for her. He discovered that she required a high level of proficiency from him, and she needed him to play in a way that inspired her. She provided strong leadership and demanded that musicians add their own creativity to the music. Though the work seemed arranged, her performances actually had to sound spontaneous and refreshing. "You can't just play the job with Carmen," Simmons quickly learned.

She was a great singer, he thought, as he kept learning more about the way she sang: He could feel her under his fingers. He kept learning about the techniques she used to imbue her songs with feeling. She offered him material he could latch on to and interpret with intelligence and finesse.

Simmons also learned about stagecraft from Carmen. For one thing, he learned that he was responsible for leading the group during the performance. One time, during a performance at the Village Gate in 1966, the piano, drums and bass were not working well together; Simmons and the drummer weren't communicating. So Simmons decided to stop playing — to "lay out," as musicians say — and let Carmen work with just the bass and drums. Afterward she told him she had been listening for Simmons above all else, and she was very irritated that she hadn't been able to hear him and lean on him.

"Don't you ever drop out again!" she warned. No matter what was going on during the performance, Carmen was always listening for Simmons to indicate where the entire group should be in a song. By that time, Simmons had already been playing for her for about five years; and his concept of accompanying kept maturing. He learned that the responsibility never shifted from him to anyone else. He became more confident about himself in the job, not by pounding to make himself understood but by pulsating — supplying the beat. The pianist can play time and harmony and imply them for the bass, the drums, and the singer. The piano player follows the singer, who leads, and the other musicians follow the piano. The pecking order developed logically from the piano's capacity for acting like an entire orchestra. Simmons, who was always interested in the orchestration as well as the pulsation, learned from listening to Duke Ellington, who was orchestrating the music while someone else in his band played the lead.

In short, Carmen taught Simmons the fine points about accompaniment. And she had enough knowledge of music and the requisites for accompaniment to give him advanced lessons. He learned that accompanists shouldn't play too much, and that they had to exercise judgment and taste in what they did play. At the same time, he learned he wasn't supposed to hold back too much. Carmen taught him that, as a musician as well as a singer, she could put the chords exactly in the right place for herself — the exact chords that she wanted. Any singer can do that better for him- or herself than any accompanist can, for singers know exactly what they are feeling. Simmons had to approximate what Carmen would have played for herself.

Carmen advised Simmons to listen to singers who accompanied themselves. He listened to them and learned what was needed and what was superfluous, managing never to give in to the temptation to try to shine at the expense of what Carmen or any vocalist might need or want. And when Carmen took over the piano bench in every set to accompany herself on a song or two, he stepped aside and listened intently. By this time she would say that she was nervous about accompanying herself, but he felt she was excellent at it. She sounded percussive and innovative, like Thelonious Monk, he thought.

When Carmen sang ballads, she stuck to the foundation of the songs — the way they were originally written. The temptation, and indeed the job for most jazz pianists, is to embellish. But the accompanist is supposed to orchestrate for the singer. Orchestrations move along to try to help the singer impart a definite meaning. Uptempo songs require less support than ballads. And there's not that much space, or silence, for an accompanist to fill in for uptempo songs.

All these lessons Carmen taught Simmons. Whatever space there was belonged to the singer. Carmen communicated her music through the spaces she wanted. If Simmons tried to move into the spaces and intruded upon her phrasing or other intentions, the singer had to wait for him to finish. Simmons had to exercise excellent judgment of taste and sensitivity to Carmen's style to know where it was appropriate for him to elaborate on what she was singing. He wanted the audience to be able to hear what Carmen was going to sing next and not be diverted by his embellishment, no matter how great the piano work might have been if it had been standing alone.

Simmons also learned not to move around a lot on the keyboard and have his notes cross over Carmen's notes, or a conflict could develop. The voice was a sensory type of instrument. It moved in a line. The piano must not be linear, though. Instead, a pianist accompanying a singer must play the chords vertically. That was the way Carmen liked him to play.

If Simmons ran across her lines and filled in all the spaces, he might ruin the suspense Carmen was trying to build as she told her stories. She achieved suspense by the way she phrased the lyrics. She wasn't just taking a breath when she left a space in a line. The space was an emphatic pause she inserted before she delivered the next sound. The pulse that Norman supplied had to be there for her all the time, but the vocal line had to have breathing spaces — pauses, with nothing intruding. When the voice stopped, the pianist had to wait for it to start again. The silence became a part of the music, and he learned to leave the silences alone. Some singers liked accompanists to fill in a lot. Simmons learned that he had to be sensitive to individual singers, with their idiosyncratic preferences, and he would utilize that knowledge when he went on to accompany other singers. Carmen was capable of using his accompaniment with only the barest essentials supplied.

Simmons was charmed and even hypnotized, as audiences were, by the way Carmen could sing so softly and slowly. She could be extremely effective when she fell absolutely still; then the audience fell still, too. "That's suspense," he said. "She can hypnotize you with one word every fifteen minutes. She knows how to deliver and use space."[2]

Simmons learned to support Carmen's great storytelling talent and enhance her acting ability. Other singers might have storytelling talent, but she was "torchy," he said. Other singers might dramatize their material, but not as heartrendingly as Carmen could do it. She could really draw an audience into her songs. Simmons learned that the key to her ability was her love affair with the words and even the syllables that supported her understanding of lyrics. She broke songs down into small portions. Carmen could slow down a word to make sure an audience was hearing precisely what she was saying and implying, and that was the way she communicated emotions. The songwriters didn't put in all the nuances of their meaning about their feelings when they wrote lyrics. Carmen could bring out the meaning behind the words — a sense of exhilaration, or joy, or profanity — just by the way she delivered a line.

In the song "Lover Man," she emphasized a negative — "don't" — that stopped the line in its tracks. Then she emphasized another word in the next line, and "lover" in the next. "She practically bites her lip to say 'lover,'" Simmons said,[3] and Carmen subtly repeated the beginning consonants of a word to serve as her improvisation; that trick of enunciation underscored the meaning of a word and made it fraught with emotion. She slowed words down and trailed off on others. She didn't linger in places where it was meaningless to pause. She spent time milking each word that could be milked. And she might soar upward on a word to imply that the meaning of the lyric was aiming at a heavenly feeling. She sang "again and again and again," not just singing the word once, to emphasize the lovemaking in a lyric. She might hit a high note at the end of a song and sustain it for a long time with no vibrato, and then, after showing absolute control in that way, she utilized vibrato. And she never hurried a song. Carmen sang it exactly the way it should be.

Critics sometimes said that Carmen was mannered — that her style was exaggerated. Simmons thought it took critics years to realize that Carmen always understood lyrics and delivered them in a sincere way. He also thought critics missed the point when they said Carmen's voice wasn't pretty. "She doesn't have a soft, gentle voice, that's true," he said.[4] Nobody would claim that Carmen had a very pretty voice, especially as she grew older and her voice showed some of the wear and tear of her smoking and constant use. Her voice was always coarser than either Ella Fitzgerald's or Sarah Vaughan's. Carmen's was guttier and grittier.

But Carmen had perfect control, and she could make audiences think at times that she had a very pretty voice, as when she gave a gentle treatment to "The Shadow of Your Smile," a pure ode to love, or "Feelin' Good," a paean to the joy of living. She could start a song like "Too Close for Comfort" softly and sweetly, and then play with words such as "plea-hease" and "tempta-haytion" to make their beauty reside in her high-styled treatment of lyrics. She could pick up the tempo in a song so that it sounded like the rapid beating of her heart, when the lyrics talked about her heart beating fast, and she could change lyrics just enough, singing "groove" instead of "leads" — and "scurry" instead of "run," praise the hipness of the "cat" being too close for comfort; her fresh ideas made the song beautiful. The quintessential jazz contralto, she could honk or bray a hard-edged, piercing line or word and end it as a whimsical, airy syllable. Perhaps most of all Carmen convinced people with her intelligence. This was the voice, which was inseparable from her style and her feeling for the essence of songs, of her middle career.

"It all comes together in her emotion, control, and knowledge of the story of the song," Simmons said. "All the singers say that the words are most important, that the story is, but they don't come out with the result. And the song is singing them. To sing the song, they must pick up high points within even a syllable to get across not just the high point of the story idea. They must isolate a syllable, or a strong word, in some kind of way to get an audience reaction.

"They have to plan ahead. Pros of all kinds do. When a tennis pro has just made a good shot, he has the next three already planned. There are climactic parts for a word, for a line, and for a whole song. And a singer has to plan that for the whole game.

"Carmen did not supply the black church element in her music that other black singers did," Simmons continued. "That used to concern her when she played black clubs until she found that black audiences ate her up. But she was not a funky-type singer. Neither was Sarah or Ella." Nor was Billie, though Billie was distinctly blues-y even when she wasn't singing a blues. "However, Billie, Ella, and Sarah had hit songs. Carmen's recording of 'Skyliner' was popular, as was her version of 'Take Five,' which she cut with Dave Brubeck. But these songs were not big hits."[5]

Carmen's style established her as one of the greatest jazz singers who ever lived, even though she never had a major hit in her life. "Carmen didn't get the wonderful bookings she enjoyed during her career because she had hot records," Simmons said. "People went to hear her sing ... with her distinctive style."[6]

Simmons also learned that Carmen's moods affected her performances. If she was happy or angry, then the audience received a happy or an angry set. She worked from her gut feeling and didn't present a routine show. Her intensity emanated from her emotionality. If she got up onstage and discovered that the audience had turned out to see her, she poured her heart and soul into her work. But if she didn't sense that the audience had come to appreciate her, she didn't feel inspired. "And she took her heart and soul and went home," Simmons said. "And if she took her intensity away with her, the audience missed something important in her show."[7]

Carmen's group knew exactly the way she was feeling when she stepped onstage. If they sensed she was feeling down, they knew they had to make the music especially wonderful for her. They had to supply her with a lift and inspiration. Music was her therapy, and her musicians sometimes had to act as music therapists. Bob Cranshaw taught Norman Simmons to stay watchful of Carmen's moods. Cranshaw knew how to make them work for her performances. If she didn't feel well, she would arrive at the job and start riffling through her book, reviewing the songs that she wanted to choose for the show. She would settle on songs the musicians hadn't played in years and discard the ones they knew well from playing them so often. Then Bob Cranshaw made it his mission to not let her have a chance to find fault with the musicians. He filled in the chorded support and embellishments she needed to put her songs across.

A perfectionist no matter what her mood, Carmen appreciated Cranshaw's efforts. Simmons recalled one musician who used to say, "Every night is Carnegie Hall." That is, every night and every set is important. That's how Carmen viewed her performances, Simmons explained. The musicians could never let themselves think they could relax and have an easy night with Carmen. If any one of them thought he was feeling short of inspiration on any night, he had to find some way to come up with it or hope somebody would do it for him.

A love interest in her life affected Carmen's performances radically. If she was involved with someone, then she was less demanding of her musicians. But if she had been all alone in her hotel room, she brought her lonesomeness or sadness or tension onstage with her. Although Ike Isaacs was gone from Carmen's life by the time Norman Simmons joined her group, Simmons knew that Carmen continued to carry a torch for Ike for a while afterwards. She sometimes invited Isaacs to have dinner with her, but he never showed up.

At the same time, Carmen increasingly exerted a charismatic influence over the press; writers perceived an aura of mystery about her personality as well as the sublimity in her artistry. But in their writings, even if the writers knew anything about Carmen's personal life, they didn't explore the possible relationship between her art and her romantic life — at least not for the public. "She stands in the light of success," wrote Barbara Gardner in *Down Beat*[8], "but with questioning eyes.... A disarming quality about Miss McRae is her unvarnished honesty. She is direct and outspoken and never could be the ultra-glamorous show business figure she envisioned herself as a youngster. She dresses conservatively and tastefully. When she dares to become shocking with colors, she's modest with the cut of the garment." Most critics praised her album *Carmen McRae: Live at Sugar Hill* (1962) on the Mainstream label's Time subsidiary as a milestone in her career. Nat Hentoff called her the best female jazz singer now working; he praised her quality of mind, intensity of feeling, compared her with Billie Holiday, cited her power, grace, wit, flexibility with the beat, and her playfulness with rhythms to develop nuances.[9]

This was the first album, Norman Simmons thought, on which Carmen's true personality blossomed. She did exactly what she wanted. No one handed her songs and told her what to do with them. It had happened often that record companies asked her to record songs she had never seen before going into the studio, and she didn't really feel familiar enough with them. But Bobby Shad of Mainstream was the Artists and Repertoire man for *Live at Sugar Hill*. He allowed Carmen to hire all her own musicians — her rhythm section included Simmons, bassist Victor Sproles, and drummer Stewart Martin — and to choose her own songs and plan every moment of the recording. She sounded more relaxed and natural than ever before on records, talking and rapping with audiences. The album captured the style she had achieved in clubs where she nurtured her loyal following.

Carmen recorded so many songs at the club Sugar Hill that there was enough material left over for several records on Mainstream — among them *In Person/In San Francisco*, the first one released, and *Live and Doin It*. Bobby Shad also culled a selection for the album *Live at Sugar Hill* that he put out on his little "drugstore" label, Time, and another little label, Hindsight, on which he released *Song Time*. "Drugstore" albums sold on racks in drugstores and five and dime stores for 99 cents. Of all the albums done live at Sugar Hill, the one with that name became one of her best sellers. Official discographers sometimes attributed these albums to different sessions in different cities, but according to Simmons, all the albums including Stewart Martin were actually recorded live at the Sugar Hill sessions: Those were the only times when Martin recorded with Carmen's group.

Throughout Norman Simmons's tenure with Carmen, he knew who her lovers were. In 1962, he observed that Carmen had a love affair with a young man she met backstage in a club in San Francisco. After the affair ended, the man remained in her life as a friend for the rest of her life. He would always deny that he had had an affair with Carmen, but just as adamantly Simmons insisted that the affair took place. The young man, who had no connection with jazz except for a love for music when he met Carmen, became a successful businessman in the jazz world as a result of his friendship with Carmen and his entree to many people through her. Another of Carmen's lovers was a highly educated, very respected musician with a teaching post at an Ivy League college in New England.

These men didn't travel on the road with her. She saw them when she could. "Carmen was frugal," Simmons said. Furthermore, some of her lovers, like the Ivy League college professor, had busy schedules and couldn't travel with her even if she had wanted them to. Since they weren't working for her, they had no practical reason or the freedom to tag along.

Although Carmen alienated some friends and lovers with her tough facade, she also held on to others who either excused her because of their great respect for her or else they never suffered a moment's discomfort from her rough side. And some friends saw only Carmen's more relaxed side.

Shirley Horn, the pianist and singer, had good, friendly relations with Carmen from the day they met in the Village Vanguard in 1962. Shirley was appearing there when Carmen went to hear the show with her friend John Levy, a well-known artist's manager, and singer Barbara McNair. Shirley was particularly excited to meet Carmen, who was a beautiful woman — "so striking to look at," Shirley thought. "I was very shy, and [thought] WOW! Carmen McRae!" Whenever Carmen appeared at Blues Alley in Washington, D.C., where Horn lived with her husband and daughter, Shirley always went to see Carmen. Their friendship would become increasingly close as years went by, after Shirley's daughter grew up, and Shirley did more touring.

Marge Costa, who had known Carmen since their childhood days in Harlem, also had a solid friendship with Carmen, but not an unruffled one. Marge had a job for the federal government. Her domineering father wanted her to stick with that job, but Carmen persuaded her to leave it in the early 1960s and become Carmen's traveling companion on the road. Marge thought they would have wonderful times together.

That New Year's Eve Marge drove with Norman Simmons, Victor Sproles, and a drummer to Chicago. Carmen flew, while the musicians and Marge froze in a van. They stuffed paper in a hole they found in the front of the van to try to pre-serve some warmth. The men drank Metaxa, the Greek brandy, to ease the burden of the non-stop drive. They finally reached Chicago, and went to a motel called 30th on the Lake. Well-rested and full of energy, Carmen greeted her friend and said, "C'mon, let's go eat." Marge was exhausted and cold from the drive. "It was so cold, I went back and got my beaver hat and scarf. That was the coldest place I'd ever been," Marge recalled.

From Chicago, they went to Phoenix, where Carmen hired "a kind of surrey with the fringe on top," Marge recalled, to drive her from her hotel room to Carmen's room. Carmen was pretty unhappy in Phoenix, because few people in her audiences knew who she was. From there the group traveled to California, as usual by van, where Marge acted as Carmen's maid, in charge of clothes and laun-dry and valet duties, at Carmen's beck and call. Marge recalled, "I couldn't stand it anymore, because the friendship was not a friendship. I was her personal maid, and that I'm not. I don't take orders very well."

In San Francisco, Marge told Carmen, "I value the friendship entirely too much, and so I'm quitting." And Marge went to stay with a friend in town. "And I never looked back," she recalled.

Marge Costa's friendship with Carmen survived. "[Carmen] forgot everything negative," Marge said. Carmen's career came first, Marge thought, and that was more important than love. "If she loved anybody, she loved Norman Simmons and me," she said. Carmen and Marge traveled together again, but not with Marge as an employee. Once they visited Jamaica, where Carmen introduced Marge to some relatives, an uncle who was a lawyer and his wife. Carmen had many relatives on that island. (They had even sponsored a parade for her when she had toured there years earlier with Ray Bryant as her accompanist.) On the road, Carmen employed people who were willing to work as roadies, valets, maids, and servants. She had one young male valet whom she liked very much, and she also had a woman who stayed with her a long time as a maid and understood the job; it was hard work.

Marge met Billie Holiday through Carmen, and Count Basie, and singers Gloria Lynne and Dinah Washington — "everyone," she would reminisce; the richness and exitement of her contacts with the jazz world helped Marge sustain the intriguing friendship with Carmen.

It was not really true that Carmen forgot everything negative, but she had neither the time nor the inclination to dwell on anything but her career. Larry Clothier, one of her best friends, would notice that although her relatives might think she neglected them and didn't give them enough money, presents, or time, she cared for them a great deal. She simply had to invest everything she earned and all her time in her career.

Carmen's longtime friendship with Larry Clothier, a tall, lanky Midwesterner, began in 1962 and lasted for the rest of her life. Clothier met her in San Francisco when she was working in a club called Sugar Hill on Broadway in the North Beach area. The club was run by some good friends of Carmen's, a husband and wife; the husband had been the doorman at the Jazz Workshop, a well-known jazz club, for a number of years prior to having his own club. At Sugar Hill, they had "a real mix of music, primarily jazz, but they also had people like Sonny Terry and Brownie McGhee, blues people, in the midst of the folk/blues era. A lot of clubs in San Francisco had similar policies; the hungry i was another one, El Matador was another," Clothier said.

Born on February 28, 1941, twenty-one years younger than Carmen, Clothier was attending San Francisco State, studying international relations and world trade, believing he would go on to law school. He was also trying to sing and work a little around the bay area. He knew Carmen McRae's work from records his elder brother owned. "As soon as he played the first tune, I was hooked. I said, 'ooookay.' Maybe it was a Nat "King" Cole tune from Carmen's early album *By Special Request* (1955). 'Suppertime' was on that album, too." Clothier decided to go to Sugar Hill and introduce himself to Carmen. "We started talking and became friends. It was pure and simple. We just talked about her music and how I felt about it. We discussed my trying to sing. Over time, during the next few years, whenever she was around, we'd always get together. She took me to a lot of places and introduced me to a lot of people.

"She was very attractive," Clothier recalled. "But we were just friends. We saw each other sporadically until about 1965, and after that, we were always in touch. She came to play at the hungry i in San Francisco that year. There was a great triple bill, and she played there for about three weeks to a month. Joan Rivers played there during that time. Carmen had Norman Simmons and Victor Sproles in her group when we first met."

Carmen seemed very self-assured and confident about what she wanted, as far as Clothier could tell in those days. "She portrayed a sense of being very self-assured and confident in what she was doing in her craft and the way she approached life. I grew to know later on that some of this outward bravado was something of a self-protective shell she had developed over time. I discovered she was not quite as steady and self-assured as she would seem on the outside. She had insecurities and foibles like all humans, but she chose to mask most of those."

Feeding the self-assured image she promoted with people were remarks she made to interviewers and musicians. Carmen told Leonard Feather for her second "Blindfold Test" on January, 1964, "Embellishing lyrics is fine, if it's just an extra word here or there, but when you make a whole new sentence out of two words that the lyricist put there because that was what he wanted and this was the way he wanted someone to interpret it, well I can't see that."[10] As high style as she was, there remained a conservative streak in her approach to songs, and she never pulled them apart as the iconoclastic and experimental musicians and singers such as Betty Carter liked to do. One musician liked to tell a funny story about the day Carmen went to hear John Coltrane playing his spiritually yearning, driven, cacophanous new music in the 1960s. Afterward she went backstage and asked him boldly and loudly, "John, what the *hell* is that?"

Onstage, Carmen was supremely collected. "Clad in neck-high, unrelieved black, Miss McRae made a visually striking appearance recently when she opened a return engagement at Shelly Manne's jazz room. Musically she was superb," wrote critic John A. Tynan about her 1964 engagement in Shelly's Manne Hole in Hollywood. In her ballads, Tynan wrote, "the singer demonstrated two qualities: an essential vibrance of tone and supreme control of her voice. Miss McRae is, in fact, perhaps the most magnificently controlled singer in jazz today."[11]

In the mid-1960s, Clothier met Carmen's mother, and observed that the women had a very close relationship. Evadne was an elegant, reserved, Jamaican "lady," he said, with a strong West Indian accent. Carmen confided in Clothier that as a young woman her mother had been an early activist for women's rights in New York City. Evadne was a seamstress at the time, and quite vocal in trying to establish better working conditions in the industry. Carmen said her mother had been militant in standing up for her own rights and the rights of others who worked around her, "and was not one to take any shit from anybody." And Clothier added with a wry laugh, "Which rubbed right off on Carmen."

Though Clothier never met Oscar McRae, her father, and thought he was probably dead by the first time Clothier visited Carmen's house, he knew that Carmen had been "really fond of her father, more so than of her mother. She respected her mother, but she was daddy's little girl, and he let her get away with a whole lot of things that her mother would not have." Clothier thought Oscar had died only a year or so before 1965. Like everyone else surviving Carmen, nobody knew precisely what had become of Oscar McRae — where he had died or what he had died from. Carmen never talked about that.

In 1963, about two years after Simmons began working with Carmen, many changes took place in her group's personnel. Bob Cranshaw and Walter Perkins left at the same time to join saxophonist Sonny Rollins's group. One of the best tenor saxophonists of his generation, or any generation for that matter, Rollins was coming out of a self-enforced retirement. Traumatized and angry, Carmen didn't speak to Cranshaw for several years. She was furious with him for leaving her with the monumental chore of training new people. But she calmed down eventually and became friendly with him again — and in some ways perhaps even more friendly than ever, because they didn't have the pressures of work over their heads. She hung out with him when their paths crossed. She put a variety of different groups together, with Norman Simmons as the anchor, after Cranshaw left. Cranshaw brought bassist Larry Ridley into Carmen's group and coached Ridley, too, about the book, so that he could avoid problems with Carmen. But Ridley didn't stay long.

Norman Simmons believes he was probably the one who drew bassist Victor Sproles into the group. Sproles played bass on some wonderful albums Carmen recorded for the Mainstream label in 1962. After Victor arrived, "the music started to pile up," Simmons said. Carmen didn't like repetition, so Simmons wrote more arrangements, and the book — Carmen's repertoire — began getting bigger. Musicians had more reading to do. Therefore Carmen decided to hire musicians who read music well. After Victor Sproles left the first time, she hired a drummer named Fats Heard and a bassist named Wyatt Reuther, both of whom could read. But although the entire group could read, it wasn't swinging. During a tour on the West Coast, Carmen confided in Simmons, "I would rather have Victor back and all those wrong notes and swing."

Simmons recalled that the group went back to New York, where Carmen hired new players, but they never got a chance to play. They went to the West Coast for their first performance with Carmen, only to discover she had hired Frank Severino, a drummer, and a friend of his who played bass. At first, Severino refused to go along with her because he was afraid to work for someone of Carmen's stature. When she hired his friend, a bass player, Severino agreed to try to travel with Carmen. So Carmen sent the bassist and drummer she had previously hired back to New York on a bus, and she bought Severino and his friend tuxedos.

She had never done anything like that before. Although Carmen and young Severino were never lovers, he had a softening effect on Carmen. She liked him from the minute she met him. She liked the way he played, too. He was not the kind of musician Carmen usually hired. For one thing, he was essentially a neophyte; he couldn't read music very well at that time. So she had to compromise all her standards. Unlike Simmons who felt his love for Carmen rested on duty and music, Severino had a strong personal relationship with Carmen. When the group traveled, the men stayed in one hotel, and she went to another: She was the boss. But Severino went to her room, took walks with her, and even bought her presents.

One time, when the group was playing at the hungry i, in the 1960s, Joan Rivers, the comedian, had an engagement there, too. The owner didn't like her, and Rivers was broken-hearted. Severino didn't know Joan Rivers at all, but he felt sorry for her and bought her some candy. Carmen had sensed that quality of empathy and sympathy in him from the start, which is why she wooed him to go on the road with her.

Carmen was less enamored of Severino's friend, the bassist. He was living on a macrobiotic diet. He looked thin, pale, and gaunt. Carmen confided in Simmons, "I don't want him dying on me." Then she fired him. Happily, Severino stayed with the group, and he and Norman traveled for about four years with Carmen. Sometimes it was just the two men driving across the country in her car, while Carmen flew. They picked up bass players in the cities where they performed. "Frankie was a feeling person. He was sweet," Simmons said. "His personality appealed to the sweet side in her — that you never saw. She didn't do anything different herself. Except the most DIFFERENT thing she did was to hire him. She had to compromise some of her ABSOLUTE CRITERIA to let him get it together. And she did it. And he did it, he got it together." Eventually, in the 1960s, Carmen re-hired Victor Sproles. He and Severino didn't get along well at all. "Neither one could read," Simmons recalled.

Simmons knew that Carmen and Frankie never had a love affair. It was always strictly a friendship. Simmons thought Carmen felt maternal love for Frankie.

In New York, Carmen had been living alone in modern, high-rise apartments — first near Lincoln Center, and then in Washington Square Village in Greenwich Village — after she and Ike Isaacs had separated and divorced. Friends who visited thought the fresh-looking, spacious apartments were splendid. The writer Gene Lees visited Carmen in her Village apartment; he and composer Lalo Schiffrin took her a song called "The Right To Love" composed by Lees. Carmen didn't want it, and instead Peggy Lee recorded it, though later Carmen sang it as well. Lees recalled Carmen's lovely apartment with a balcony and her entertaining way with her guests. She told them that her little dog could sing. They laughed and said, "Oh, come on, Carmen." "Oh, yes," she said. And to prove it, she played the piano. The little dog just sat still and did nothing. But when she hit a song that the dog recognized, it began to howl.

Though others admired her New York lifestyle, by 1966 Carmen was fed up with the pace of life in New York. She was sick of hailing cabs and combating all the other pressures of life in the great metropolis. She was yearning to put down roots someplace; the gypsy lifestyle of a troubadour on the road amused her less and less. She was only happy when she reached her destination, stepped onstage, and felt welcomed by the audience. Furthermore, her parents had moved to a community near Los Angeles, as had some aunts. Carmen decided to move to the West Coast to be close to them and to find an oasis of peace and quiet. She found it in a house of her own set far back from the road, high on a hill, overlooking a canyon, at 2200 Summit Ridge Drive. Soon Carmen's mother, who was widowed after Carmen moved to L.A., was living with her.

Marge Costa recalls visiting Carmen's beautiful house where she swam in the pool. Carmen had a lush garden and a gardener to tend it. "She grew marijuana in the backyard and hung it up in the closet to dry," Marge recalled. "I asked her: 'Aren't you worried? The planes are flying over. Suppose they see it?'"

"Fuck it," Carmen said.

"Bless her heart. She wasn't afraid of anything," Marge said. "I had a grand time with her. I had a rich life around jazz because of Carmen. She was almost like a protector. She wouldn't let anyone say anything against me. But she could say anything she wanted. If she said something rough, I would leave. When she got on my nerves, I would say, 'Goodbye, Carmen.' Then we'd get back together.

That's what friends do. They love you in spite of your faults. Sassy (Sarah Vaughan) asked me how I could stand Carmen, and I answered, 'That's what friends are like, Sassy.'"

But usually Marge stayed home, having learned the hard way that Carmen on the road focused totally on her career, not on the rewards of friendship. Marge got a job as a public health administrator and educator in the Washington, D.C. area and went to see Carmen perform at places easily reached by short trips on airplanes, trains, or cars — New York, Philadelphia, or Atlantic City.

Much of the information in this chapter comes from interviews with Bob Cranshaw, Norman Simmons, Walter Perkins, Larry Clothier, Marge Costa, Gene Lees, Shirley Horn, and Billy Taylor.

[1] Gleason, Ralph, "Carmen McRae Joins The Elite," *Times Mirror*, published in the *Journal American* (May 13, 1961).

[2] Gourse, Leslie, *Louis' Children* (New York: Quill/William Morrow and Company, 1984).

[3] Ibid.

[4] Ibid.

[5] Carmen McRae recorded on an album featuring the very popular song "Take Five," by the Dave Brubeck Quartet. The album sold more than a million copies. The Dennis Brown discography says she recorded it in a live performance at Basin Street, New York, where she worked on September 6, 7, and 8, 1961, with Dave Brubeck on piano, Paul Desmond on alto saxophone, Gene Wright on bass, and Joe Morello on drums. The Bruyninckx discography says this session was recorded on September 6, 1961. Both discographies say this song was recorded for Columbia.

[6] Gourse, op. cit.

[7] Ibid.

[8] Gardner, Barbara, *Down Beat* (September 13, 1962).

[9] Hentoff, Nat, "Carmen McRae: A Mystery Solved," *HiFi/Stereo Review* (December, 1962).

[10] Feather, Leonard, "Blindfold Test," *Down Beat* (January, 1964).

[11] Tynan, John A., *Down Beat* (September 10, 1964).

CHAPTER SIX

Mixing Business with Pleasure

In 1966, another man came into Carmen's life, François Vaz, a French-born guitarist. Vaz had heard much of Carmen's star status; fine reviews of her work appeared regularly.

Ralph Gleason once again used his syndicated column in the *Times Mirror Syndicate* to praise Carmen as a singer, a storyteller, and an actress. "She is ... utterly in a class by herself in any corner of the vocal world, jazz or otherwise," he wrote.[1] Burt Korall in the *Saturday Review* called attention to the way she had remained untouched "by the negative aspects of that sought-after devil: Success." Carmen had never pursued superstardom and chose instead to try to keep evolving as an artist, he said.[2]

Helen McNamara of the *Toronto Telegram* called her "Charmin' Carmen" for her performances at a club called The Town and praised her distinctive style, especially when she accompanied herself at the piano. "Miss McRae has long since developed into a highly stylized and completely original singer, who can range widely and wildly from brusque, raw sounds to pure high notes. The effect is sometimes disconcerting but never dull. One never knows quite what to expect," wrote McNamara, a generally conservative but perceptive critic.[3] The following May, when Carmen played at Toronto's Colonial Tavern, a reviewer criticized her a bit for her slow treatment of one song. But "Miss McRae is also to be commended for her rare ability to hush a nightclub audience just by employing in her vocal phrasing dramatic pauses which speak volumes," wrote Peter Harris in his column, "Nightclubs."[4]

Carmen met Vaz when she was working in the Riviera Hotel in Las Vegas in December, 1966. Vaz was playing in singer Lou Rawls's group at Caesar's Palace.

Carmen and Vaz had an instant attraction to each other; they simply "fell in love."

"We should try to work together," Vaz told her. "Otherwise we will almost never see each other."

"No, that's not a good idea," Carmen responded. "I know me. You just stay with Lou. We should see each other from time to time."

"Not a good idea," Vaz said. "We travel too much. Let's try to make a go of it."

At first Vaz, who had been born on June 19, 1931, making him eleven years younger than Carmen, didn't think about any of the differences between them. "It was beautiful," he said. "All relationships are beautiful when they begin." Vaz would always treasure a few photographs of them from their first New Year's Eve together; they were very happy, sitting at a table in a club with a couple who were Carmen's friends.

Right away Carmen went on a diet and began to lose weight. Although Vaz had thought her very attractive anyway, he decided she looked even better when she lost ten pounds quickly, then lost another ten pounds. And her face was radiant.

"The first job we played together was at the hungry i in San Francisco in January, 1968," Vaz reminisced. By this time she had been living on the West Coast for about a year. She took Vaz to her house. Norman Simmons, who was staying there, too, had already noticed how much Vaz had ingratiated himself with Carmen. Simmons began to feel that she had found someone else to rely upon musically, and so Simmons decided to leave the group sometime soon. He also wanted a chance to catch up on what the rest of the jazz world was doing and to use what he had learned in a different situation.

As it turned out, François Vaz would leave the group before Simmons did. The problem, as Simmons assessed it, was that a war broke out between Carmen and Vaz when Carmen told him that she wasn't going to take him along to a gig at London's Playboy Club and then to Germany. Simmons was in the house at the time that the fireworks began. Vaz insisted that Carmen take him to England and Germany.

Vaz had left his job with Lou Rawls — he had given up that security for Carmen. He felt that now she couldn't leave him behind. Carmen fought the obligation, because it was going to cost her money that she didn't want to spend. She really couldn't afford to take Vaz with her and make enough of a profit. But she gave in, and Vaz went along to London. While Simmons thought that Carmen was frugal, Vaz opined she could be stingy with others, though not with herself. Vaz's opinion was closer to the truth.

After their trip to England and Germany, Vaz and Carmen fought all the time. No doubt the battle was about who was going to rule the roost. The group that went to London with Carmen included John Heard on bass, Frankie Severino on drums, and François Vaz on guitar. On this tour they played with a number of different bass players along the way — Red Mitchell, Ron Carter, and Ray Brown among them.

After the European tour, and back in Los Angeles, Carmen recorded an album called *The Sound of Silence* for Atlantic Records in June, 1968, with a big band which included Jimmy Jones, the pianist and arranger, and trumpeter Shorty Rogers, also a musician and arranger, as well as Vaz.

Whatever quarrels Carmen and Vaz had, their relationship continued to develop. In 1968, on *The Mike Douglas Show* in Cleveland, just after their return from London, Carmen introduced the band and said, "This is my husband, François Vaz." She said the same thing at the Monterey Jazz Festival, announcing "I needed a guitarist, and so I married one."

Vaz recalled that, "Everyone laughed with us, not at us." Though they never actually married, they had decided to use the story as a surprise.

Vaz had good memories of 1968. They played Marty's on the Hill in Baldwin Hills in Los Angeles, and Lurlean's in Chicago, owned by Carmen's friend, Lurlean Hunter, a singer whom Carmen admired so much that she played there mostly as a favor, not for the money. "Count Basie came," Vaz recalled about the gig. "And we worked in Mister Kelly's in Chicago, and then in New York City. We did the Village Gate in the summer of 1968." Although Vaz didn't recall their playing anywhere else in New York that summer, a young pianist and composer, Bertha Hope, the widow of the innovative bebop pianist Elmo Hope, recalled hearing Vaz and Carmen at the Club Baron at 138th Street and Seventh Avenue in Harlem.

"And she treated him roughly," Hope recalled, referring to Carmen's behavior on the bandstand. "Carmen said, 'This is my pianist, my bassist, my drummer,' and introduced them by their names, 'and oh, Lord have mercy, this is my husband, the guitarist.'" Carmen's voice dropped down low when she said that. It had been on the rise for the others. Hope was shocked at the way in which Carmen put him down in public. "It didn't seem like the right thing to do in front of an audience. I didn't need to be privy to that," she said.

While Vaz didn't concentrate on that sort of thing, he did recall that he and Carmen had some very rough spots as well as some very beautiful times during their tempestuous love affair.

"We had hassles just like any couple has. I have a marvelous picture of her, which she dedicated to me and said I was the most wonderful thing in her life, the greatest thing that ever happened to her in her life. And as for the bad things, I think I'm the one who said something nasty to her. We were working at La Concha in Puerto Rico. For my birthday Carmen offered me a trip to St. Thomas nearby. Just before that happened, well, Carmen had to have her sleep. That was very important. She needed very heavy curtains. She wouldn't stand for daylight when she went to bed." Carmen became very angry with Vaz because the curtains weren't thick enough in their room in Puerto Rico. He pointed out that there was absolutely nothing he could do about them. After all, he wasn't the hotel's decorator.

Furthermore, he recalled, "I was called Mr. McRae. I remember the ex-husband of Peggy Lee saying people did the same thing to him. I was making arrangements. Oscar Cohen was handling her business, her bookings. But as far as accommodations were concerned, or a reheasal set up, it was left up to me. It was a strange situation because Norman Simmons was her musical director. (Normally the musical director arranged for rehearsals, sound checks, and other such matters.) So I was doing a job which was not very easy.

"At times I had to take the musicians' side against Carmen. I told her, 'First I'm a musician.' She said, 'First you're my man.' I said, 'But if you're unfair, I must take the musicians' side.'"

Sometimes Carmen was just in a bad mood, he said, "as anyone can be without any specific reasons mentioned. She would be very sullen. She had a very strong personality. When she would get angry, she would be silent. That would automatically come about. And it just spread. No matter how many people were around. So basically it was great musically, but I must say that Carmen was right (to resist the suggestion) when I asked could I work with her."

After the gig in Puerto Rico, Carmen did take him to St. Thomas for his birthday celebration, but she was sullen and unhappy the whole time. They spent a miserable day together.

When they stayed at Carmen's house in California, Carmen's mother snubbed Vaz. "Carmen's mother didn't particularly appreciate my presence," Vaz recalled, "which didn't make things very easy. She was domineering. And unfortunately she was sick and dying of emphysema." Vaz met some of Carmen's good friends: Sylvia Pierce, the ex-wife of pianist Nat Pierce, Sarah Vaughan, and other singers.

Vaz felt that sometimes Carmen "had difficult times with people because she was very forward." Vaz opined. Part of the reason for that, he believed, was because West Indians could be very tough. He had already been married and divorced from a West Indian woman, with whom he had had two children, by the time he met Carmen. "Anything she had to say." Vaz continued, "came with a cutting edge, a razor blade, so her relationships were generally pretty stormy. And the only one who seemed to survive that was Sylvia. But years later when I talked to Carmen, she said she and Sylvia had fallen out. I was surprised because they were very, very tight."

Vaz also recalled that Sarah Vaughan visited Carmen when they played at the hungry i. Vaughan and Carmen got along very well, he said, because they had some of the same tastes, including a liking for cocaine.

Norman Simmons also knew Carmen as an extremely independent soul. Once she and several girlfriends, the wives of musicians Eddie Higgins and Ed Thigpen, and Sarah Vaughan, were driving in a car and a bunch of men were following in another car. Carmen got out, confronted the men, and got rid of them. "They were wild, independent females," Simmons recalled with a hearty laugh.

He also had memories of Carmen's shy, quiet side. One night in a dressing room, she said to him softly, sounding like a little girl, "Stop screaming at me," instead of shouting back at him aggressively.

But Carmen's relationship with Vaz was simply too stormy. "The most difficult thing is for two people who are together in the same business and see each other every day," said Vaz. "On top of that, it was a weird thing for Carmen because she was paying me as a sideman, and I guess that after a while it got to her. And she was staying in expensive hotels, and my salary didn't allow me to stay in the same hotel. It started at the Village Gate. We had separate dwellings.

"She could be a very difficult person, and she could be tender at times," Vaz added. "But her voice was like her, like a diamond, rough with cutting edges. And she was very careful about the choice of her musicians. She wouldn't stand for any kind of mistake, which happened very seldom.

"We split up in the fall of 1968, after a gig at Lurlean's in Chicago. I have a touching picture of myself with Carmen from those last days. She was singing a ballad, and she held one of my hands which meant I couldn't play while she was doing so. Some friends took the photo. I also have a couple of very nice pictures taken at Mister Kelly's on our near last gig. Those I care about, and those are the only ones I have."

After they split up, *Jet* magazine published two lines about the couple, saying, in their "People" column, that Carmen McRae and her guitarist husband of a few months, François Vaz, "are not hitting on those mellow notes anymore. Miss McRae bluntly told those who were interested in the windy city, we're not together anymore."[5]

With Vaz, who had earned some good reviews during his tenure with Carmen, gone from her life, Carmen had to face the assessments of how underappreciated she was. In a *Down Beat* article written by Samm Mitchell, Ella Fitzgerald was quoted as saying "Rating by talent, a thousand beautiful things should have happened to her."[6] But Carmen had to keep earning her hosannas from gig to gig, review to review.

By 1969, and perhaps as early as late 1968, Carmen had left Associated Booking Corporation. So many times when the group arrived in a city, nobody knew she had come to town. There was no advance publicity. Carmen finally decided to hire a manager who would coordinate all the aspects of her career, including booking, publicity, and recording.

At first she hired someone who did not work out. He stayed with her only very briefly. He promised to book her into rooms with big orchestras and to take her out of the club world. And he did manage to achieve that, as Simmons recalled.

Norman Simmons left Carmen in 1969. Carmen was very upset with Simmons for leaving. She wanted him to stay. But he decided it was finally time for him to try something else. He had worked so closely with her for so long that he felt he had lost his own identity. No other job offers had come to him after a while with Carmen because people knew he wasn't free to take them. His job with Carmen had become like a marriage. It was also the most important growth period of his career.

Members of her groups for years to come would feel the same way about her. Working with Carmen was like studying at the knee of a master; her group was an informal training school. Simmons felt that he had been close enough to a great artist to have absorbed some of her knowledge, which she took the time to share. He didn't believe she had as much patience with training other pianists after him. Norman used the education Carmen had given him when he went on to play with many of the best jazz singers of the century. Finally, Simmons worked with Joe Williams for several decades, until the end of Williams's life in 1999.

After Simmons left Carmen's group, he received a letter from her which he considered quite "nasty." She wrote that he had been paid for writing arrangements, and he had failed to write an arrangement for Duke Ellington's tune, "Satin Doll." She was very angry with him about that. He was astounded. "Everyone knows that song, or should know it," he said. "Can you imagine someone not knowing it?" Carmen had never had a written arrangement for it, because none of the musicians in her groups had ever needed one.

Norman did understand why Carmen was so angry, even bereaved, at his departure. It was a great strain for her to reorganize her group constantly. Singers like the confidence they feel when they find a musical director who will stay in the job forever because it takes a lot of energy for a leader to break in new people. "It's like breaking up a marriage, when a musical director leaves, and a group leader has to take in new people and get it happening," said Simmons. "With me, she could lay up there asleep in her room while I rehearsed the group. But changes happen. Carmen had trouble with that." Simmons would find that Joe Williams could handle change better. "He could do a lot of jamming. He could throw something together right quick. He wasn't so precise." A few years after he left her, Norman and Carmen did become friends again.

"Of all the singers, Carmen was my sweetheart because of her artistry and her elegance, and because she passed it on to me. She was very together, a very strong woman. Strong is a funny word. We use it to imply resistance. In reference to Carmen, I mean she's together, straight-ahead and honest with herself." Carmen wasn't going to let anyone penetrate her space, push her around, or impose upon her. She was earthy and blunt at any cost. Simmons thought she had both a strong character and personality. "Things you might criticize her for — being hard on musicians — she knows those things about herself. She is demanding," Simmons said, assessing his former boss long after he left her. "Something in Carmen's character and carriage carries over to the music. She doesn't let anyone stomp around in her life."

It isn't clear whether Carmen behaved in such a mercurial, volatile, and cranky way for any one reason. She had started out in the music world with a quick temper, as Dick Katz remembered. She lived on the fast track in more ways than one. She was accustomed to meeting slick, opportunistic people who loved the seductive, sometimes rough ambience of the nightlife. And it was difficult to find true love in such a milieu. Billy Taylor thought Carmen, like Billie Holiday, Ella Fitzgerald, and Sarah Vaughan, was unhappy because she never had a happy, lasting love relationship or marriage — "what most of us think of as a normal life," he said. Because of that failure, the singers had "different bad reactions. Someone keeps slapping you in the face, you have to say 'hold it,' or even start slapping back," said Taylor. Carmen hadn't been a bit difficult when she had first been married to Klook in the 1940s, Taylor remembered. Drummer Chico Hamilton, one of the legions of jazz musicians who met Carmen at different stages of her career, recalled her as a friendly woman when she was Klook's wife. But later on, Hamilton would say succinctly, "She became evil."

Hamilton thought Carmen hated men. He went to hear her sing a set at the Rainbow Grill in New York, in the 1970s, and in his opinion, all her ballads were about how terrible men were. But actually her repertoire contained multitudes of subjects and attitudes about love relationships. With a formidable reach, firm grasp, and at times a piercing quality to her voice, she encompassed the whole spectrum of American popular song. She was equally at home singing the uptempo song "A Foggy Day," and gargling words for "Sunday," extolling the joy of meeting her lover on that one day out of the whole week, and asking "What Kind of Fool am I?" using, by turns, a delicate, tender sound and a firm voice, and interpreting "Midnight Sun," in which she played with the last word "sun," and the bitter lyrics of "Woman Talk" and "Trouble Is a Man" and the witty "You Aint Gonna Bother Me No More." In between songs, she blithely tossed out lines such as: "You know what it is. I haven't had a drink, that's my problem," and: "You know what I just realized — how butch a woman can become when she is wearing pants. Now can you see me doing this with a dress on?"

Other friends knew that Carmen liked to smoke a great deal of marijuana; that had been true since her salad days in Harlem. She also spent money on other refreshments, cocaine among them. It may be that the drugs altered her patience quota. The years of hard knocks on the road had battered her, too, everyone said, as they did most musicians. But women leaders were particular targets for many music business people, and even other musicians. She would have had to become wary at the very least, even if she didn't necessarily have to develop the hair-trigger temper that made her seem unfriendly and even merciless on occasion. If some people settled on the notion that she hated men, others thought she simply targeted anyone who annoyed her. It may also have been that Carmen's intense involvement with lyrics increasingly possessed her. As much as she owned songs, they also owned her.

Norman Simmons saw Carmen's development as simply the norm for an artist. "When you're young, you have a dream to get someplace. There's a certain intensity in that climb. Then later, you have the dealings of the business world to contend with. And you reach a plateau and become disenchanted and bitter. Life onstage is okay, but offstage it's a drag," Simmons explained.

But sometimes Carmen's bright, social side predominated. She liked to entertain friends at small dinners which she cooked herself in her house in Los Angeles; occasionally — not often — she threw big parties for them. One of her large parties was a birthday party, to which she invited her friend Marge Costa and important people in the jazz world, such as guitarist John Collins, her friend and neighbor, artists' manager John Levy, and the very successful composer, arranger, and alto saxophonist Benny Carter, who wrote such tunes as "Key Largo" for the movies, as well as the eminent critic Leonard Feather, all of whom came with their wives. Carmen's manager-to-be, Jack Rael, thought Carmen didn't really like Feather, though she respected him. (She didn't like many people, Rael would also say.) Annie Ross, one-time mistress of Carmen's first husband Klook and singer with the group Lambert, Hendricks and Ross, came to the party, too. Annie Ross didn't know the other people there well, and she didn't like it when Carmen told her to sing and entertain the other guests. Though Carmen hadn't warned Annie Ross, Carmen had definitely planned to insist that Annie sing. "That really got my back up," Ross recalled.

Marge Costa felt that Carmen had no regrets about offending people. Carmen didn't think there was anything wrong with the way she behaved. When Marge had problems with Carmen, Marge simply walked away and returned later. She valued Carmen's friendship, admired her, and didn't want to hold any grudges. The good simply outweighed the bad. But quite a few friends and acquaintances passed in and out of Carmen's life after a squabble or an insult had irritated or even devastated them.

Despite these harsh moment, it was just as normal, even ordinary, for Carmen to get together with girlfriends, hang out for an evening, and have a really good time. Carmen managed to keep some warm friendships for her whole life. For instance, all through the years, Carmen and Sarah Vaughan remained close; they would telephone each other and tease each other about the men in their lives.

One night in the late 1960s, when Billy Taylor had been playing in a club on Bleecker Street in Greenwich Village, Carmen and Sarah went to hear him. During a break, he sat with them at a table, and asked them about chords.

He said, "How do you get the harmonies that you want from accompanists?"

Sarah said, "By not ever asking for them."

Carmen said, "Right. If I ask for a raised ninth, I never get it. I get anything but."

Taylor thought both singers had "fantastic ears." When he played for Carmen, he played "just some pianistic harmonies," he said, and she would find some "fantastic notes and say 'that worked.'" Taylor would say, "I know it does."

"Her thing, as harmonically sophisticated as she was, was lyrics. She handled the most subtle lyrics; she approached lyrics differently than Sarah did. Carmen combined so many elements that were important in that era. Rhythmically she was very secure; she swung. And in her group, if she wanted that to happen, you would hear that. So she wasn't leaning on another instrument, she was really very aggressively making that kind of feeling happen. And yet she was one of those singers who had so much control that she could sing behind the beat, whatever she wanted rhythmically. She was unique. She could do things rhythmically, melodically, and harmonically that no one else could do. She could take a song and own it."

That night, Taylor asked Carmen and Sarah which of them was the better piano player; both were known as expert pianists.

"I am," both said together.

"I've got her," said Carmen.

"Don't believe it," Sarah said, and they laughed.

The two singers loved to laugh together and parry with each other. If there had ever been competition between them, and if there would at times be more in the future, as some people close to Carmen believed, their friendship and camaraderie survived and overrode all.

Much of the information in this chapter comes from interviews with Norman Simmons, Marge Costa, Billy Taylor, Annie Ross, François Vaz, Jack Rael, Larry Clothier, and Bertha Hope.

[1] Gleason, Ralph, The Rhythm Section, "Carmen McRae — An Ecstatic Singer," *Times Mirror Syndicate*, published in the *New York Post* (April 17, 1966).

[2] Korall, Burt, "McRae, Maye and Lee," *Saturday Review* (April 29, 1967).

[3] McNamara, Helen, "Charmin' Carmen Fills the Town," *Toronto Telegram* (March 14, 1967).

[4] Harris, Peter, "Nightclubs," *Toronto Daily Star* (May 22, 1967).

[5] "People," *Jet* (*c.* end 1968). The exact date of the article could not be verified prior to publication.

[6] Mitchell, Samm, "Carmen McRae," *Down Beat* (December 12, 1968).

CHAPTER SEVEN

Manager Jack Rael Steps In

Beginning in the early 1970s, Carmen's friend Larry Clothier began to undertake little jobs for Carmen. "Just on a piecemeal basis," he recalled. "I booked a few things, arranged a few dates." Carmen began suggesting that Clothier might want to manage her one day. He did not have the experience, of course, at the time. But he was becoming familiar with her personality and was learning about music and the music business from her. "She and I sang together a lot in private, not performing onstage. We sang one time for a luncheon in Scandinavia, an impromptu thing. We did 'Two for the Road' by Leslie Bricusse and Henry Mancini one time." They also sang together for fun in Carmen's living room, when she would play the piano for them.

Clothier learned that Carmen didn't have a lot of "interchange," as he called it, with her relatives on the West Coast. She wasn't continually attentive, but when she had the time and inclination, she did things for them; she was fond of them. "I think Carmen appeared to be this famous bitch relative who could have done more and shared the wealth. The relatives can hardly ever see the expenses, the overhead, that goes along with being famous," he added.

"She had a lot of women friends. She liked gay women and straight women," Clothier said. She also had many straight and gay male friends. Though Clothier saw many gay women around her, he never saw any suggestion of homosexual activity brewing with her, certainly not in public. "Some people make it quite evident in public what they intend to do in private. I never saw that in Carmen ever," he said. He and Carmen, however, talked about every possible subject under the sun, and homosexuality in relation to many people both of them knew of course came up as a topic.

However, it was known in jazz circles that Carmen had affairs with both men and women. Because Carmen's bisexuality was a sensitive subject, some people who knew her didn't want to comment about it a great deal — or even at all. They regarded it as Carmen's private business. But as Bob Cranshaw would later reflect, "People knew; we know with each other. People just knew Carmen went both ways. It's just better not to get into it. I knew what she was about when I was with her, and I never got into it, because she was so kind and beautiful to me. I was one of the gentlemen who respected her. I knew a lot of things. But we had respect for each other. She was a gas, a happening lady," he said.

One artist's manager — not her own but a friend of Carmen's — said, "That's the facts of life. Everyone who knew her knew that. It's not a big deal. It was generally acknowledged in the business that this was the way it was."

Marge Costa was even more candid and forthcoming: "Carmen had bisexual affairs. She said that everything there was to do in life, she had done. And she would say that in clubs. 'Anything you can do, I can do, and I have done it,'" Marge reminisced. "She had a close relationship with Billie Holiday. Carmen was not a prude. I never saw her in bed with anyone, but she dug men, and she dug sex, period. I believe that she was bisexual."

That was the general consensus among everyone who knew her by this time. Marge continued: "I just don't think she had access to the right kind of man, and she would get a weak man who liked the fast life, the entertainment life. Carmen was not going to give up her singing and traveling for the kind of man she needed. I think she was basically lonely."

Not everyone agreed with Norman Simmons, who had given the subject a great deal of thought and said: "Sure. I knew she had bisexual relationships. Sometimes bisexuality is a convenience. I knew a lot of women who had bisexual relationships. For female singers, it can be difficult to find a man. And the longer the women are out there, the worse it gets. You chose this career, and that's part of the price. You can get to the point where you don't have a choice.

"Singers are a hard group of people to deal with, and no man really wants a singer for a wife. The average man doesn't want a wife who's gone all the time, and temperamental, and a prima donna. Most (men) are hired by singers, and managers, and paid by the singer. That kind of stuff wasn't exactly cut out for women, and when they do it, they make a sacrifice, and it develops a tremendous amount of ego. It's just extremely demanding. You're married to the business. A man needs a masculine identity, and you can't have that with a singer. Singers go through a lot of stress. They're prima donnas. Some guys do jump in but wind up taking advantage of them one way or another, taking advantage of the situation one way or another....

"I knew Carmen for a long time. Basically she was a normal woman. Being in show business, you have more opportunities, but your life is more public, too. Other women, their lives are not public. So you don't know about [their sexuality]. They experiment when they're young, and if it works, and you need it later on in life, there it is. And understanding between women can be a little closer than between a man and a woman. At least with two women, there's a little more basis for understanding about where it's coming from, especially as life gets more difficult as you get older. Women invest themselves in men by taking care of them. And as time goes on, women need to be taken care of. Men don't understand why you need to be taken care of instead of them. Problems come up from that."

There were times when women pursued Carmen and asked for introductions to her, hoping to become intimate with her. Jack Rael, her manager, remembered a hustler asking for an introduction to Carmen. Carmen told Rael, "Forget about it." Her sexuality was not uppermost in her mind, her career and music were her priorities.

"She did a lot of thinking," Larry Clothier explained, "mainly about herself. She was self-centered, selfish, all of those things that anyone who had achieved what she did would be. Especially for a woman to pursue this business of being a singer, and it's maybe even harder in the jazz world, you have to be centered and single minded. She was pursuing a career and dedicated to it and knew what she wanted to do and was able to focus on it to the exclusion of nearly everyone and everything else around. I wasn't around in the early parts of her career, but when I met her, she had already arrived at a certain plateau. By then she had more responsibilities. And it's not easy.

"She was so unique and talented. I don't think she ever felt that insecurity about her craft. Carmen knew what she could do. She knew she could sing in tune, while so many others can't sing in tune and don't really know what they're doing. They have to battle with that plus the outside forces everyday. Carmen, in the same way as Sarah Vaughan, didn't have to battle with those demons. She knew she had the artistic range to do what she wanted to do. It must really be difficult for much less talented performers. She didn't have to battle with the gods and the lack of generosity, too. Carmen never had any illusions about her vocal instrument. It wasn't as beautiful as Sarah's or even Ella's, but Carmen had some other things that Sarah didn't have. Sarah knew that, too. Carmen could illuminate you with her rap."

In his book *Notes and Tones*, a collection of interviews done by her friend, drummer Arthur Taylor, Carmen had ample opportunity to air her views on myriad subjects to a much greater degree than when she spoke to audiences during her performances. On October 30, 1970, in Cologne, Germany, she talked to Taylor about her piano playing as a means to get where she wanted to go as a singer.[1] She believed that whatever she knew about the piano was extremely important to her career. "Without (knowledge of the piano,) I would perhaps not even be singing, or if I had become a singer, it might not be as impressive as whatever it is I do now."

Onstage — and Carmen felt this was of paramount importance — she sang for herself. She also sang for her musicians because she needed them to play competently behind her, to communicate the way she wanted them to with the audience. "So it is really a combination of doing it for everyone ... musicians, myself, and audience," she said. Carmen very much wanted the musicians to like what she was doing and not just play for the money, so that they would be sincere. And she spoke of her love for the music business — a love that apparently transcended all the difficulties she faced on a gig-to-gig basis. "It's such a beautiful business we're in," she said. She drew inspiration and guidance for her direction from her audiences. If they liked what she was doing, they let her know, and she listened to them. She paraphrased Louis Armstrong's credo, which was "I'm here in the interests of entertainment."

Did she categorize herself as a jazz singer?, Taylor asked. She was "jazz oriented," she said, but she only wanted to be categorized as a good or bad singer. She had started with the intention of being a singer. "But it was awfully hard ... to play and not to improvise in some sort of way on the melody. If doing that made me a jazz singer, then yes, that's what I am." She also expressed puzzlement about exactly what constituted a jazz singer. She had heard many people such as Ray Charles, Nancy Wilson, Tony Bennett, Frank Sinatra, and others who improvised and "who are all making exorbitant amounts of money," she said. They were called pop singers, but they never sang a song the way it was written. Still, they weren't called jazz singers. She didn't know if it was a question of how much improvising they did or something else. "I don't understand it," she said.

Carmen also spoke of her love for contemporary music, because she would never have wanted to spend her whole life singing eight bars and a channel, or bridge, and eight bars, and 4/4 time and 3/4 time. She loved other time signatures, such as 7/8 time and 5/4 time, and was delighted to have Beatles songs to perform, not just tunes about moon and June to choose for her repertoire.

Carmen responded to many questions by Taylor about politics, travel, and her favorite musicians; she picked bebop founders Charlie "Bird" Parker and John Birks Gillespie — she always called him affectionately by his real name and not Dizzy. She loved the Kenny Clarke-Francy Boland band — a particularly brilliant European band that included some Americans — and Miles Davis, trumpeter Freddie Hubbard, Cannonball Adderley, and even Blood Sweat and Tears were among her favorite groups. She loved music she could communicate with, she said, and she couldn't communicate with the avant-garde. It left her cold. "If there are six people in a group and all six are playing something different, there is no way for me to know who to concentrate on or what's going on." And she spoke of how happy she was when young people showed up in her audiences and let her know they dug her bebop-rooted music. She was particularly pungent in her opinions about avant-garde jazz and the publicity surrounding musicians and their drug use. All her answers gave insight into Carmen's keen intellect and introspection.

To Taylor's question about the publicity surrounding musicians and their drug use, she gave an extremely candid answer, "... You've got to use something to be in this business. It's very hard to get by without drinking or smoking or whatever people feel they physically need to make it." She thought that people could come from fine, normal families and still need help to cope with the stresses of the music business. She thought it was foolish for anyone to try to destroy himself, "but I do believe some sort of stimulant must be used by those who feel they need it in order to survive," she said. She felt very proud of the "cats" who had gotten too far into drugs and then saved themselves and walked away. She didn't try to make excuses for musicians who hadn't overcome their habits. She actually said: "If you can't rule yourself, you should go and take a gun and kill yourself, because that is better."

Taylor wanted to know about her technique; did it change when she was doing a recording, or a radio show, or a club date or a concert? Carmen said yes. If she was alone in a radio studio with technicians, or doing a TV show in front of an audience, or a concert with only the audience present, or playing in a recording studio with only musicians and technicians, each situation demanded certain energies and different approaches from her. She preferred to sing for concert audiences. She disliked television, because she couldn't see all the people she was singing to, though she enjoyed taking part in a panel on a television show.

Carmen didn't think she did her best work in a recording studio, because, she said, "I never know the song until I record it and start doing it, and six months later it's right." That was exactly what Norman Simmons had noticed. They were often given twelve songs to learn and record rather quickly. "But you don't know them until later," Carmen said. Her live recordings at Sugar Hill for Mainstream had circumvented that handicap. Critics may have liked her earlier recordings, but she said she changed songs radically and arrived at her most mature interpretations only after she had been singing them for a while in clubs.

And with modesty, she told Taylor that she hoped her interview would be worthy of standing alongside the others he was conducting for his book. Taylor asked her if she was religious. She mentioned having left behind her early Catholic training. As for an organized religion, she said, the only one that appealed to her was the Baha'i faith: Dizzy Gillespie had talked about it to her. "But I don't know," she said, though she knew she wasn't an atheist. "My main concept of anything we can consider godly would be to treat my fellow human beings, regardless of what color or creed or religion they might practice, as individuals. Let me put it this way: A lot of individuals are not human beings. I'd rather treat an individual the way I get vibrations from him as a human being. Consequently, I have to practice it myself. I cannot expect my fellow brother or sister to be decent if I don't try to be." She knew that she didn't like some people and some people didn't like her, and believed when people felt that way, they should stay away from each other because life was too short for anyone to have to tolerate a person one didn't like. It wasn't fair to give anyone that burden.

Privy to Carmen's innermost thoughts such as these, Larry Clothier continued analyzing Carmen day-by-day. The longer he knew her, the more he learned about her. "On some levels she had a very highly developed intellect. She praised Billie Holiday's reading of lyrics. She thought no one could read a lyric like Billie. Sarah Vaughan was more basic in her thought processes. Not stupid, she was very sophisticated about some very sophisticated subjects. She had a sophisticated understanding of the street. Carmen knew all about that, too, but Carmen had a much wider view of things. She was more interested in the world. And she could handle her own affairs. Sarah knew pimps and gangsters, and she was comfortable in saloons with the night people. Sarah was insecure about things outside music." Carmen was comfortable in many circles.

She was, for example, comfortable with Larry Clothier, who was essentially a white farm boy, born in Kansas, about 25 miles from Hutchinson on Highway 50, precisely "in a farmhouse three or four miles outside of Sylvia, Kansas, in the middle of a snowstorm," he liked to say. He was always interested in going places and seeing things. But he didn't have any idea of where these places were. Carmen taught him a great deal.

But Carmen's choice as her manager at this time in her career was a savvy, experienced man who had been wheeling and dealing in the music business for over two decades. Milwaukee-born Jack Rael had been a saxophone player who had worked with a band in Madison, Wisconsin all through his college days. After earning his diploma, he went to serve in the army for three years in the early 1940s. When he was discharged, he went back to playing the saxophone.

While in Tulsa, Oklahoma for a one-nighter on October 20, 1946, he heard a wonderful young singer on the radio. "There was this girl singing her ass off," he recalled. Rael telephoned the station to find out who the singer was, this superb country and western singer, and was told, "That's our local girl, Clara Ann Fowler, sponsored by Page Milk."

Jack Rael went to meet Fowler, this woman eight years younger than he, "a poor country girl, who grew up as one of eleven kids in a house that had no indoor toilet." By the following December, Rael had given up playing the saxophone and devoted all his time to managing Clara Ann, whose name was changed to Patti Page. Rael invented overdubbing, he said, for which he received an award. "Bill Putnam was the engineer. I told him what to do. He said, 'It's never been done.' There was only acetate at that time. I said, 'Why can't we record with another disk?' We needed another voice on the record, and we had no budget. The technique worked. The song was 'Confess.' We followed it with 'The Tennessee Waltz,' which she overdubbed. And she was on her way, the number one singer in the world for fifteen years. We traveled together. We never married."

This was long before Carmen McRae began to build her career. But eventually she did, and she, Patti Page, and Jack Rael shared the same accountant. Patti also had a hairdresser, Bruce Vanderhoff, that Carmen McRae used. Peggy Lee was friendly with him, too. Peggy Lee and Patti Page arranged for Jack Rael and Carmen McRae to meet around 1970 or 1971.

The first meeting between Carmen and Rael took place in Rael's office in New York City — two rooms on the top floor of the Plaza Hotel. A friend of Rael's, Norman Rosemont, who managed singer Robert Goulet, helped secure the little office for Rael. "Carmen came up there, and we talked, and it was fine."

He said to her, "What are you doing?" And she told him. Rael told her that he produced all of Patti Page's records.

Carmen said, "Do you think you'll have time for me?"

"Why not? It will be a hobby," Rael responded.

Rael said he didn't think he and Carmen ever had a contract in all the years that he worked with her, until 1989. "I would take her word for anything. She was very honest."

Before she hired Rael, Carmen had already acquired her secretary and accountant, an attractive white woman named Jan March who lived in Los Angeles and was about ten years younger than Carmen. Jan March remained with Carmen for the rest of her life and become executrix of Carmen's will.

In some ways, Rael kept his distance from Carmen. He didn't socialize with her a great deal, in part because he knew how rough she could be, but also because she couldn't afford the expense of his going along on her tours. He knew her financial situation well and didn't fault her for trying to keep her costs down. Years later he would look back at the list of what he had done for her and feel proud of his accomplishments.

When he began managing her, he started her with a salary of $2,500 to $2,750. "It wasn't chopped liver in those days. It went up to $25,000 a concert."

One of the first engagements Rael got for Carmen was at the Rainbow Grill atop the RCA building in New York. The reviews for her performance there were superb. The *Down Beat* critic wrote "Opening her program with a graciously romping 'I Love The Life I Live,' Miss McRae made it very plain that she does." And "Miss McRae becomes more than a singer. She delves into the realm of the actress, using her hands, face, and body with taste and control. And her interpretation of 'The Folks Who Live On The Hill' ... was handled with the care of someone who has deep respect for the material, as she virtually built that 'house on the hilltop high' out of nimble phrasing." For the closing of the tune, she began "down in the diaphragm and ended in the head, as her voice rose higher and higher until it diminished and disappeared, presumably somewhere on the other side of the hill. The audience applauded loud and long with loud bravos."[2]

Then she sang a country and western tune written by Jimmy Rowles, called "The Ballad of Thelonious Monk," with the great Monk portrayed as a cowboy for a dash of humor. And then there was "Alfie" and "I Cried For You" and "Just a Little Lovin'," the title of her new Atlantic album at that time — altogether a heady brew of a set.

Carmen did some television around that time — all the usual shows she had been appearing on for years. Arranging for her recording contracts, too, in 1971, Rael booked Carmen's group at Donte's, a club in the valley in Los Angeles, where she played for $900 against 100 percent of the door. "And we took in $2,500 for the week."

At Donte's, Carmen cut one of Rael's favorite recordings, one of the two he produced for her, *The Great American Songbook*, on November 6, 1971. He loved it because of the musicians she used, particularly the great guitarist Joe Pass, and because Carmen herself was "so loose," Rael said. The exceptional accompanist Jimmy Rowles played for Carmen for that date, and so did bassist Chuck Domanico, with whom she worked often throughout her career, and a drummer named Chuck Flores. She sang the ballads she loved, and which she interpreted with her usual improvisatory genius — songs such as "Body and Soul," "At Long Last Love," "I'll Remember April," "Day By Day," "Satin Doll," and others, at least thirty songs, most of which were eventually issued on the Atlantic label. Later people reading her sessionography would be astounded at how many songs she had recorded.

She also played the Monterey Jazz Festival in 1971. And she had a big following in Toronto, where Rael booked her. She played the Hyatt House in Atlanta and did well, and the Plaza Hotel in New York, which had a little room where most people got paid about $1,500.

During the next year, 1972, Carmen started to earn more money, beginning with a week at Century Plaza in Century City, where she worked for three weeks and received $4,000 a week. In Philadelphia she also earned $4,000 in a club; she went to Baltimore in 1972, too, and played the Playboy club circuit. Carmen traveled to Seattle, Washington, then Portland, Oregon, for $4,350 a week; within a few weeks she earned $12,500. She had never earned that much money before. She did a television show in December for $3,750, and then she played in a club in Denver, Colorado, and another one in San Francisco.

Among Carmen's recordings that year was a lovely album, *Carmen*, done with guitarist John Collins, who had grown up with her on St. Nicholas Avenue in Harlem. He had had no idea, when they were youngsters, that she would become a very famous singer; he knew only that she played the piano.

Collins was part of the charmed circle of people who never had any problems with Carmen. Collins had an easy time with Carmen, he said, because: "I would tell her off. Well, I could. We understood each other. She would always tell me, 'John, there's only a few of us left.' She came to visit me at my house, too. One time I was going to a Los Angeles Jazz Society concert, and she came to my house to see Eddie 'Lockjaw' Davis. He was very sick with cancer at the time.

"It was wonderful to record with her. She gave me quite a bit of leeway because we were friends. I went into the studio, and she said, 'John, I want you to play your ass off.' That was her instruction to me. We had that kind of rapport. She could be abrasive to people if they caught her at the wrong moment. Then anything might happen. I used to tell her that I thought of her as Mabel Mercer [for the great singer of popular songs who emigrated from England to the U.S. by way of Paris, where she had starred at Bricktop's club in Montmartre and introduced many of Cole Porter's songs to the world]. That's what I called her. You could never think of a tune that Mabel didn't know. Carmen was the same way. Carmen's repertoire was amazing."

In 1973, Carmen worked in the Rainbow Grill for almost a month, prompting Margo Jefferson of *Newsweek* magazine to include Carmen in an article about the resurgence of interest in jazz in the country. "There's the wry elegance of Carmen McRae's voice," Jefferson acknowledged.[3] It was at the Rainbow Grill that the venerable *New York Times* critic John S. Wilson noticed Carmen scolding her pianist and turning her back on the audience for a while. When she turned back to face her fans, she seemed befuddled for a moment, as if surprised to find the audience still there. But then she recovered her aplomb and put on a show. Wilson disliked this display of temperament, and thought she was quite mannered at times on some songs. Throughout the years, Wilson would vacillate between calling Carmen the greatest jazz singer in the world and putting her down as among the most mannered. However, that was the only type of negative criticism she ever recieved, and it came along infrequently.

At one point Rael decided that if Patti Page was such a big star in Japan, Carmen ought to try to become one there, too. So he booked her for $7,000 a week for three weeks, plus transportation round-trip for herself and her trio, and her accommodations and expenses — "and that really started to explode us in Japan," he recalled. She played just one hotel that time; in Japan they had dinner shows, which included a performance costing $200 a person — a lot of money in those days; of course now it costs $2,000 a person.

"And she was on her way. That was good money in those days. Carmen wasn't as hot as Sarah Vaughan. Sarah had Dave Garroway [the broadcast personality] and he did it." By playing Sarah's recordings on his Chicago-based network NBC radio show constantly in the 1940s, Garroway gave the great diva a priceless boost. Carmen had no world-famous mentor in her corner.

Every time Carmen played in New York, she attracted the attention of John S. Wilson and his sensitive, pungent opinions. He noted that an audience for her concert at Avery Fisher Hall in March, 1975, liked her "in whatever role she cast herself — a vocal acrobat using swoops, dips, and staggers in the Sarah Vaughan manner; her casual but emphatic recitative style that, consciously or unconsciously, carried echoes of Sophie Tucker; her informal, earthy discourses between numbers...." He also took issue with her trademark style — "a flat, take it or leave it delivery that drains the lines of some songs of melodic content or an approach to uptempo, swinging songs ... that is so deliberately disinterested that their inherent swinging qualities disappear. But she balanced this with an exploratory vocalism that redeemed ... overdone songs" and imbued them with color.[4]

Rael and Carmen made a great team. "I had her in Toronto July 10 to 23, 1975, and in Winnipeg on the 24th, and in Vancouver on July 26 and 27," he said. "And what do you think she made for those three Canadian dates? $20,000. It took her one week. Then she was back in Las Vegas in August, then in Chicago, where she played in different places, and then Montreal, and in Sweden — she was big in Sweden — and on a cruise ship, and at Playboy clubs for one show a night, and then back to Japan in 1975 for two weeks for $25,000 for one engagement lasting from July 2 through the 15th."

There were myriad gigs, some of which Carmen made the connections for herself. For fifteen years, saxophonist Red Holloway owned a club called the Parisian Room on La Brea at Washington Street in Los Angeles. He wanted Carmen to work there, and he began inviting her in 1972, when he bumped into her on a street in Manhattan.

"No," she said, "Those people are so noisy. I'll cuss them out."

"I don't think they'll be noisy," he answered.

"I'm not coming," she insisted.

It took Holloway three years to convince her to try his club. She finally agreed in 1975 with the proviso: "If I have to deal with all that noise and bullshit, I'll walk offstage."

"Okay," he said.

When she did her first set of the two sets scheduled nightly at the Parisian Room, an audience filled the club. People were very quiet. At the end, they gave her a standing ovation. She told them, "Red has been trying to get me here for three years. I said 'no, there's too much damn noise.' Now I have to eat those words. You're the greatest audience anyplace. I love you."

Carmen went back to work at the Parisian Room every year, her last dates taking place in late 1982, just before the club closed its doors in February, 1983. She always brought her own trio and always packed the house for the entire week. Holloway knew that people talked about how raucous Carmen could be, but at the Parisian Room, "she didn't lose her temper once," he said. "She was a very nice lady, Carmen. I didn't know an awful lot about her. You don't know real intimate details unless you are hanging around. We were on speaking terms but didn't go out." That wasn't necessarily Carmen's fault. By his own admission, Holloway was "a loner," and didn't like to become too involved with people. "Sometimes you hook up with someone and get in a whole lot of trouble you wouldn't ordinarily get into on your own," he explained. He didn't even know that his friend, Ike Isaacs, the bassist, had once been married to Carmen. But Holloway did know that Carmen behaved with a bright attitude and good manners every time she played his club.

Carmen's connection with Red would lead her to do an album, *Fine and Mellow: Live at Birdland West*, with him for Concord in December, 1987, in Long Beach, California, with Red on tenor saxophone, John Clayton on bass, Jack McDuff on the organ, Philip Upchurch on guitar, and Paul Humphrey for the drums.

According to their agreement, Rael received 15 percent of the gross of Carmen's fees as his payment. Carmen paid for all her other expenses, including musicians, who she paid well and on time. None of them ever complained about their salaries. Despite her temperament, many of them stayed with her for years; one of the longtermers was pianist Marshall Otwell.

In 1976, a friend of Otwell's, bassist Luther Hughes, auditioned for her group. She told him, "I have a list of bass players a mile long. What I really need is a piano player. If you bring a piano player, okay." So he brought along Otwell in 1976. "She was one of the people I had always wanted to play with," Otwell recalled.

It took quite a while for Otwell to understand Carmen, whom he considered a perfectionist. "Her level of concentration when playing music was something I hadn't encountered before. I had to learn how to concentrate that intensely and keep things as she wanted them. She was not a young woman at that point, and she had some pretty firm ideas about how it should go and what was necessary. Basically I was learning to accompany on her job ... I was in my early thirties, thirty-two or so to start, and I stayed eight and a half years. Her way of communicating could be so shocking that it was very stressful at first.

"If she would say: 'You stupid motherfucker, why did you do that?' she meant: don't play that G there, or something like that. Typical overstatement. And the first time someone directs that at you, it's shocking. Your first reaction is: 'She is really angry at me.' And her surface emotions often were turbulent. She was a volatile person. And she appeared to be very upset about things. It could be anything she didn't like — a musical detail, something going on in a hotel, an arrangement with a club owner. Her exterior was not what we now call professional, which is unemotional and placid, as we say in the business world. And so I had to kind of learn how to read that, because I did learn that it didn't mean what it appeared to mean. She and I developed a pretty close relationship. We were pretty good friends with a pretty good working relationship.

"I got to understand what I could do for her and what I couldn't, and she understood the same," Otwell said. "And still, after many years it could be that at any point in the middle of a performance she was capable of turning and trying to humiliate someone, me included. It kind of got better. At one point, I had been with her about two years, and I was checking something out before we went onstage; part of our routine was we would check to see we had the same list of tunes. And this day she was really ragging about the performance the night before. She was much more emotional than she needed to be. Somehow during that conversation a little light went on in my head. I thought the worst thing she could do was fire me, and that might be the best thing. I walked out. After that she almost never did that to me again. She had been testing and pushing me for two years. What was my limit? Apparently that's what I had to do. That's the surface aspect of Carmen that people are most familiar with."

By this time, Carmen no longer stayed with Norval Perkins and his family when she went to Washington to play. Donna, Norval's daughter, knew that Carmen's fame had increased and noticed that Carmen had changed with her fortunes. She was still kind to her relatives, but she had less time, and perhaps even less energy or patience, to spend with them. Her musicians noticed she was beginning to show mild respiratory problems, too. When Norval went to Los Angeles, he stayed at Carmen's house. But when Carmen went to Washington, she always stayed in hotels, usually at the Watergate. Most often Carmen met the Perkins family in the clubs and concert halls where she played. She always put tickets aside for them or saved tables, and she instructed people to be very considerate of her family.

Donna had always loved the way Carmen treated her like a grownup throughout the years. "We talked about my mother and father. We would laugh about their shortcomings," Donna recalled, "and we had our little confidences and understandings about how we viewed those two. I didn't talk about her music to her. I had questions, but I felt as if I didn't want to ask her something dumb, and I would save those questions for daddy. Instead I would ask her something bland, like 'Are you going to be able to sing "Miss Brown To You" tonight?' She might say she had her stuff set up one way, and she would do another song instead. Or we might simply ask her what her stuff for the night would be. I never asked her how long she practiced. That was small talk to her, not interesting to her. She wanted to know about you.

"I think performers are curious about people who lead normal lives. 'How do you get to school?' 'Do you wait for the bus every day? I couldn't stand waiting for the bus every day,' she would say. And she would ask me about whether I had a boyfriend. She would let me be in her dressing room, just the two of us. She let me be the last one to leave. She didn't mind my being there when everyone else had to leave. She would do some kind of meditation, calming herself. She always had a beautiful handkerchief that she grabbed and took onstage. It wasn't for wiping sweat. It was almost like a piece of jewelry.

"As time went by, she became more casual onstage." Carmen didn't dress as elaborately, in sequins or lame and wearing high heels, as she had done when she was younger and slimmer. "Her dressmaker sewed caftan-type muumuus. They were in." Donna remembered that Carmen eventually began to wear even more informal clothes. "She wouldn't go slumming in (ermines) and pearls — that was one of her songs, 'The Lady Is a Tramp,' and she wouldn't be trying to show off around poor people. They don't want her to be all bummed out either. But she was comfortable.

"Carmen wasn't into small talk and niceties. I recall her being a little brusque with people. People are going: 'Carmen, Carmen!' She would smile, sign her autograph, and they would ask her where she was going next, and if she didn't feel like talking, she would say: 'Get them out of here,' right in front of them. Some of that comes with age. You want what you want when you want it. We [her relatives] kind of knew not to crowd her. Early on, we used to be all around her. And we understood: You get to a point where you have your own entourage. She would take care of her family and make sure we were in the front row. She took care of that always. There could be 20,000 people in the hallway, and Carmen would say, 'Let them in, that's my sister, let my sister in,' and upset people who had been waiting for autographs for 20 minutes.

"I followed her musical career. I loved her style. English was my major, and I loved how she phrased and paid attention to the sentiments being expressed in her music. She was an actress while she was singing. That, for me, was completely enthralling. I thought she was a consummate actress. Even though she smoked cigarettes, she never was high or drunk onstage; she never did anything to hurt herself. She would always tell them in the clubs about the air conditioning. (She wanted it on sufficiently high to help her with her breathing.) She was very concerned about keeping her voice healthy. We didn't have the same view of smoking then as we would have later. Then there were elixirs or things she used to smooth her voice. She would have lemon and honey in her dressing room.

"I don't think she was a bitchy person, but her musicians probably thought so because she was demanding and exacting; she was always hearing everything, every note, that everyone else was playing. Onstage she remembered your name; she was a gracious and grateful person to audiences, and she gave complete credit and a little history and anecdotes about who wrote the music.

"She was always on time even when she would stay at our house. She had a time, two hours prior to a performance, that she had to go to the place to perform. She never ran into the place where she was performing with her mink coat. She never ran in. She was always there on time. You could tell that from her shows. Her shows ran completely by her plan. She took requests from the audience, and she had already practiced what they were going to ask for. If the audience brought up something that the musicians weren't ready for, she would go to the piano and play her own accompaniment. She would always have a little part of her show where she was playing. I thought she was always good to her musicians; her standards of excellence they respected."

Though Carmen's relatives managed to stay in good standing with her, some musicians, even those who had worked with her happily, found themselves on precarious footing at times. As one of her sidemen in her later groups would say, for no apparent reason she was simply moody. When Dick Katz went to see her playing at a mid-Manhattan club, Jimmy Ryan's, in the mid-1970s, he was already well aware from gossip on the jazz world's grapevine that she spoke in a negative way about piano players. Before she came out onstage, as her group was warming up the audience for her, Katz went and sat in for her. Listening behind the scenes as he played introductory music, she didn't know who was playing. When she arrived on the bandstand, she recognized Katz and said, "I knew someone back here could play." But she didn't say hello to him; she didn't ask how he was; she didn't introduce him to her audience.

In 1977, Harvey Siders, writing a cover story about Carmen for *Jazz* magazine, did a thorough job of defining both Carmen's appeal and her temper. He wrote about the stares and glares that Carmen gave to any backup musician whom she considered errant for the night. Siders loved her "quest for perfection" because he felt she was maintaining high standards to pass to the next generation of jazz singers. "She picks the material, sets the tempos, and has every right to expect the correct (chord) changes and voicings behind her so she can concentrate on the lyrics and shape the unique phrasing that has made her the only singer in captivity who can belt them out in italics."[5]

Carmen explained her sometimes all-too-public ire with her musicians. She didn't like embarrassing musicians, she said. "But I concentrate very hard on what I'm doing up there, and so should they. They're getting paid very good money for what they're doing." She felt they had no excuse for not getting the music right, since they rehearsed everything, she said, "to death."

Siders recalled one performance she had recently given at the Playboy Club in Los Angeles, where she excoriated the bass player onstage. Afterward, calling the musicians to a "command performance" of her scolding backstage, she explained to Siders that she told them: "'You're playing shit tonight. What's goin' on?' And I reminded them: Look, if I do somethin' wrong, I'll get out of it somehow. If *you* do somethin' wrong, I don't know where the hell I'm at. So concentrate. I don't intend to do another show like that!" She also explained that she reprimanded her pianist, Otwell, for not playing a chord in a particular way that she might need to be able to get from one song to another. "I'm not paying them to make me look like an idiot. I pay them to make me look good," she said to Siders.

"She may win through intimidation on occasion," Siders wrote, "but for the most part she wins through expertise."

Carmen had established a reputation for having no pre-performance jitters. Her friend Sarah Vaughan became so nervous before nearly every performance that she verged on hysterics, claiming she just couldn't go onstage, she couldn't do it, she couldn't continue. Carmen's overdone reprimands to her musicians, both on and offstage, constituted a form of nerves; she took them out on others instead of herself. The intensity with which she approached and imbued her music and lyrics grew with each passing year; her musicians could depend upon her for excessive emotionality in her approach to her every moment as a performer. Carmen was very hard on herself, too, claiming to Siders that she hadn't made an album yet that really satisfied her.

There were times when Carmen's musicians could bask in the glow of her approval, of course. One such instance was her live performance with Sarah Vaughan and her trio and the Los Angeles Philharmonic Orchestra at the Hollywood Bowl, on August 13, 1977. Carmen praised the whole proceedings, including her sidemen Andy Simpkins on bass and Joey Baron on drums, to the skies — "and you'll hear it in the album (*Blue Note Meets the L.A. Philharmonic* on the Blue Note label, which had arranged to record the proceedings.) "The charts were by Bill Holman. What more need I say?" Siders perceived the performance as a cutting contest between Sarah and Carmen, and so did *Los Angeles Times* critic Leonard Feather, who wrote that Carmen, with her lesser vocal instrument, ("Miss Head Voice," Feather called her,) had bested the gloriously endowed Sarah Vaughan, "Miss Chest Voice."[6]

To Siders, Carmen revealed herself as exceptionally picky and opinionated — familiar with and open to a wide variety of tunes from all fields of popular music, from the Beatles to bossa nova — and concerned about the future of jazz singing. "It's a disappearing art," she said. "The young, upcoming singers aren't singing pure jazz. At least I don't hear them." At that time she was, for the most part, correct, because new jazz singers weren't getting many chances to work. Young instrumentalists would not begin to step into the limelight until the early 1980s, when Wynton Marsalis's popularity, nurtured by Columbia Records, started paving the way for them. Siders concluded that "her conversation is liberally sprinkled with italics.... She constantly stresses certain points.... It's colorful, lively, dramatic, filled with humor and pathos, and it rivets your attention. All of which neatly sums up Carmen's vocalizing."[7]

Asked about her personal goals by Siders, she said she was hoping to improve her recording career and finally come up with a hit record that "makes it on the charts. 'Cause I'm tired of working so goddam hard. I wanna be able to pick and choose my gigs. And if I get me a record that makes any kind of noise, I just might be able to do that."

The hit record that would earn a Grammy award and a million dollars continued to elude her. But her fees were excellent. Jack Rael had booked her into Las Vegas for $7,500 a week in 1974 — "good money in those days," he said — and for a tour of Europe in November, 1975, and in Australia in 1976 for $22,000 for a week, and in Sweden in 1977 for three weeks for $17,000 a week plus expenses. She worked in Caesar's Palace with Bill Cosby in 1979 in Las Vegas, then in Tokyo again in June, 1979 for $27,000. "It got better and better as it went along," Jack Rael summed up, "once you got the ball rolling."

For a woman who never won a Grammy, though she would have seven nominations altogether, Carmen was cutting a wide, flamboyant swath through the jazz world.

Much of the information for this chapter comes from personal interviews with Larry Clothier, Jack Rael, Red Holloway, John Collins, Donna Perkins Potts, and Marshall Otwell.

[1] Taylor, Arthur, *Notes and Tones* (New York: Perigee Books, 1977). All material from *Notes and Tones* is included in this footnote.

[2] Tolnay, T., "Caught in the Act," *Down Beat* (May 13, 1971).

[3] Jefferson, Margo, "Jazz Is Back!" *Newsweek* (December 24, 1973).

[4] Wilson, John S., "Carmen (McRae) Sings In A Variety of Roles," *New York Times* (March 11, 1975).

[5] Siders, Harvey, "Perfectionist Carmen McRae," *Jazz* (Fall, 1977).

[6] Feather, Leonard, *Los Angeles Times* (August 1977).

[7] Siders, op. cit.

CHAPTER EIGHT

Globetrotting

C armen's reviews were in effect awards. The *New York Times's* John S. Wilson, then the dean of jazz critics, wrote cannily about Carmen all the time. In September, 1979, he remarked on the development of her "personal, idiomatic style" by the way she mixed elements of jazz and cabaret singing and pared down the material. "It is a style that, largely because of its bare bones quality and her rather astringent manner of delivering a line, can sometimes seem chilly and impersonal. But at the Village Gate where she is appearing ... Miss McRae has everything in balance — her material, her approach and her delivery — and she creates an atmosphere that is warming, appealing, and communicative...."[1]

In the past, Wilson said Carmen had sometimes seemed too intently hip for his taste. But at the Gate she went in the exact opposite direction, and even took the trouble to explain to the audience the genesis of the song, "Send in the Clowns." She told the audience that the song was about "rushing clowns out to cover disasters at a circus," thus clearing up the mystery of that song's meaning. Audiences had no doubt long been puzzled by the lyrics. And the song "had a deeper, more powerful effect than it usually does in its superficial, nightclub presentations," wrote Wilson in his review. For years Sarah Vaughan, by sheer dint of her magnificent voice and astounding vocal acrobatics, convinced audiences of the emotionality of this song, but it was Carmen who brought out the deeper meaning of the piece and made it an unforgettable experience.

Wilson also praised the way Carmen enunciated and subtly altered words and made her parlando, or half sung-half spoken material, swing. And he loved the poignancy of her interpretation of a Paul Williams song, "Loneliness," which Wilson called "tailor-made" for her eccentric style. (Carmen, with her restless, inquiring mind, kept searching for new material and sang more Williams songs as well as other tunes by composers not usually included in jazz repertoires.)

For Carmen's mid-December, 1979, engagement at Marty's at Third Avenue and 73rd Street in New York City, then the leading jazz supper club on the Upper East Side, Wilson lauded her again and discussed Carmen's fascination and indebtedness to Billie Holiday. Carmen explained the powerful effect Billie's friend-ship and support had supplied, as well as the way Carmen had spent a long time early in her career imitating Billie. "I thought I was not a very good talent and I had to feel that what I had to say was going to be appreciated," Carmen told Wilson.

It wasn't until Carmen apprenticed in Chicago in 1948 that she began to step out from behind the shadow of Billie's gardenia (the traditional flower that Billie began wearing in her hair to cover up a curling iron accident.) "I was doing my own thing, maintaining my own audience, and out came Carmen," she said about herself.

In the twenty-five years since Carmen had won the *Down Beat* critics' poll New Star Award, she had undergone many changes. "Nothing stays the same. I've lived. I've been to different countries, met different people. You have to change. I don't think my voice is as good as it was in 1954 or 1955. But I've learned of some depths that I did not know I had. Now I feel that I'm really interpreting songs, that I'm a little bit of an actress. It's important that people believe in what I'm doing." Wilson interviewed Carmen in Marty's little dressing room behind the bandstand. And so for Carmen, the lyrics were "numero uno." "The melody may not be good in spots, but I can change that. On uptempo things, you just pop your fingers and concentrate on rhythm."

Carmen spoke of loving the bass most of all. "I depend on the bass rhythm in ballads to give me inspiration." She named some of her favorite bassists — Andy Simpkins and Ray Brown, who had done a spectacular, eerie duet for the murder scene for the original soundtrack of the movie *In Cold Blood,* as well as playing accompaniment to singers. Carmen also spoke about the great European bassist Niels-Henning Orsted-Pedersen. As favorite accompanists on other instru-ments, she named drummer Roy Haynes, who had played for Sarah Vaughan's trio for years, pianist George Shearing, and trumpeter John Birks Gillespie — Dizzy — whom she always called by his real name.[2]

On May 23, 1980, in the *Baltimore Evening Sun,* writer Ernest Freda called Carmen "one of that exclusive first name trio of jazz singers,"[3] meaning Ella Fitzgerald, Sarah Vaughan, and Carmen, who were usually cited as the three greatest jazz singers of the twentieth century (sometimes Anita O'Day was included in that group too).

Stephen Holden followed ably in John S. Wilson's path at the *New York Times* in 1981, by praising Carmen's interpretations of the ballads "My Foolish Heart" and "I'd Rather Leave While I'm In Love" for their "rich psychological" content. "In these songs, both of which confront ... emotional commitment, Miss McRae pretended to be a fortress of strength momentarily touched by romantic inclina-tion. Her blend of cynicism and tenderness lend a rare illumination to the lyrics."[4]

Carmen's career was so illustrious within the jazz world that Burrill Crohn, a fledgling documentary film producer in 1981, thought of her first as the hostess and narrator for his seven-part series for television on women in jazz. His friend, bassist Harvie Schwarz, warned him, "She's a wonderful professional, a great singer, but if you mess up, you'll be in big trouble, especially if you're a man." Crohn faced up to the challenge. Paid about $5,000 for her participation, Carmen hosted three of his videos, Marian McPartland the other four.

Crohn gave Carmen the script for the first video when she was staying at the Sherry Netherland hotel during an engagement at Lincoln Center in New York. She was "nice and polite," he said, when she received the script. He sent a limousine to bring her from the hotel to a club called The Other End on Bleecker Street in Greenwich Village, where he was going to do his filming. In the throes of "doing everything for the first time in his career — writing, producing — some things fell between the cracks," he reflected. "Other people were helping. But there was no makeup person."

As soon as Carmen arrived at The Other End, she asked, "Where's the make-up person?"

When she discovered that Crohn didn't have one, "she looked at me like I was a worm," he recalled. "We had to get into the limo and go to the Sherry Netherland. From that time on she ignored me. I was sweating bullets. I was a wreck. She got her own makeup, and we started to work. Every time I gave a direction, she ignored me. I came out of that thinking I was never going to be a filmmaker. It was harrowing. There was no compassion, no forgiveness. She was working with amateurs, and she didn't like that. But to her credit, she could have walked out. She stayed there and did the job she was hired to do, and she did it very well in spite of the tension between us."

Overweight, she nevertheless dressed herself beautifully in a muumuu that covered her from her neck to her ankles and gave the impression that she was voluptuous. (She always wore high-necked dresses to cover the pale, jagged scar on her chest from an accident with boiling oil that occurred when she was a child.) She was wearing slippers because her feet hurt, and so she said to Crohn: "Promise not to shoot my feet." But a long shot showed her old white slippers. Carmen did her own makeup, and her hair was a little frizzy and stood up no matter what she did with it. It looked fine, Crohn thought. "And the show came out good. We did good. But behind the scenes, it was pretty terrible."

However mixed Carmen's feelings were about traveling, or any other annoyance or event that took her away from her secluded house in California with its spectacular canyon view, she continued to live her life on the road with her group. Marshall Otwell remained her accompanist; her favorite drummer Joey Baron, who adored her, and who had played with her occasionally in California, most notably in the concert with Sarah Vaughan and the Los Angeles Philharmonic, recommended drummer Mark Pulice to her in 1980, and Pulice and bassist Jay Anderson began playing for her at the same time.

Otwell figured the group worked about half the year, for about seven weeks at a time, and then had the same amount of time off. One of the places they worked was the Henry Street Settlement House on the Lower East Side of Manhattan, where Carmen performed for an audience of young people who couldn't afford the uptown clubs and paid only $5 to hear her. She loved performing for budget audiences. So in the summer of 1982, at the settlement house, she showed up in purple colored pants and a bright red sweatshirt with a gigantic white flower embossed across her chest. She looked very athletic and ready to reach out to the casual, sporty audience.

At age sixty-two, Carmen still had a chiseled, Levantine face. Nothing had lowered the eyebrows peaking over the bridge of her sharp nose, and no scowl had left a wrinkle in her brow. She kept her vocal and physical mannerisms to a minimum, and her style was lean and strong. For "Sophisticated Lady," her aristocratic nose pointed somewhere toward Mecca, transcending the impression of her sweatshirt. "Do Nothing Till You Hear From Me" followed, with its tag line assuring you that she would not be in touch; the target of her tune had ruined someone's dream, and so he could sit there and wait for nada forever, said Carmen. A jet-propelled "Foggy Day in London" came next, evoking the supersonic Concorde, then the latest status symbol for the traveler who had done and seen everything.

She sat down on a stool to sing a highly embellished interpretation of "Everything Must Change," and at the end, when she sang about crying, she was actually crying. Toward the end of the set, she did a very fast "Thou Swell," with some of the best vocal improvisation ever heard. When she tried to get offstage, people yelled their encore choices at her. She said, "Get it out, or you'll get gas." And she sang her own choice.

A few weeks later, she sang some of the same songs in a very different setting; her version of "Everything Must Change" was even more embellished for the well-to-do audience at Marty's on the Upper East Side. But she seemed to have less real enthusiasm for the performance. She didn't let her hair down as she had done for the kids at Henry Street.

In the eight years that Otwell traveled with Carmen, he went to Japan with her seven times, and to Europe for the summer festivals, and to New York, as well as to many out-of-the-way places. One especially out-of-the-way place was the fifth floor of a building in Sydney, Australia, atop a Chinese restaurant on the first two floors, a casino on the third floor, and a dance hall on the fourth floor. Ordinarily the group found wonderful pianos in the places where they played. But Carmen couldn't abide the Sydney club's piano. For the first time she exercised her option, which was always written in her contracts, to insist on a good piano. The next day, Otwell and the club owner went looking for a new piano in the stores.

"The piano is very important to her music," said Otwell. "She does a lot of things with her trio, and her songs are soft and slow, and the piano has to be very orchestral. If you have a piano that isn't well in tune or doesn't have good, resonant strings, you can't play simply and have it work. You can't play two notes and let them ring and have any impact, whereas if you have a good piano, you can do all that. And I always felt that what was required behind her was to play as simply as possible." Years later, when he went back and listened to his recordings with her, he always wondered why he played so much, why he sounded "so busy." "I was always trying to play this pristine kind of backdrop," he recollected.

Otwell was almost never aware of the racial difference between himself and Carmen, unless she chose to make a remark to the audience. Sometimes, when the group would play the blues, Carmen would say, "Not bad for a bunch of white boys." She wasn't color blind, Otwell knew, but he didn't feel she ever discriminated against him or displayed anger toward him because he was white. "It was either because of something musical or something I did," he said. Yet he did have a sense that she resented whites, or at least had some negative feelings against them. He could understand her attitude, though, which wasn't an aggressive hostility. It was more of the feeling: "We've been so mistreated." But he didn't try to analyze her attitude about race. He felt the sensitivity about it in general in the country by 2000 was different than it had been in the late 1970s and early 1980s; everyone had become much more sensitized, perhaps overly so, to racial matters, or questions, by the 1990s, he said.

He noticed she had many friends around the country, including many gay and straight women, but he never was sure if she had a lover or partner of either sex. He thought there might have been possible candidates for romances of a sort with Carmen, but he also had the idea she might have "been past that point in her life."

For the most part she concentrated on her career and treated all men and women with equal interest as long as they fit in with her plans and mood about her career. When a jazz fan named Burt Westridge, a stranger to Carmen, approached her when she was playing at Buddy Rich's club near Madison Square Garden and asked her to sign a petition to support the jazz radio station, WRVR, she agreed. She signed the petition with cordial, good cheer during a break in her show. "She was very pleasant and charming," Burt recalled. She gave people a little time to explain their business with her, and if it made sense to her, she let them linger for a few minutes. But she generally didn't like intrusions from anyone, man or woman, by this time.

If there was one constant in her life, it was that when Carmen was working, she focused completely on her show and matters that came up in the club, and nothing else really caught her attention. Otherwise she was guided by her completely unpredictable moodiness.

When Carmen played at the Blue Note, still one of the most glamorous clubs in New York, in the early to mid-1980s, Dick Katz, whom she had given short shrift at Jimmy Ryan's a decade earlier, went to see her again. She greeted him by saying, "I knew all the piano players would be here." That was the extent of her conversation with him. Dick felt she emanated a bitterness; she lacked warmth.

Anyone catching her on the wrong day came away with a jaded view of her, said people who traveled with her for long periods of time. Above all, they knew she was moody, and just as liable to vent her feelings on men as on women, and on musicians as on non-musicians. Her behavior had nothing to do with her sexual orientation. Carmen herself had told one of her lovers how upset she was to learn that people talked about her as if she were gay. "I really dig men," she told the lover.

Jack Rael didn't care if her affairs were with gay women or not; he knew that some of Carmen's women friends took advantage of her. One even stole luggage and some clothes from Carmen's house. It was strange to think of Carmen as a victim, but that is exactly what she was at times, and that was part of the reason why she became so tough and could seem so cavalier with other people's feelings. She was warding them off, afraid of their potential for damaging her in some way. As Norman Simmons had noticed admiringly, she didn't let anyone stomp around in her life.

Marshall Otwell was intrigued by what he perceived as the sweet, warm person buried deep within Carmen, and "her exterior, emotional self was fighting with that person most of the time," he said. He glimpsed Carmen's sweet side only occasionally, when she extended herself to try to do something nice for people, "here and there." Most of the glimpses he had were of what she gave to her audiences. "Carmen was about relating to an audience. She had a way of making an emotional connection with an audience. It was unlike anything I've ever seen. She was a wonderful singer and a gifted musician, but in my perception, her real gift was getting her own special personality over to the audience. Not making them love her; that might not be quite the right way to say it. But she could move an audience to feel what she was saying and singing. In some sense, I almost think of her as a great actress. If we had jazz opera, she would have been a great opera star."

Offstage, Carmen stifled her powerful inner warmth, although she did reach out to Otwell several times to bring him into her personal life. She invited him, along with two other people, to her house for Christmas dinner one year. "It was like a little family," he said. He brought his girlfriend at that time. Carmen's good friend Sylvia Pierce, pianist Nat Pierce's ex-wife, came to dinner. Otwell observed that Carmen and Sylvia were close friends; Sylvia took care of Carmen, understood the singer's volatility, and accepted her as she was. "Sylvia was a very forgiving friend to Carmen," he said.

Otwell lived in Laguna Beach, south of Los Angeles. If the group played a late gig in Los Angeles, Carmen said to him, "Take a spare room, because we have an early flight in the morning." She made breakfast for him, too. "She really liked food; she liked to cook and to eat," he said. She also had favorite restaurants to eat in and took him along. At times her relationship with him seemed very normal, relaxed, and trusting, and she had a great sense of humor. All over the world, she had friends who came to see her perform and invited her to their homes. She had friends in London who always took her to dinner, and she took Otwell along. "She was a treat, I miss her," he reflected years later, and he laughed softly to himself at one of his memories of her.

"We were in an airport between jazz festivals," Otwell said. "Dizzy Gillespie was traveling with us. She and Dizzy were great pals. We were sitting on a little bench in the airport, waiting for the flight. Ten yards away, soldiers with automatic weapons for security purposes were lined up against a wall, staring straight ahead, in the at-ease position. Dizzy put a little hash pipe in my hand. 'Here man,' he said. It just cracked me up. He and Carmen were pushing this hash pipe between them. I don't know if it was made of bone or stone. We were staring straight at these soldiers. I took a couple of hits with Carmen and Dizzy. But I was just so surprised."

Otwell would eventually reflect that his favorite album done with Carmen was *You're Looking At Me*, a tribute to Nat "King" Cole in 1983 for the Concord label. She culled through Nat's repertoire painstakingly to select the songs she wanted to do, and she patiently listened to other people's opinions. Someone suggested she consider "Don't Let It Go to Your Head," which Nat may have been the only one ever to record. Though Carmen didn't choose that one, she politely listened to a recitation of its lyrics and others she didn't know well.

Mark Pulice was only twenty-two years old when he began working with Carmen. At first he found her very pleasant, he recalled. But he soon learned that it was difficult to figure out what she wanted. Although she didn't necessarily explain to him, he knew if he wasn't giving her what she wanted, because "she had The Ray. We called it The Ray," he said. "She glared at you if you weren't playing what she wanted. And if you listened to music with her, and she liked you to do that, you could figure out what she wanted. Once you figured it out, you could get along just fine with her."

"We hung out with her on the road. We would go to a movie or have dinner. She liked to go out and have fun. But as she got older and sicker, she stayed in her hotel more. It was hard for her to get around. She had problems with breathing. There was no third set with Carmen."

When he began working for her, when she was sixty, she walked through airports. But over the years, her breathing problems really began to manifest themselves. She used wheelchairs to move through airports. Despite her handicaps, the group traveled throughout the United States, as well as to Europe and Japan a few times a year, to Argentina several times, and to Rio. In each place, they played in top clubs. Carmen began performing seated on stools. Critics remarked about this but never asked her why. As a younger woman, she had sometimes sat on stools to perform. Now she did it all the time.

Pulice liked the women Carmen had working for her behind the scenes. At first there was a woman, later replaced by her sister, Shirley Thomas; Shirley became a mainstay of Carmen's staff. Several other people worked for Carmen on and off. They did pretty much everything for her: They sent for her food, packed her clothes, got her cigarettes, and did anything that she didn't want to do herself, "which was borderline everything," Pulice recalled. Larry Clothier noticed the same thing. Carmen wouldn't even get up and walk across a room to get a glass of water if she could have someone else do it for her.

"She was probably harder for those people behind the scenes than for the musicians to deal with," Pulice said. "We were only working for her for a couple of hours a night, but from the ladies she hired, she required her stuff her own way all the time. She wanted comfortable hotels, nice dressing rooms, stuff that stars wanted. And if she didn't get it, she pressed until she got it. She liked thick curtains and quiet in the mornings. Breakfast came late for her. She ate bacon and eggs. She ordered up that kind of stuff in the afternoons. She liked to watch soap operas. Eventually we got her interested in basketball, the Lakers; she watched that. If we were watching that, she would call us and ask, 'Are you watching?' Baseball was a big passion of hers. She did not do sports herself."

On April 15, 1986, Pulice was part of the group that made the album *Live in Tokyo*, comprised primarily of ballads, recorded live at Kan-ihoken Hall and released on the Lobster label. The concert was taped for a video, too, but unfortunately it did not become generally available. Pulice had a copy, however, and loved it, considering it a very fair representation of what the group did with her. (Another video, made many years earlier for Ralph J. Gleason's television show, *Jazz Casuals*, would become commercially available in 1999 on the Rhino label, and that, too, would present Carmen at her best and most typical in a live performance. She was seated for that video, and so her choice of performing while sitting down in her later life never seemed particularly peculiar.)

In 1986, Marshall Otwell went through a sea change. He became interested in writing software. The urge to do it swept over him the way that learning to play music had done when he was younger. At age forty, he found the challenge of software so exciting that he had to make a change in his life. After eight years of traveling, he had gotten burned out by the lifestyle anyway. He wanted to get into what he perceived as a real business. "The music business is a real business, too," he said, "but you kind of have to be a genius and obsessed to survive in it. Carmen definitely was that."

Again Carmen had to go through the ordeal of changing her musical director. This time Larry Clothier, who was managing her by then, invited Eric Gunnison to play piano for her. Larry had known Eric for several years. Carmen auditioned him on the grand piano in her living room, listened to a couple of tunes, and said, "You're hired. You leave for New York in about a week." Gunnison would play with her for the next five years.

He noticed her pronounced bouts of difficulty in breathing, sometimes because of the weather, if they were in a hot climate with a lot of humidity. "It seemed to get worse as the years went by." They cancelled some performances because of her breathing difficulties. But she always recovered and sang again.

From the start, Gunnison and Carmen got along very well in their working relationship. He learned a lot by listening to her, especially when she played a couple of tunes for herself at the end of every set. The first summer he toured with her, beginning in June, 1986, they went to Europe with Carmen's trio that time consisting of Ray Brown on bass, Mickey Roker on drums, plus assorted horn players including tenor saxophonists Johnny Griffin and Stanley Turrentine, and the vibist Milt Jackson. When they reached the Antibes festival in the south of France, they were invited to Bill Cosby's cabana at the Hotel du Cap. There he put out a spread of food and drink, "and the whole trio went to the cabana. It was very interesting, because Cosby was laughing so hard at Ray Brown and Mickey Roker, and so was Carmen. I never saw her have a better time. All of them had stories about various musicians, and the lifestyles of musicians, and someone had done this or that. Just the way they told their tales was very funny. I never saw Carmen that happy again. She was definitely enjoying herself with those guys."

Gunnison was thrilled to meet the people she introduced him to. Then thirty years old, he knew some of the repertoire when he joined her, and what he didn't know he learned in a hurry. He wanted to keep that gig.

Shirley Horn, the singer and pianist who had met Carmen briefly in the Village Vanguard in 1962, had worshipped Carmen as a great jazz singer. Horn had stayed home in Washington to raise her daughter. In the early 1980s, Horn began traveling a lot, and she and Carmen met regularly at the North Sea Jazz Festival in The Hague, Holland. Horn began looking forward to the festival as much to hang out with Carmen as to play there. "We got up at seven or eight in the morning, had breakfast, and talked all day long," Shirley said.

In California, when Horn played at the City Grill in the old Hotel Roosevelt, Carmen went to hear her perform. Carmen owned many of Horn's records and knew something about her life. When in Washington, Carmen would visit Shirley at home and they would eat together. And when Horn went to play in California, she brought along seasoning to cook her food that Carmen liked — greens, fried catfish.

Shirley Horn had a slow, almost soporific style of singing, and her piano playing was exalting. "It was the music that brought us together," Horn would recollect. "I have a lot of her records. I don't think we learned much from each other about music, but I learned a lot about her, when she told her life story, about the good times, the bad times; she'd had an interesting life, she'd been around, she knew a lot of people. I learned a lot about life. She and Shirley Thomas (by then Carmen's traveling companion and helper — essentially a valet) told funny stories. I sat for hours listening.

"When Carmen talked about the men in her life, she kind of put them all down," recalled Horn, who was happily married to the same man all her life. "She talked more about Kenny Clarke, and she was flattering to him; she didn't give him such a hard time. Kenny seemed to fare the best in her memory. I had the feeling that Carmen had loved him."

Carmen's breathing troubles persisted, though they didn't interfere with her sitting down, having cocktails, and breaking bread with Horn. Several times Carmen tried to stop smoking, but she never succeeded for long.

Scott Colley had met Carmen briefly in 1982 at the Los Angeles Jazz Society awards ceremony, where Carmen presented an award to Jimmy Rowles, with whom Colley was then playing. Colley himself received a young talent award. By 1986, he had made his way around the jazz scene enough and impressed enough people so that he was recommended to audition for Carmen's group. "I showed up at her house and played maybe one tune, just with her singing and my playing the bass for a ballad. She never actually told me that I had the gig. Her management sent me the itinerary and tickets the next day, and then we were doing tours and weekend things, the Fairmount hotels in the U.S. and things like that. I was in college at the time, at Cal Arts, the California Institute of the Arts, in Los Angeles. It sort of worked out that I would do some touring with Carmen and try to keep school together at the same time. I don't think it was until a year or so later, when Larry Clothier began managing her, that we did more things, especially Japanese and European touring."

Colley indicated the difference of opinion, or of memory, about exactly when Larry began managing Carmen fulltime, though in any case it was in the mid- to late 1980s. Jack Rael definitely recalled acquiring a non-singing role for Carmen as the madam of a whorehouse in the movie *Jo Jo Dancer, Your Life is Calling*, starring comedian Richard Pryor, released by Columbia Pictures in 1986. Carmen played Pryor's grandmother, one tough businesswoman. The producer-director thought of Carmen for it and telephoned Rael, and that's how the deal came about. Rael didn't pursue the part. Carmen had never given much thought to trying to do more movie work after filming *The Square Jungle* in 1955. She preferred to concentrate on her singing, and furthermore, she knew there weren't many good parts available for African-American actresses at the time.

Colley's first experience of recording with Carmen came when the group went back to New York and did a recording called *Any Old Time* for the Denon label in 1986. When Colley listened to the recording later, memories flooded him, for he had been both happy and scared to be around those musicians.

Colley thought Carmen respected her trio at that time and showed the men her warm side. "My experience with her was great. She told us to listen to her, and I learned so much from playing with her, especially for ballads and for her phrasing on ballads. They were a lesson every night and really made songs into conversations. She had a way of pacing that was incredible.

"My favorite moments with her were when she did 'you done me wrong' kind of lyrics, as she did for the *Any Old Time* album for Denon."

Colley did a fair amount of hanging out with Carmen, drinking and eating, in the first years he worked for her, but in the last few years, she withdrew; she wasn't feeling very well. Colley's relationship with Carmen's music continued onstage. "She had this incredible sense of time and pacing, and she had an incredible way of playing the piano. Vocally she would phrase way behind the beat, in the way that Brazilians do quite a bit, and Billie Holiday, too. Carmen had such a center you could hear from her piano playing. That was a great lesson for me; that the music should be centered on the form, and at the same time have this element of freedom in the phrasing. Her phrasing was very much like (guitarist) Jim Hall's and other instrumentalists'. They have such an incredible sense of time and freedom, and also the patience for a lyric, like there's no hurry to get it out, it's all based on this group communication that shows the musicians are listening to everything that's happening all the time.

"When you were playing with Carmen, you were aware she was listening to you and reacting to you all the time. I've had that same experience with all my favorite improvisers. She was just so completely centered. That was most obvious when she sat down by herself at the piano."

Colley left Carmen in about 1987; a variety of bassists played with her thereafter.

Information for this chapter came from Dick Katz, Larry Clothier, Jack Rael, Shirley Horn, Mark Pulice, Eric Gunnison, Scott Colley, Marshall Otwell, and Burrill Crohn.

[1] Wilson, John S., "Jazz: Carmen McRae," *New York Times* (September 14, 1979).

[2] Wilson, John S., "Carmen Salutes Billie Holiday," *New York Times* (December 14, 1979).

[3] Freda, Ernest, " Carmen McRae: She's On First Name Basis With Style," *Baltimore Evening Sun* (May 23, 1980).

[4] Holden, Stephen, " Pop: Carmen McRae Doubles With Stanley Turrentine," *New York Times* (July 9, 1981).

CHAPTER NINE

Working Hard to Maintain Her Stardom

C armen and Jack Rael would have many shouting matches through the years, yet they continued to work together until at least 1985, with only a few breaks in their professional relationship. The alliance was to their mutual benefit financially. Rael was especially proud when he booked her as a replacement for Sarah Vaughan in a tribute to Dizzy Gillespie at Wolftrap in the 1980s, negotiating a $30,000 fee for Carmen — the most money she had ever made for one performance.

Rael reflected that he had liked all the albums she made since 1975 for the Blue Note label; the first, *I Am Music*, with Roger Kellaway as pianist, arranger, and conductor, and Dave Grusin, playing on only a few tracks, with a studio orchestra. All the tunes on the album were rather obscure; they were not among the most popular of American standard pop songs. They included such rarely heard tunes as "Faraway Forever," "I Ain't Here," "Who Gave You Permission?," and the title tune. Her second album for Blue Note, *Can't Hide Love*, had a number of well-known jazz and studio musicians, including trumpeters Snooky Young, Bobby Shew, Oscar Brashear, and Blue Mitchell; trombonists George Bohanon, Maurice Spears, Grover Mitchell, and Ernie Tack; reeds men Jerome Richardson, Ernie Watts, Pete Christlieb, Don Menza, and Jack Nimitz; and rhythm section players Joe Sample, Chuck Berghofer, Harvey Mason, and Larry Bunker. The tunes covered a wide spectrum, ranging from the pop standard "The Man I Love" to Thad Jones's "A Child Is Born," a favorite in the jazz world. Succeeding albums for Blue Note contained a mixture of obscure songs that never became a prominent part of the pop or jazz repertoires as well as a collection of well-known pop standards.

It was her third album for Blue Note, *Carmen McRae at the Great American Music Hall*, which turned out to be a very good seller, probably the best-selling album of her entire career over the long haul. The personnel included her dear friend, Dizzy Gillespie, as well as Marshall Otwell on keyboards, with Ed Bennett on basses, and her favorite drummer, Joey Baron, a well-known studio drummer who rarely traveled away from home base in those days; he didn't play with Carmen as often as she would have liked.

Many of the tunes were very familiar to audiences, among them: "Them There Eyes," "On Green Dolphin Street," "On a Clear Day," "Miss Otis Regrets," "Too Close for Comfort," "Old Folks," "Time After Time," "I'm Always Drunk in San Francisco," which Carmen liked to do, and "Don't Misunderstand," "A Beautiful Friendship," "Star Eyes," "Dindi," "Never Let Me Go," "T'Aint Nobody's Business If I Do," "Only Women Bleed," which was another song that Carmen favored, and "The Folks Who Live on the Hill." The eclectic repertoire and the excellent music attracted fans for Carmen.

Rael found many qualities in Carmen that amused him. For starters, after he booked her in Sao Paulo, Brazil in November, 1984, she enjoyed it so much that she took him there with her for three weeks the following September. Carmen liked everything about Brazil — the food, the people, and the music. The owner of the hotel where the group stayed provided individual suites for Jack and the musicians as well as for Carmen. The food was gratis and fine, and so were the accommodations on the planes coming and going. She did one show a night for five nights.

"We had beautiful luggage when we went to Brazil, Louis Vuitton luggage," Rael recalled about the trip in 1985, on which he took his wife. "I had to leave a few days early for some other acts I had going. And I got torn apart by the people at the airport to see what I was bringing in from Brazil. They were ready to rip the lining apart."

When he spoke to Carmen by telephone, she asked, "How was your trip?"

"The trip was okay. But be careful," he said. "They went through us with a fine-tooth comb."

She said, "Oh. I'm loaded with stuff," and she dumped it down the toilet. When she went through customs, the agents didn't even look in her pocketbook. "She liked cocaine, pot, and she grew marijuana herself," Rael recalled, "and whoever came to visit her had shit for her. When you're a star, you don't have to worry about that. People always bring you stuff to impress you."

Another time Rael booked Carmen on the cruise ship, the *Norway;* she did many cruises, some on the *Rotterdam,* which she loved, in the 1970s, and some on the *Norway,* which she didn't like at all, in the 1980s; the *Norway* wasn't elegant enough for her taste. But she did the cruises in the company of many other famous jazz musicians, most of them black, including her friend, John Birks.

For one cruise on the *Norway,* for which she earned about $15,000, Carmen took along a black drummer; her regular trio's drummer was ill. "Carmen was introducing her musicians," Rael recounted about one of her performances late in the cruise, "her piano player, and her bass player," and then she mentioned the name of the drummer, "and I've been on this ship five days," Carmen said, "and I ain't seen this nigger till now."

Rael was so shocked and amused that he nearly fell out of the balcony. "Only Carmen could say that," he said. Needless to say, everyone laughed, including the other black people on the cruise.

Carmen enjoyed the good life. She owned two Mercedes Benz cars, one a dark brown, 1976, four-door sedan, and the other a station wagon. She had those cars for years, though she very seldom drove them herself. "And her license plate said KMBA," Rael recalled, "which stands for 'Kiss My Black Ass.' She could be funny. She could be even funnier when she had hip people in her audiences. When she started doing a phrase that was way out, she could be funny."

In 1985, Carmen paid Jack Rael almost $85,000, which meant that she had earned close to three quarters of a million dollars. "She spent it and paid taxes, that she did. The accountant looked after her," said Rael about Jan March, who was also Carmen's secretary.

In 1986, Carmen earned a good deal of money in Switzerland, Finland, Rome, and Japan. Sometimes she went twice a year to Japan, often recording while she was there. Rael said: "That's what built up her CDs."

Rael and Carmen could work together in complete agreement and calm, but there were many times they did not. When she was recording in Long Beach, California, Rael didn't approve of some aspect of the proceedings. And "she was there with a few of her girlfriends, who took advantage of her always." He and Carmen had a shouting match about the record date he didn't like. "That's when I finally left," Rael said.

For a while Carmen was managed by a man named Kim Harstein, who had managed other well-known musicians, and then Carmen asked Ray Brown, the bassist, to manage her. But Brown was always on the road and hard to reach. Devra Hall, artist's manager John Levy's girlfriend, who worked for him, and later became his wife, arranged some matters for Carmen in this period. Hall and Carmen got along very well.

"She was finicky," Hall said, "but if you knew what she wanted, and if you could give it to her, she was fine. She hated stupid questions; she hated to repeat answers to questions like: Where were you born? What was your relationship with Billie? She wanted people to do their homework about those sorts of things." Hall, in arranging interviews for publicity purposes, coached reporters in advance so they could come up with varied questions and not repeat each other and irk Carmen.

Hall once set up an interview with a writer whom Carmen had abruptly hung up a phone on a few years earlier. Carmen had been tired from an afternoon concert in one city, and she faced a club gig in New York that night.

Though she had told the writer to call that evening, Carmen didn't want to be bothered by anyone. She didn't explain; she just slammed the phone down. Now Hall wanted Carmen to talk to that same writer for a magazine article. The writer tried to avoid the situation, confiding to both Hall and Rael, "I'm afraid of her." But they cajoled her.

When Carmen got on the phone, she asked the writer: "Don't I know you? Have we ever met?"

"No," the writer said, although they had actually met once.

"Are you sure?" Carmen said.

"Yes," said the writer.

Carmen said, "I think I wasn't very nice to you one time."

The writer said, "Well, you didn't know who I was at that time, and you didn't know what I would do to you."

Carmen said, "YES!"

"So let's forget it," said the writer.

After that, they went to work peaceably.

"Carmen didn't have a charming personality," said Hall, "but she could be charming when she felt like it, as long as you didn't interrupt her soap operas. Though some people thought she was difficult, if you stood up to her, she would respect you. If you didn't, she lost respect. Tell her what she had to do, and she backed down."

Once, for "Desert Island Disks," a radio show on KCRW-FM, Carmen had to come up with a list of ten records she would take with her to a desert island. Hall and Carmen went through all Carmen's old records, "and she got involved and enjoyed it," Hall recalled. That was in the mid-1980s.

For a while, around this time, Carmen went back to Jack Rael for management. She had already broached the subject with Larry Clothier, but he was busy working for Sarah Vaughan's traveling group. Furthermore, Carmen's fear of strangers, or aversion to them, became stronger as time passed; it hadn't abated. As a result, she hadn't approached anyone else but Clothier. And he didn't take on the job of Carmen's management right away. He thought about it carefully.

"Subsequently," Clothier recalled, "we were hanging out, and she said, 'We're both getting older. So let's.' She was mad at Jack (Rael) for something. 'I'm going to ask you again.' So I said, 'Yes.' We had been doing a lot of business together, bookings, tours, but Jack was still her manager, she was still paying Jack. Anyway, she and I were close friends. She knew that I knew her and had no illusions. And she knew me and what I would do. She would tell people I was her friend. She had always done that, and that had opened many doors for me."

Larry Clothier sometimes thinks it could be said that he really began managing Carmen in 1983, and sometimes Jack Rael recalls that his management ties to Carmen weren't really severed until 1989. Rael was actually in touch with her throughout the 1980s and 1990s, though the full responsiblity for Carmen's management passed to Clothier in the 1980s.

Essentially, Clothier continued Carmen's program that had been started by Rael. "We did a lot of overseas work, all over Europe, and in Japan, and Brazil. Occasionally, she still went to Toronto and Montreal, but she spent a lot of time in Italy, Spain, France, and Holland. She went to the North Sea Jazz Festival a lot of times in The Hague, Holland," he recalled. She also went to Cuba in the company of Dizzy Gillespie and other musicians.

The fees in those years continued at about the same level that Jack Rael had established as reasonable to expect, but there were no hard-and-fast rules about them. Sometimes Carmen received $25,000 for a concert, sometimes much less. "In this business," Clothier said candidly, explaining the situation exactly as most performers and managers have found it, "there's no standard fee. You tailor your expectations to what the situation will stand. Maybe you'll get $50,000 in one situation, and then you go into some other situation where that's ridiculous. There's just not that kind of revenue there. You go into the Village Vanguard for one fee because it's a good thing for you to appear there, but you get more money in another place."

Rael would say that Carmen's most important albums were done in the 1980s, and they included several which Larry Clothier arranged — one primarily of standards recorded live and culled from six shows she performed with Betty Carter, *The Carmen McRae/Betty Carter Duets*, accompanied by pianist Eric Gunnison, bassist Jim Hughart, and drummer Winard Harper, at the Great American Music Hall in San Francisco, on January 30, 1987, and released on the Great American Music Hall and Bet Car/Verve labels.

While preparing to do this album with Betty Carter, Carmen was appearing at New York's Blue Note. According to singer Annie Ross, Carmen delivered a lackluster set without much enthusiasm. Carmen summoned Ross from a ringside table to the stage to sing.

Ross said, "I don't want to do that."

Carmen said from the stage, in a sarcastic tone of voice, "Ain't nobody twisting your arm."

Ross thought, "Shoot! Fuck you, I'll get up and sing."

Then Carmen called other people to the stage, finally calling Betty Carter.

"Naturally they were well-rehearsed and knew what they were doing," said Ross.

Though Ross described it as a lackluster set, Carmen and Betty got a lot of applause. After the set, Ross went up to Carmen's dressing room and found Carmen sitting alone, head in hands, looking in the mirror. "That's such a sad picture of a lady alone," Annie Ross thought. In Annie Ross' opinion, Carmen had "a lot of anger in her. It was probably from the stresses of life on a woman out in a man's world at that time."

Another time, Carmen was appearing at Donte's in Los Angeles. A Hollywood producer was throwing a dinner party for Annie Ross along with Paula Prentiss, Richard Benjamin, and Mike Nichols. Since Annie Ross had promised Carmen that she would go to see her show at Donte's, Ross excused herself from the party in her honor and went to see Carmen perform. Carmen didn't even say hello. After the show, Carmen told her, "I'll drop you off where you're staying."

Ross was staying at a friend's house in the canyons, which were "dark and scary at night," she said.

Carmen's modd quickly changed, and she rushed Ross into the car and said, "I ain't nobody's goddam chauffeur." Carmen then drove Annie Ross to "this black canyon, with no street lights, and there wasn't a front light on the house. I had a key to the house. I opened the car door and got out. By the time I got to the front door, Carmen was gone. Boy, was she angry. Other times she could be just delightful, but I don't think she was a happy person. I thought she was wonderful. But, boy, was she weird. But she sure had a distinctive, beautiful sound, and I loved the way she played piano."

Carmen managed to have a tiff with Betty Carter, too, soon after they made their album together. Carmen made a caustic remark about Carter's singing, and Carter took such umbrage that she went to Carmen's next Blue Note gig and sat at a table without applauding. But that very night they mended their fence and began talking again once the gig had ended.

All these quarrels were in marked contrast to Carmen's relations with some younger singers, who called her the professor, or the chief, and sometimes visited her in her Los Angeles house. Among the younger, accomplished jazz singers who adored Carmen for the aid and advice she passed along freely were Carol Sloan and Helen Merrill. Both were Carmen's buddies and loved her without reservations.

The album that followed after the live recording with Carter was *Carmen Sings Monk*, a tribute to the music of Thelonious Monk. She was backed by pianist Larry Willis, bassist George Mraz, and drummer Al Foster, all first-rate musicians, and tenor saxophonist Charlie Rouse, a veteran of Thelonious Monk's famous band. Carmen recorded a few tracks of the album for the RCA Novus label live at the Great American Music Hall in San Francisco on January 30 and February 1, 1988, and the rest were done in a studio. The Monk songs she chose were especially challenging: "Straight, No Chaser," "In Walked Bud," "Ruby, My Dear," "Well, You Needn't," "Blue Monk," "I Mean You," "Pannonica," "Rhythm-a-ning," "Ask Me Now," "Monk's Dream," "Round Midnight," "Ugly Beauty," and "Reflections." Carmen had been unsure whether she could do such an ambitious project — Monk's music was so difficult. She had considered doing it for years. Larry Clothier kept insisting and encouraging her. Despite all her physical limitations by this time, she was one of the only singers, if not the only one, who could bring off an album of such demanding harmonies, rhythms, and lyrics.

The album was one of Carmen's most ambitious ventures. Most of the songs had convoluted melodies and lyrics. Six songs had lyrics written by Jon Hendricks, with others by Sally Swisher, Abbey Lincoln, Bernie Hanighen, and Mike Ferro. Few of the songs were easily accessible, with the exception of the kicky, plucky "Well, You Needn't," named "It's Over Now" on the album. A listener really had to pay attention to Carmen's deft work. Titles were changed to avoid copyright problems. "Straight, No Chaser" became "Get It Straight." "In Walked Bud" became "Suddenly," "Monk's Dream" was changed to "Man, That Was a Dream."

Preparing to record the album, Carmen had spent hours and hours in her car, in hotel rooms, on the road, in bed at night, listening to Monk's music assiduously, living with it, trying to figure out "how the melodies were really meant to go," as she told Nat Hentoff.[1] "In fact, nothing went where you thought it was going to go," she said. However, her knowledge of the piano helped Carmen understand the construction of Monk's music. "I'm sure that Monk never had a vocalist in mind for his songs. If he had, he wouldn't have made them so hard," she said.

Hentoff thought she sounded as if she really enjoyed the experience of being stretched to perform Monk's music. Her rhythm, phrasing, and authoritativeness helped her put the album across. To promote it, Carmen made herself accessible to the media, allowing bookings on the *Today Show*, CBS's *This Morning*, *Live at Five*, *Good Day*, *CNBC News*, VH-1 *Visions*, and granting interviews to the *Wall Street Journal*, *Associated Press*, and *Life* magazine, among others. The album became Number One on Gavin Jazz and ranked high on other charts, including 14th place on Billboard (Debut) as reported by the RCA Novus label during the week of June 5, 1990. This was Carmen's debut album on the RCA Novus label. "More than merely being in tune with Thelonious Monk's music, throughout her career McRae has captured the off-kilter flavor of Monk's lines in an especially Monkish way," wrote the idiosyncratic critic Will Friedwald in the *Village Voice*, June 19, 1990.[2]

While Carmen was undertaking her most intellectual venture on recordings, her friend Sarah Vaughan was showing signs of slowing down. She, too, found the long walks through airports arduous, and she had to stop to rest and catch her breath often. In the fall of 1989, Vaughan arrived from a week at Blues Alley in Washington, D.C. for a week at New York's Blue Note — the usual clubs where Vaughan, Carmen, and other headliners in jazz played. Vaughan's right arm was swollen and bandaged; she couldn't sign autographs. Just before her opening night at the Blue Note, Vaughan received the word from a doctor. She had lung cancer. The news devastated her, and yet she went onstage to entertain. One old friend from the Earl Hines band came by to say hello and told her he had glaucoma. She commiserated with him, saying she had it, too. But she didn't mention her life-threatening ailment. However, by the end of the week, the stress weighed so heavily upon her that she couldn't go onstage anymore.

Carmen and Larry Clothier arrived in town to go to the Blue Note to hear Sassy. They flew in from Savannah, Georgia. Carmen was fatigued from the plane trip, so on the day she arrived, she decided to rest in the hotel instead. Larry Clothier went as Carmen's emissary, but discovered that Vaughan had cancelled the night's shows. She hadn't told anyone what was bothering her, but the club management knew she had spent frantic hours on the telephone, talking to people.

Soon Vaughan called a meeting of her friends at her hotel and told them the truth. The Blue Note asked Carmen if she would fill in that night. Carmen refused. Nobody knew that she, too, was feeling ill with respiratory problems. They were different from her friend's, but nevertheless she had to husband her energies. The Blue Note management was fit to be tied. Clothier wanted her to do the job, but to no avail.

Vaughan went back to her own lovely house in Hidden Hills, California, an exclusive, hilly enclave. Some of her close friends — those who knew the truth — visited her. Carmen called Vaughan and made a date to visit. They spent an afternoon together. Carmen could see that Vaughan felt severe pain. But not once did "Sass" mention her cancer. Carmen never brought it up, either. They talked about the good old times, when the two young and slender singers had been full of dreams and energy. They recalled their later meetings on the road, when Carmen flew from Los Angeles to San Francisco just to catch one set by her friend in performances, and Vaughan did the same for Carmen. They talked about the days when they had hung out together, drinking and gossiping at tables alone in clubs, keeping their fans at bay, and attracting attention when people recognized them as two jazz divas. But the reality of Vaughan's cancer was too painful for them to mention.

That was the last time Carmen ever saw her friend alive. On April 4, 1990, Sarah Vaughan died at home. Carmen kept working.

Information for this chapter came from Jack Rail, Larry Clothier, Annie Ross, Shirley Horn, Devra Hall, and Carmen McRae.

[1] Hentoff, Nat, "On Records: McRae Sings Monk," *Wall Street Journal* (September 26, 1990).

[2] Friedwald, Will, "Blew Monk," *Village Voice* (June 19, 1990).

CHAPTER TEN

Carmen's Blues

The pathos of Carmen's final visit with Sarah Vaughan emerged in the song "Sarah" from Carmen's album *Sarah: Dedicated to You*. In the song, Carmen sang of "Sarah" going to heaven where she joined Billie Holiday and Dinah Washington. They were already settled in, and Dinah insisted on singing lead. "Sarah" said that was fine with her, she was new there.

When the record was being planned in 1990 for its February, 1991 release, Shirley Horn heard about it. She remembered that once when they were hanging out, Carmen had said, "We'll record together one day. Or we'll work together." So Horn called Larry Clothier and told him: "I'm a good accompanist, and I want to play for her."

Clothier told Carmen, who called Horn. They discussed the project as a possibility. A few months went by. Carmen called Horn again and said, "What's going on with you? I want you to do a tribute to Sarah with me."

The two singers made a list of songs. Over a period of months, Carmen would forget the list that Horn had made and ask for it again, wanting to know what Horn would sing.

Horn said, "I'm not singing, I'm just accompanying." They recorded at a studio in New York. Carmen often performed the final song on the CD, "Sarah," in her nightclub and concert gigs, and everyone cheered for the emotionally wrenching piece about "Sarah" joining the other great singers of the twentieth century. Carmen owned it; that is, she sang the definitive interpretation of it, and nobody else could hold an audience spellbound with it as Carmen could.

On her annual trip to The Hague, where Carmen and Horn hung out together, Carmen met a young singer, Denise Jannah. Jannah came away from this meeting with a very different impression than Annie Ross had wrested from her last meetings with Carmen. In July, 1990, the Surinam-born Jannah, who had moved to Holland to study, and who eventually set up home base in Utrecht, and with the support of many music world insiders had built a career as a teacher and jazz singer, went to hear Carmen perform at the North Sea Jazz Festival.

Carmen's concert was scheduled for the Jan Steen Zool, a big room in the huge Congress building where the festival takes place every July. Denise knew the announcer for Carmen's concert and persuaded him to get her backstage to Carmen's dressing room. "It was nothing fancy, just an ordinary, plain, clean room, and she was by herself," Jannah recalled. "I told her how much I enjoyed her concert and always had enjoyed her work, and I told her about myself, that I was a singer. She asked me what I was doing. I said that I was in a show, *A Night at the Cotton Club*, and in it I did such and such tunes, including 'Black and Blue.' She asked me how many refrains I did. I told her. She said there were more. She took them out of her briefcase and gave them to me to copy.

"I asked her if she was teaching. She said, 'no,' she wasn't. I said I would have loved a lesson."

Carmen said, "Whenever you feel like what you're doing is right, stick with it. Follow your instincts." Jannah was grateful for the supportive tip.

In 1991, Carmen was again booked to play at the Blue Note in New York City. Mark Pulice knew she was having problems with breathing that week. Her lines were short; she never held a note. Although her difficulties were nothing more than usual, one night she actually had to quit the gig early. And on the last night she worked, although the audience was absolutely unaware of her distress, Carmen had great problems breathing.

"That was the last night she ever worked," Pulice recalled. "We were supposed to do one of those early morning shows, but she couldn't make it."

Carmen finished her second set of the last night of her engagement at the Blue Note in May, 1991, then she climbed laboriously to the dressing room upstairs. Afterward she went back to her hotel on the Upper East Side with her assistant and traveling companion, Shirley Thomas. In the middle of the night, Carmen could no longer breathe, and she was rushed by ambulance to Lenox Hill Hospital. That was the first time drummer Eric Gunnison, who had played with her from 1980 until her last gig in 1991, had ever seen her sick enough to enter a hospital.

Carmen lay in a darkened room in the hospital for days, waiting for permission to go back to California. Once back in California, she entered a hospital again. According to Gunnison, the doctors put a ventilator down her throat and ruined her voice. She never regained it at its full strength.

Larry Clothier got another impression regarding the outlook for the resumption of Carmen's career. According to him, doctors told her she could do her exercises, quit smoking, and go back to work. Clothier believed them and encouraged Carmen to take care of herself so she could return to singing and enjoying life. But she didn't commit herself to rehabilitation. She had no interest at all in moving, never mind exercising. She liked having people wait on her hand and foot. Jack Rael thought Carmen was simply tired of all the effort her career had entailed for so long. Mark Pulice and other musicians went to her house a couple of times. They saw she could walk around if she wanted to, though she had a little machine, a motorized chair lift, that transported her up and down a half-flight of stairs. "She smoked until the day she died," Pulice said. " She smoked about a pack a day."

Larry Clothier was, at times, beside himself at his inability to get Carmen to work herself back into shape. He loved her and blamed her infernal laziness for refusing to face up to the chore. He knew she could conquer her problems if she only wanted to. A young singer, Vanessa Rubin, decided to do a tribute album to Carmen for the Novus label while Carmen was still living and could enjoy the attention. Rubin believed that Carmen was simply "tired," she said, and that Carmen didn't want to work anymore.

One night Carmen went out to dinner with Clothier and a few other friends to see a show in a club. When she went to the ladies' room, she huffed and puffed as she walked slowly across the floor.

Five years after breaking up with Carmen, François Vaz had gone back to France to live and had married a French-woman. They lived in the south in Anduze, near the city of Nîmes, and they also had a villa in St. Martin. Vaz had not been in touch with Carmen for years and had no idea that she was sick, but he decided to telephone her on her birthday in 1993. She was absolutely delighted to hear from him and invited him to visit her at her house, he said. He said he was in France. She told him she really appreciated his call.

Jack Rael, on the other hand, knew very well that Carmen was sick. She frequently called him to come and fix the rabbit ears of her televison set — simply to move them around to improve the reception. She didn't want to get out of bed herself and do it. But sometimes when Rael actually traveled all the way from his house in Rancho Mirage, where he lived in retirement, to see her, she sent down the message that she didn't want him to come upstairs.

Carmen did grant an interview to James Gavin for a video and an article in the *Village Voice* published in early 1995. She came down to the crew on the chair lift from her bedroom. "She looked drained of color and sounded weak," wrote Gavin. But makeup helped. And soon Carmen began to look more like herself.

"And did she talk!" he wrote. She told her life story over again, praised Lady Day and Sarah Vaughan, dismissed Mel Torme and Nancy Wilson — and said she hadn't loved her first husband Kenny Clarke. She claimed she had actually been born in 1918. She said there was no harm in her barbed tongue. "I've never pushed anybody down the stairs or shot anybody. Now how much can you do with just words?" she asked.

Gavin and his crew were curious to know whether she could still sing on that November day in 1994; Carmen said she didn't think so but decided to show them what she could do. She tried "Ain't Misbehavin'" by Fats Waller. Gavin thought she sounded a bit rusty but unmistakably still Carmen — "gutsy and acerbic."

he wrote. "At the end, we cheered, telling her how good she sounded. 'Aw, I sound like shit,' she muttered, turning her face away." She thanked the crew for deciding to include her in a documentary "before I'm dead," she said, and disappeared up the chair lift to her bedroom.[1]

Sandy Jordan, widow of the saxophonist Clifford Jordan, who had died soon after recording some of the Thelonious Monk tracks with Carmen for her tribute album to Monk, received a call from Carmen at this time. "A year after Clifford died," Sandy recounted, "Carmen was sick herself, yet she called and asked, 'How are you making it with this?' That was a human thing to do, and endearing."

In January, 1993, Carmen appeared in a wheelchair for the National Association for the Advancement of Colored People's award show, during which Dianne Reeves sang to her. Carmen received an award. Then the National Endowment for the Arts gave Carmen a $20,000 lifetime achievement award in January, 1994, presented at the International Association of Jazz Educators convention in Boston. Larry Clothier accepted the award on her behalf, since Carmen was too ill to go herself. This award said that Carmen's career was distinguished by "her instinctive feeling for rhythm, her skillful vocal technique, her innovative scat singing, as well as her relaxed manner of presentation."[2]

Carmen desperately needed the award money by then. She had already taken out mortgages on her house. She had never won a Grammy award, although she had been nominated seven times for albums including her tributes to Billie Holiday, and Nat "King" Cole, and the McRae-Carter Duets. She had won a Billie Holiday Award from the French Academy du Jazz in the last decade of her life. But Carmen had no smash hit albums; the closest approximation over time was *The Great American Song Book* album done live at Donte's in 1971.

In October, 1994, Carmen suffered a stroke and was taken to the Cedars of Lebanon hospital in Los Angeles. But she was soon discharged and went home. A month later, Carmen lapsed into a coma, and on November 10, 1994, she died at home. The obituaries quoted her as saying: "All I want to be remembered for is my music."[3]

Shirley Thomas was with Carmen when she died. (About nine months later, Shirley Thomas had a heart attack and died, too.) Carmen's house had been mortgaged to help Carmen with her financial situation, said Jack Rael, and what little money was left over to be salvaged after Carmen's death went to her secretary, accountant, and executrix, Jan March. Furthermore, there was very little money in royalties from recordings coming to Carmen. Marge Costa knew that Carmen died of emphysema, from which she had suffered for years. "She also had hypoglycemia. She had everything, asthma, bronchitis. How she could sing is more than I can understand. She could get off the stage and cough and cough and not breathe, and go back on and sing her heart out. She smoked to the end of her life. She tried to quit, but never successfully, and anyway it was too late," Marge Costa said.

According to Carmen's wishes, she was cremated, and her ashes were buried at sea, in the Pacific Ocean, off the coast of Los Angeles, by Jan March. That was all Carmen wanted.

Marge Costa thought there should be closure and threw a memorial party for her life long friend. It was held at Marge Costa's house in Wheaton Woods, Maryland. "When I told anecdotes about her, it was fun. We had her videos, albums, and cassettes."

"I miss Carmen, I do miss Carmen," said Costa. "We had a good time. And she was a kind of special person. She was so talented she would have to be different and difficult. But we were friends. I have all of her albums."

In Holland, Denise Jannah had recorded her first album. She was going to send Carmen a copy, but never got a chance to. "One day I was in the wings in a small theater in Terneuzen, in the south of Holland, and about to go on, with my group already onstage, and all of a sudden I heard the emcee announce Carmen's death. It completely threw me off ... thirty seconds later I had to go onstage, but I was a bit shaky, and I told the audience I was startled, and I dedicated the concert to her. I sang 'Lady Sings The Blues' a capella. I asked for a minute of silence and got it. It was very intense. I was sending a signal to her wherever she was, thank you thank you thank you."

Information for this chapter comes from Shirley Horn, Denise Jannah, Larry Clothier, Jack Rael, Mark Pulice, Marge Costa, and others.

[1] Gavin, James, "The Woman We Loved," *Village Voice* (January 3, 1995).

[2] O'Haire, Patricia, "Carmen McRae Remembered as Top Jazz Stylist," *New York Daily News* (November 12, 1994).

[3] Ibid.

Carmen and Lee Konitz.
Photo: Raymond Ross.

Carmen and Lee Konitz sitting in with Sonny Canterino, Dave Bailey, Bill Crow and unknown pianist at the Half Note, New York, November 11, 1964. Photo: Raymond Ross.

Clark Terry and Carmen. Photo: Raymond Ross.

*Performing at
the Five Spot Café in
January, 1965.
Photo: Raymond Ross.*

Carmen and Dizzy Gillespie relaxing in the sun at the Newport Jazz Festival, 1965.
Photo: Raymond Ross.

Performing at the
Newport Jazz Festival
in July, 1965.
Photo: Raymond Ross.

Carmen at the piano and Rod Taylor in a publicity image for Hotel, *1967.*

Performing at the tenth anniversary of the Half Note Club at the Village Theater, 1967. Photo: Raymond Ross.

Late night New Year's Eve at the hungry i club in San Francisco.
François Vaz is sitting to the right of Carmen.
Photo courtesy of François Vaz.

Performing at Town Hall,
September, 1969.
Photo: Raymond Ross.

On a panel discussion about Billie Holiday held at the
Library for the Performing Arts Auditorium, Lincoln Center, New York,
with Roger "Ram" Ramirez, A.B. Spellman, Artie Shaw, 1973.
Photo: Raymond Ross.

Carmen and her good friend Joe Williams.
Photo © Herb Snitzer.

Performing at the Blue Note,
December, 1983.
Photo: Mitchell Seidel.

Publicity shot of Carmen McRae in
Jo Jo Dancer, Your Life Is Calling,
Columbia Pictures, 1985.

Carmen in 1989.

Carmen McRae: A Selected Discography

This section has been compiled by the author from several sources, and features a selection of albums on which Carmen was the leader. Recording sessions, where known, are indicated by their corresponding Sessionography number.

BOY MEETS GIRL, recorded in New York, 1955, released on the Decca label. (9)

BY SPECIAL REQUEST, recorded in New York, 1955, released on the Decca label. (10)

TORCHY!, recorded in New York, 1955, released on the Decca label. (14, 15, 16)

BLUE MOON, recorded in New York, 1956, released on the Decca label. (17, 18, 19)

AFTER GLOW, recorded in New York, 1957, released on the Decca label. (23)

MAD ABOUT THE MAN, recorded in New York, 1957, released on the Decca label. (24, 25, 26)

CARMEN FOR COOL ONES, recorded in Los Angeles, 1957, released on the Decca label. (29, 30, 31)

MAHOGANY HALL STOMP: TIMEX JAZZ SPECIAL, (various artists) recorded in a live television performance, Chicago, 1957, released on the Decca label. (32)

BIRDS OF A FEATHER, recorded in New York, 1958, released on the Decca label. (36, 37, 38)

PORGY AND BESS, (various artists) recorded in New York, 1958, released on the Decca label. (41)

BOOK OF BALLADS, recorded in New York, 1958, released on the Kapp label.(42)

INVITATION, probably recorded in New York, c. 1959, released on the Official label. (43)

WHEN YOU'RE AWAY, recorded in New York, 1959, released on the Kapp label. (44)

SOMETHING TO SWING ABOUT, recorded in New York, 1959, released on the Kapp label. (45)

IN LONDON, recorded live at the Flamingo Club, London, England, 1961, released on the Ember label. (47)

CARMEN MCRAE SINGS LOVER MAN AND OTHER BILLIE HOLIDAY CLASSICS, recorded in New York, 1961, released on the Columbia label. (48)

JINGLE BELL JAZZ, recorded in New York, 1961, released on the Columbia label. (49, 50)

SOMETHING WONDERFUL, recorded in New York, 1962, released on the Columbia label. (53, 54, 55)

IN PERSON/IN SAN FRANCISCO, recorded live at Sugar Hill, San Francisco, 1962 and 1963, released on the Mainstream label. (56)

LIVE AT SUGAR HILL, recorded live at Sugar Hill, San Francisco, 1962, released on the Time label. (57)

CARMEN MCRAE, recorded live at Sugar Hill, San Francisco, 1963, released on the Mainstream label. (58)

SONG TIME, according to Norman Simmons, recorded live at Sugar Hill, 1963, released on the Hindsight label. (59)

BITTERSWEET, recorded in New York, 1964, released on the Focus label. (60)

SECOND TO NONE, recorded in New York, 1964, released on the Mainstream label. (61)

HAVEN'T WE MET?, recorded in New York, 1964, released on the Mainstream label. (62)

WOMAN TALK, recorded live at the Village Gate, New York, 1965, released on the Mainstream label. (63)

LIVE AND WAILING, recorded live at a concert in New York, 1965, released on the Mainstream label. (64)

LIVE AND DOIN' IT, recorded in San Francisco, 1965, released on the Mainstream label. (65)

FOR ONCE IN MY LIFE, recorded in London, 1967, released on the Atlantic label. (67, 68, 69)

CARMEN MCRAE AND HERBIE MANN, recorded in New York, 1967, released on the Atlantic label. (70)

PORTRAIT OF CARMEN, recorded in Los Angeles, 1967, released on the Atlantic label. (71, 72, 73)

THE SOUND OF SILENCE, recorded in Los Angeles, 1968, released on the Atlantic label. (74, 75, 76)

LIVE AT CENTURY PLAZA, recorded live at the Century Plaza, Los Angeles, 1968, released on the Atlantic label. (79)

CARMEN MCRAE WITH THE NORMAN SIMMONS TRIO, recording location unknown, 1969, released on the Hindsight label. (80)

JUST A LITTLE LOVIN', recorded in Miami, 1970, released on the Atlantic label. (83)

NOVEMBER GIRL, recorded in London, 1970, released on the Black Lion label. (86)

CARMEN, recorded in Hollywood, 1971 to 1972, released on the Temponic label. (88)

THE GREAT AMERICAN SONGBOOK, recorded live at Donte's, Los Angeles, 1971, released on the Atlantic label. (89)

IT TAKES A WHOLE LOT OF HUMAN FEELING, recorded in Los Angeles, 1973, released on the Groove Merchant label. (90)

MS. JAZZ, recorded in New York, 1973, released on the Groove Merchant label. (91)

AS TIME GOES BY, recorded live in Tokyo, 1973, released on the Japanese Victor label. (92)

I AM MUSIC, recorded in Los Angeles, 1975, released on the Blue Note label. (93)

CARMEN MCRAE AND HER TRIO LIVE, recorded in Belgrade, 1975, released on the Jazz Door label. (94)

CAN'T HIDE LOVE, recorded in Los Angeles, 1976, released on the Blue Note label. (95, 96, 97, 98)

CARMEN MCRAE AT THE GREAT AMERICAN MUSIC HALL, recorded live in San Francisco, 1976, released on the Blue Note label. (99)

LIVE AT THE ROXY, recorded live at The Roxy, Los Angeles, 1976, released on the Blue Note label. (100)

RONNIE SCOTT'S PRESENTS CARMEN MCRAE LIVE, recorded live at Ronnie Scott's Club, London, 1977, released on the Pye label. (101)

BLUE NOTE MEETS THE L.A. PHILHARMONIC, recorded live at the Hollywood Bowl, 1977, released on the Blue Note label. (102)

I'M COMING HOME AGAIN, recorded in New York, 1978, released on the Buddah label. (103)

LESS IS MORE, recorded live at Shelly's Manne Hole, Los Angeles, *c.* 1970s. released on the Night Music label. (104)

JAZZ GALA '79, recorded live at the Theatre du Casino, Cannes, 1979, released on the America label. (105)

TWO FOR THE ROAD, recorded in New York, 1980, released on the Concord Jazz label. (106)

RECORDED LIVE AT BUBBA'S, recorded live at Bubba's, Fort Lauderdale, 1981, released on the Who's Who label. (107)

YOU'RE LOOKING AT ME, recorded in San Francisco, 1983, released on the Concord label. (108)

FOR LADY DAY, VOL. 1 AND VOL. 2, recorded live at the Blue Note club, New York, 1983, released on the RCA Novus label. (109)

LIVE IN TOKYO, recorded live at Kan-iho-ken Hall, Tokyo, 1986, released on the Lobster label. (110)

ANY OLD TIME, recorded in New York, 1986, released on the Denon label. (111)

THE CARMEN MCRAE/BETTY CARTER DUETS, recorded live at the Great American Music Hall, San Francisco, 1987, released on the Great American Music Hall and Bet Car/Verve labels. (112)

FINE AND MELLOW: LIVE AT BIRDLAND WEST, recorded live at Birdland West, Long Beach, 1987, released on the Concord label. (113)

CARMEN SINGS MONK, recorded live at the Great American Music Hall, San Francisco, 1988, released on the RCA Novus label. (114, 115)

SARAH—DEDICATED TO YOU, recorded in New York, 1990, released on the RCA Novus label. (116)

Carmen McRae: A Selected Sessionography

T his section is based on several existing sessionographies — one by Walter Bruyninckx, another by Tom Lord, and a third by Denis Brown of England. Brown's sessionography is to date unpublished. Carmen herself told interviewer W. Royal Stokes that her first recording was done with Mercer Ellington's band. Only Denis Brown includes that recording in his sessionography. However, because Carmen mentioned it, it is included here. The primary source of discographical information here is Lord's book.

Album titles included in the body of the Selected Sessionography are derived primarily from Lord's sessionography. Not all the sessions have album titles, though most likely some of those sessions were released as albums, not necessarily in the order in which they were recorded.

Another list of album titles exists in the *All Music Guide to Jazz* published in 1998 by Amazon.com Books. Information in that list for Carmen McRae diverges at times widely from the Lord list of album titles, record labels, and dates. The material included in this Selected Sessionography, although not all-encompassing, seems to be reliable, according to research done by the author of this book.

Although Carmen also made other recordings during the 1940s, little is known about them. Some may never have been released, and so they have been omitted from this Selected Sessionography. While Brunynickx notes that Carmen worked with Benny Carter's band in 1944, and Count Basie's band in the 1940s, too, none of the existing sessionographies mention any recordings she may have made with those bands.

Carmen made many recordings, according to her own memory, for a small, independent label, Stardust. They circulated in a limited way. The recordings preceded and may have helped lead to her job as an intermission pianist and singer with the house band at Minton's Playhouse in 1953. Carmen also recorded for Venus, Bethlehem, and Decca, distinctly different labels. The Decca jazz recordings are, of her early work, the ones most readily available today.

In several cases, the existing sessionographies disagree about the musicians with whom Carmen recorded in the mid-1950s, when her career was becoming more established. Lord's book was chosen as the primary source because it is the most recently published sessionography, and its information seems to be the most reliable. In some cases, I have added a little of my own information, when I know it is more accurate than here to fore published data.

George Avakian, the noted producer, directly contributed some of his memories of the era in the recording world, too, to this sessionography. So did pianist Dick Katz, flutist Herbie Mann, writer and saxophonist Bill Simon, and accordianist Mat Mathews and his wife Paulette Rubinstein, then called Paulette Girard.

A record label has been mentioned, where known, for each entry; the same recordings may also have been released on other labels at the same time or subsequently, but only the first label release is mentioned here. For formal, discographical information, please refer to the existing published discographies, particularly the Lord book.

The discographies are:

1. *The Jazz Discography, Vol. 14*, by Tom Lord, Lord Music Reference Inc., 1996, distributed by North Country Distributors, Cadence Building, Redwood, N.Y. 13679.

2. *70 Years of Recorded Jazz, 1917-1987*, by Walter Bruyninckx, privately published by the author, Lange Nieuwstraat, 2800 Mechelen, Belgium. Some entries in this older discography differ markedly from Lord's.

3. Unpublished but probably available on request is Carmen McRae, in *The Great Vocalists-Discographies series*, by Denis Brown, 22 Passey Road, Moseley, Birmingham, West Midlands, B13 9NU England. There may be a small fee for this 69-page pamphlet, in which some entries differ markedly from Lord's.

Instruments are noted as follows: trumpet (tpt), trombone (tbn), alto sax (as), baritone saxophone (bar), soprano saxophone (sop), clarinet (cl), bass clarinet (b-cl), flute (fl), alto flute (al-fl), piccolo (pic), oboe (oboe), fluegelhorn (flghn), cornet, tuba (tub), accordian (accord), violin (viol), viola, cello, vibes (vib), piano (p), organ, keyboards, electric piano (elec-p), synthesizers, celeste (celeste), marimba (mar), bass (b), drums (d), percussion (perc), guitar (g), harp, leader (ldr).

(Because of a lack of corroboration from other discographers, several recordings listed in Brown's discography up through 1953 are omitted in this sessionography. The omissions are not intended to dispute Brown's findings.)

Carmen McRae is the leader on all the sessions listed below unless otherwise noted:

1. *This entry is adapted from Brown. Both Brown and Bruyninckx state that Carmen recorded under her married name of Carmen Clarke at this time:*
MERCER ELLINGTON (leader) and His Orchestra, Kenny Dorman, Bob Williams, Ray Copeland, Eddie Boozier (tpt), Red Kelly, Dan Minor, Charles Stovall (tbn), Jackie Fields, Curby Alexander (as), Freddie Williams, Alva McCain (ts), Harry Webster (bar), Luther Henderson (p), Bill Pemberton (b), Heywood Jackson (d), Carmen McRae (vcl).
New York, May 17, 1946, label unknown.
Moon Mist (unissued)
Pass Me By

2. *This entry is included because of information in a 1955 publicity brochure from Associated Booking Corporation:*
With Unknown Personnel.
New York, date unknown, Stardust Records.
In Love In Vain
Autumn Nocturne
Foggy Day
Wanting You

3. With Unknown Personnel.
New York, date unknown, Venus Records.
Old Devil Moon
Tip Toe Gently
(*Author's Note: Some rumors say that Venus was a subsidiary label belonging to Bethlehem, but it's more likely that Venus was a small, separate company from both Stardust and Bethlehem. The two songs mentioned here as appearing on Venus also came out as a Bethlehem release. They may — or may not — have been the same recordings.*)

4. *This entry is adapted from Bruyninckx and Brown:*
With Herbie Mann (fl, ts), Mat Mathews (accord), Mundell Lowe (g), Wendell Marshall (b), Kenny Clarke (d).
New York, October 6, 1954, Bethlehem.
Easy To Love
Tip Toe Gently*
If I'm Lucky
Old Devil Moon *
(* *Associated Booking Corporation notes these songs were originally done for Venus Records.*)
(*Author's Note: Because of information from Mat Mathews, the author believes that 1954 was actually the release date, not the recording date for Bethlehem. Carmen recorded for Bethlehem before Stardust, according to Mathews. The same applies to the dates for the Bethlehem recordings mentioned below.*)

5. With unknown personnel.
New York, October 8, 1954, Decca.
They All Laughed
Keep Me In Mind
Ooh! What'cha Doin' To Me
If I'm Lucky
(*Author's Note: For that same date, Lord, giving no personnel, lists the same songs. Brown, giving no specific personnel, says Carmen recorded those songs on October 8, 1954 with the Jack Pleis Orchestra, New York, on the Decca label.*)

6. *This entry is adapted from Bruyninckx and Lord:*
With Tony Scott (cl), unknown vibes (1) Dick Katz (p), Osie Johnson (d).
New York, December 1954, Bethlehem.
You Made Me Care
Last Time For Love
Too Much In Love To Care (1)
(*Brown lists the personnel as:* Tony Scott [cl,

ldr], Dick Katz [p], Skip Fawcett [b], Osie Johnson [d].)

(Author's Note: It is valuable to draw attention to the discrepancies between discographies, which further explains why some claims for her early recording career are excluded.)

The following entries are adapted from all three discographers:
7. With Tony Scott (cl).
New York, December 1954, Bethlehem.
Misery

8. With the Jack Pleis Orchestra,
and the Dave Lambert Singers on (1).
New York, February 21, 1955, Decca.
Get Set (1)
Whatever Lola Wants
Am I The One To Blame?
You Don't Have To Tell Me

9. *This entry has been adapted from Lord and Brown:*
With Sammy Davis, Jr., and the Jack Pleis Orchestra.
New York, spring 1955, Decca.
A Fine Romance
I Go For You

10. *This entry has been adapted from Lord:*
With Dick Katz (p), Billy Strayhorn (p on 1), Carmen McRae (p on 2), Mundell Lowe (g), Wendell Marshall (b), Kenny Clarke (d).
New York, June 14, 1955, Decca.
Just One Of Those Things
Sometimes I'm Happy, Sometimes I'm
 Blue
Something To Live For (1)
Love Is Here To Stay
I Can't Get Started
This Will Make You Laugh
Suppertime (2)

All the following entries are adapted from Lord, unless otherwise noted. In some cases Brown and Bruyninckx differ markedly in details:
11. With the Mat Mathews Quintet,
Herbie Mann (fl), Mat Mathews (accord), Dick Katz (p), Mundell Lowe (g), Wendell Marshall (b), Kenny Clarke (d).
New York, June 16, 1955, Decca.
My One And Only Love
Yardbird Suite
Give Me the Simple Life
I'll Remember April
You Took Advantage Of Me

12. With the Mat Mathews Quintet,
Herbie Mann (fl), Mat Mathews (accord), Dick Katz (p), Mundell Lowe (g), Wendell Marshall (b), Kenny Clarke (d).
New York, 1955, Coral.
Love Is Here To Stay
How Many Stars Have To Shine?
Sometimes I'm Happy
I Can't Get Started
Just One Of Those Things
My One And Only Love
I'll Remember April
You Took Advantage Of Me
Until The Real Thing Comes Along
A Room With A View

13. With the Jack Pleis Orchestra.
New York, 1955, Decca.
Tonight He's Out To Break A New Heart
Come On, Come In
The Next Time It Happens
Come Down To Earth, Mr. Smith

14. With the Jack Pleis Orchestra,
plus 10 strings.
New York, December 16, 1955, Decca.
Speak Low
But Beautiful
If You'd Stay The Way I Dream About You
My Future Just Passed

15. With the Ralph Burns Orchestra.
New York, December 29, 1955, Decca.
Last Night When We Were Young
Midnight Sun
Yesterdays
Good Morning, Heartache

16. With the Jack Pleis Orchestra, Joe
Wilder (tpt), Andy Ackers (p), Danny Perri
(g) added.
New York, December 30, 1955, Decca.
I Don't Stand A Ghost Of A Chance With
You
We'll Be Together Again
I'm A Dreamer, Aren't We All?
Star Eyes

17. With the Tadd Dameron Orchestra.
New York, March 28, 1956, Decca.
Blue Moon
I Was Doing All Right
I'm Putting All My Eggs In One Basket
Nowhere

18. With the Jimmy Mundy Orchestra.
New York, March 29, 1956, Decca.
My Foolish Heart
Lush Life
Until The Real Thing Comes Along
Laughing Boy

19. With the Jimmy Mundy Orchestra.
New York, Mar. 30, 1956, Decca.
Summer Is Gone
Lilacs In The Rain
All This Could Lead to Love
Even If It Breaks My Heart

20. With the Jack Pleis Orchestra.
New York, May 4, 1956, Decca.
You Don't Know Me
Never Loved Him Anyhow
Skyliner *
If You Should Leave Me
(Author's Note: This song was a very big hit,
possibly the biggest Carmen had.)*

21. With the Jack Pleis Orchestra.
New York, September 4, 1956, Decca.
The Party's Over
Namely You

22. With the Jack Pleis Orchestra.
New York, *c.* February 1957, Decca.
It's Like Getting A Donkey To Gallop
How Many Stars Have To Shine?
As I Love You
So Nice To Be Wrong

23. With Ray Bryant* (p) except for (1) on
which Carmen plays piano, Ike Isaacs (b),
Specs Wright (d).
New York, March 6 or April 18, 1957, Decca.
*(Author's Note: Other discographers list the
pianist as either Bryant or Ronnell Bright,
but it was definitely Bryant, who clearly
remembers the date. He played regularly in
Carmen's group at this time.)*
I Can't Escape From You (1)
Guess Who I Saw Today*
My Funny Valentine
The Little Things That Mean So Much (1)
I'm Thru With Love
Nice Work If You Can Get It
East Of The Sun
Exactly Like You (1)
All My Life
Between The Devil And The Deep Blue Sea
Dream of Life**
Perdido (1)
(Author's Note: Carmen recorded this song
before Nancy Wilson did. Wilson had the hit.)*
*** Carmen wrote this song.*

24. With the Jack Pleis Orchestra, Charlie
Shavers (tpt), Ray Bryant (p),
Ike Isaacs (b), Specs Wright (d), (unknown
tbn, reeds, plus strings.)
New York, June 18, 1957, Decca.
Zigeuner
I'll See You Again
Some Day I'll Find You
I'll Follow My Secret Heart

25. With the Jack Pleis Orchestra.
New York, June 19, 1957, Decca.
If Love Were All
Mad About The Boy
World Weary
A Room With A View

26. With the Jack Pleis Orchestra.
New York, June 20, 1957, Decca.
I Can't Do Anything At All
Never Again
Poor Little Rich Girl
Why Does Love Get In The Way

27. With the Jack Pleis Orchestra.
New York, *c.* July and August, 1957,
Decca.
Rich Man, Poor Man
Coax Me
Passing Fancy

28. With unknown trio.
Recorded live, location unknown,
December 2, 1957, Calliope.
My Funny Valentine
Exactly Like You

29. With the Fred Katz Orchestra, Buddy
Collette (fl, as), Warren Webb (oboe),
Justin Gordon (b-cl), George W. Smith
(cl), Joseph Gibbons (g), Ike Isaacs (b),
Specs Wright (d), plus 13 strings.
Los Angeles, December 5, 1957, Decca.
You're Mine
I Remember Clifford
A Shoulder To Cry On
Weak For The Man

30. With the Fred Katz Orchestra, Bill
Green, Harry Lee (fl), George Smith (cl),
Mahlon Clark, Justin Gordon (b-cl), Ike
Isaacs (b), Specs Wright (d) added.
Los Angeles, December 16, 1957, Decca.
All The Things You Are
After I Say I'm Sorry
If I Were A Bell

31. With Frank Flynn (vibes, mar), Larry
Bunker (vibes), John Towner Williams, Joe
Marino, (p, celeste), Fred Katz (cello-l), Ike
Isaacs (b), Specs Wright (d).
Los Angeles, December 16, 1957, Decca.
Any Old Time
What's New
Without A Word Of Warning
The Night We Called It A Day (1)

32. With Ray Bryant (p), Ike Isaacs (b),
Specs Wright (d).
Recorded during a live television perform-
ance, Chicago, December 30, 1957, Decca.
A Foggy Day
They All Laughed

33. With the Jack Pleis Orchestra, Charlie
Shavers (tpt), Ray Bryant (p), Ike Isaacs
(b), Specs Wright (d), unknown tbn, reeds,
plus strings.
New York, March 5, 1958, Decca.
Invitation
Moon Ray
Low And Behold

34. With the Fred Katz Orchestra, Ray
Linn, Pete Candoli (tpt), Milt Bernhart,
Bob Enevoldsen (tbn), Vince DeRosa
(flghn), Calvin Jackson (p), Billy Bean (g),
Tommy Johnson (tub), Red Mitchell (b),
Larry Bunker (d).
Los Angeles, April 21, 1958, Decca.
I Get A Kick Out Of You

35. With the Jack Pleis Orchestra.
New York, *c.* late July 1958, Decca.
I'll Love You
I'll Love The Ground You Walk On
How Many Stars Have To Shine?
It's Like Getting A Donkey To Gallop

36. With the Ralph Burns Orchestra,
Irving "Marky" Markowitz (tpt), Fred
Kelin, Donald Corrado, Dick Berg, Tony
Miranda (flghn), Ben Webster (ts), Don

Abney (p), Mundell Lowe (g), Aaron Bell
(b), Ted Sommer (d), Ralph Burns (d).
New York, August 4, 1958, Decca.
Mr. Meadowlark
Skylark
Bye Bye Blackbird
Flamingo
A Nightingale Sang In Berkeley Square
When The Swallows Come Back

37. With Irving "Marky" Markowitz (tpt),
Al Cohn, Ben Webster (ts), Don Abney
(p), Mundell Lowe (g), Aaron Bell (b),
Nick Stabulas (d), plus Ray Charles and
five singers.
New York, August 6, 1958, Decca.
His Eye Is On The Sparrow
The Eagle And Me
When The Red Red Robin
   Comes Bob Bob Bobbin' Along
Georgia Rose

38. With Barry Galbraith, Mundell Lowe
(g), Don Lamond (d), Nick Stabulas (d).
New York, August 8, 1958, Decca.
Bob White
Baltimore Oriole
Chicken Today, Feathers Tomorrow
Summertime

39. With the Frank Hunter Orchestra,
Don Abney (p), Joe Benjamin (b), Charles
Smith (d).
New York, October 1958, Kapp.
Play For Keeps
Which Way Is Love
Show Me The Way
Talk To Me

40. With unknown accompaniment.
New York, 1958, Kapp.
Don't Cry, Joe
The More I See You
Big Town
What Has She Got?

41. With the Jack Pleis Orchestra.
New York, October 29, 1958, Decca.
My Man's Gone Now
Summertime

42. With the Frank Hunter Orchestra,
Don Abney (p), Joe Benjamin (b), Charlie
Smith (d).
New York, December 1 and 2, 1958, Kapp.
By Myself
The Thrill Is Gone
How Long Has This Been Going On?
Do You Know Why?
My Romance
Isn't It Romantic?
If Love Is Good To Me
When I Fall In Love
Please Be Kind
He Was Too Good To Me
Angel Eyes
Something I Dreamed Last Night

43. With the Belford Hendricks Orchestra.
Probably New York, *c.* 1959, Official.
It's So Much Fun
Belonging To You
I Go For You
Oh, Look At Me Now

44. WITH THE LUTHER HENDERSON
ORCHESTRA, directed by Belford Hendricks.
New York, March 3, 4, and 10, 1959, Kapp.
I'm Glad There Is You
I Only Have Eyes For You
Ain't Misbehavin'
When You're Away
I Concentrate On You
Ev'ry Time We Say Goodbye
If I Could Be With You
When Your Lover Has Gone
I'll Be Seeing You
Two Faces In The Dark
Willingly
The More I See You

45. With the Ernie Wilkins Orchestra, Art Farmer, Jimmy Maxwell (tpt), Ernie Royal replaces Maxwell on (1), Richard Williams, Al Stewart, Lennie Johnson (tpt), Jimmy Cleveland, Billy Byers, Mickey Gravine (tbn), Paul Fauline (b-tbn), Vinnie Dean, Phil Woods (as), Porter Kilbert (as) replaces Woods on (2) Zoot Sims, Budd Johnson (ts), Sol Schlinger (bar), Dick Katz (p) Tommy Williams (b), Floyd Williams (d).
New York, November 10 – 12, 1959, Kapp.
I See Your Face Before Me
A Sleepin' Bee
Comes Love
Three Little Words
It's Love (1, 2)
How Little We Know (1, 2)
You Leave Me Breathless (1, 2)
Love Is A Simple Thing (1)
Falling In Love With Love (1)
That's For Me (1)
Alone Together
I Couldn't Care Less

46. With the Belford Hendricks Orchestra.
New York, September 14 and 15, 1960, Mercury.
Wonderful One (unissued)
Hard To Get
It's So Much Fun
I Might Say
Oh Look At Me Now
Envy
The Very Thought Of You

47. With Don Abney (p), Kenny Napper (b), Phil Seamen (d).
Recorded live at the Flamingo Club, London, England, May 1961, Ember.
I Could Write A Book
Body And Soul
Thou Swell
Round Midnight
A Foggy Day In London Town
Don't Ever Leave Me
　(Napper and Seamen out)

Moonlight In Vermont
Day In, Day Out
Lover Man
Stardust
They Can't Take That Away From Me

48. With Nat Adderley (cornet), Eddie "Lockjaw" Davis (ts), Norman Simmons (p), Mundell Lowe (g), Bob Cranshaw (b), Walter Perkins (d).
New York, June 29, 1961, Columbia.
Travellin' Light
I Cried For You
I'm Gonna Lock My Heart
Lover Man
Them There Eyes
God Bless The Child
Yesterdays
What A Little Moonlight Can Do
Miss Brown To You
My Man
Strange Fruit
Some Other Spring
　(Adderley and Eddie Davis out)
(Author's Note: For this album, Norman Simmons, who had just come to work as her regular accompanist, arranged all of the songs in this highly praised recording that was a tribute to Billie Holiday.)

49. With Norman Simmons (p), Bob Cranshaw (b).
New York, June 29, 1961, Columbia.
The Christmas Song
(Author's Note: The Lord discography lists Simmons as playing cello on this date, but Simmons is strictly a pianist.)

50. With Nat Adderley (cornet), Norman Simmons (p), Mundell Lowe (g), Bob Cranshaw (b), Walter Perkins (d).
New York, June 29, 1961, Columbia.
I'm Gonna Lock My Heart
If The Moon Turns Green
Lover Man

51. With unknown accompaniment by (p), (b), and (d).
Location unknown, *c.* 1962, Columbia.
Am I Going Out Of Your Mind?
Baby, Baby

52. With the Marty Paich Orchestra.
Los Angeles, February 6, 1962, Columbia.
How Does the Wine Taste?
So Long
Night Life

53. With the Buddy Bregman Orchestra.
New York, June 22, 1962, Columbia.
Just In Time
Give A Little, Get A Little
Come Rain Or Come Shine

54. With the Buddy Bregman Orchestra.
New York, June 22 and July 11, 1962, Columbia.
Medley: Blow, Gabriel, Blow, and All Through The Night
Anything Goes
Medley: Getting To Know You and
    Hello, Young Lovers

55. With the Buddy Bregman Orchestra.
New York, July 11, 1962, Columbia.
Long Before I Knew You
Medley: If This Isn't Love and
    Look To The Rainbow
The Great Come And Get It Day
A Wonderful Guy
Medley: Don't Cry and I Like Ev'rybody
Warm All Over
There Never Was A Baby Like My Baby
Something Wonderful

56. With Norman Simmons (p), Victor Sproles (b), Stewart Martin (d).
Recorded live at Sugar Hill, San Francisco, September 27 and October 13, 1962, and September 2 and 21, 1963, Mainstream.
Sunday
What Kind Of Fool Am I?

A Foggy Day
I Left My Heart In San Francisco
I Didn't Know What Time It Was
Let There Be Love
This Is All I Ask
Thou Swell
It Never Entered My Mind
Make Someone Happy

57. With Norman Simmons (p),
Victor Sproles (b), Stewart Martin (d).
Recorded live at Sugar Hill, San Francisco, September 27 and October 13, 1962, Time.
Sunday
What Kind Of Fool Am I?
Foggy Day
I Left My Heart In San Francisco
I Didn't Know What Time It Was
Let There Be Love
This Is All I Ask
Thou Swell
It Never Entered My Mind
Make Someone Happy

58. With Norman Simmons (p),
Victor Sproles (b), Stewart Martin (d).
Recorded live at Sugar Hill, San Francisco, 1963, Mainstream.
Spring Can Really Hang You Up the Most
Bye Bye Blackbird
Solitude
I'm Gonna Laugh You Right Out
    Of My Life (Carmen in, Simmons out)
Medley: Long Before I Knew You
    and Just In Time
Round Midnight
I Got It Bad And That Ain't Good
My Ship Is Coming In

59. With the Norman Simmons trio, Simmons (p) Victor Sproles (b), Stewart Martin (d).
Recorded live at Sugar Hill, San Francisco (according to Norman Simmons), 1963, Hindsight.
I'm Gonna Lock My Heart

Thou Swell
Fly Me To The Moon
Miss Brown To You
Make Someone Happy
I Left My Heart In San Francisco
Just A Gigolo
Just In Time
Guess Who I Saw Today?

60. With Norman Simmons (p), Mundell
Lowe (g), Victor Sproles (b), Curtis Boyd (d).
New York, May 20, 1964, Focus.
When Sunny Gets Blue
How Did He Look?
Guess I'll Hang My Tears Out To Dry
The Meaning Of The Blues
If You Could Love Me
Spring Can Really Hang You Up The Most
Second Chance
If You Could See Me Now
Here's That Rainy Day
I'm Gonna Laugh You Right Out Of My Life
Ghost Of Yesterday
I'm Lost
Come Sunday
Cutie Pants

61. With John Bello (tpt), John Messner,
Charles Small, Chauncey Welsch (tbn),
Tony Studd (b-tbn), Dick Berg, Jimmy
Buffington (flghn), Phil Bodner (fl, al-fl, cl,
oboe), Shelly Gold (fl, al-fl, oboe), Barry
Galbraith (g), Norman Simmons (p),
Richard Davis, Victor Sproles (b), Archie
Freedman (d), George Devens, Phil Kraus
(perc), George Bianco (harp), Ariane
Broone, Frederick Legawiec, Carmel Malin,
Joe Malin, Vera Morganstern, David
Nadien, Raoul Poliakin, Max Polikoff,
Tosha Samaroff, Jack Zayde (viol), Alfred
Brown, Harold Furmansky, David
Mankowitz, Manny Vardi (viola), Maurice
Brown, Alta Goldberg, Charles McCracken,
George Ricci (cello,) Peter Matz, arranger
and conductor; Don Sebesky probably

arranged four songs where noted below,
according to Norman Simmons.
New York, August 1964, Mainstream.
In Love In Vain
Where Did It Go?
The Music That Makes Me Dance
    (probably arranged by Don Sebesky)
Because You're Mine
Too Good (probaby arranged by Don Sebesky)
Once Upon A Summertime
The Night Has A Thousand Eyes
Cloudy Morning
    (probably arranged by Don Sebesky)
Blame It On My Youth
Winter In May
    (probably arranged by Don Sebesky)
My Reverie
And I Love Him
Alfie

62. With Burt Collins, Mel Davis, Bernie
Glow, Jimmy Maxwell, Jimmy Nottingham
(tpt), Wayne Andre, Bill Watrous (tbn),
Paul Faulise, Tony Studd (b-tbn), Don
Butterfield (tub), Ray Alonge, Dick Berg,
Jimmy Buffington, Earl Chapin (flghn,)
Phil Bodner (fl, al-fl, cl, oboe, pic, as, ts),
Barry Galbraith (g), Norman Simmons (p),
Richard Davis, Art Davis (b), Mel Lewis,
Ed Shaughnessy (d), Doug Allen, Phil
Kraus (perc), Margaret Ross (harp),
Bernard Eichen, Arnold Eidus, Leo
Kruczeki, Charles Libove, David Nadien,
George Ockner, Gene Orloff, Raoul
Poliakin, Aaron Rosand, Tosha Samaroff,
Michael Spivakowsky, Jack Zayde (viol),
Charles McCracken, George Ricci, Harvey
Shapiro, Anthony Sophos (cello), Don
Sebesky (conductor, arranger.)
New York, 1964, Mainstream.
Life Is Just A Bowl Of Cherries
Who Can I Turn To?
He Loves Me
Sweet Georgia Brown
Don't Ever Leave Me

Gentlemen Friend
Haven't We Met?
It Shouldn't Happen To A Dream
Limehouse Blues
I'm Fooling Myself
Love Is A Night Time Thing
Fools And Lovers

63. With Ray Beckenstein (fl), Norman Simmons (p), Joe Puma (g), Frank Severino (d), Jose Manguel (bongo).
Recorded live at the Village Gate, New York, November 1965, Mainstream.
Sometimes I'm Happy
Don't Explain
Woman Talk
Kick Off Your Shoes
The Shadow Of Your Smile
The Sweetest Sounds
Where Would You Be Without Me?
Feeling Good
Run, Run, Run
No More
Look At That Face
I Wish I Were In Love Again
(Author's Note: Additional personnel on this album was Paul Breslin, bass.)

64. With unknown personnel.
Recorded live at a concert in New York, 1965, Mainstream.
You Better Go Now
Love For Sale
If I Could Be With You One Hour Tonight
Miss Brown To You
Perdido
Too Close For Comfort
Midnight Sun
Traveling Light
Love Is Here To Stay
(Author's Note: This was probably also done live at the Village Gate, at the same time the previous album was done, according to Norman Simmons, and simply released as a different album.)

65. With Norman Simmons (p) Victor Sproles (b), Stewart Martin (d), and others.
San Francisco, 1965, Mainstream.
Nowhere
Trouble Is A Man
That's Why The Lady Is A Tramp
My Ship Has Sailed
I Only Have Eyes For You
I Guess I'll Hang My Tears Out To Dry
   (Carmen plays piano for herself.)
A Sleeping Bee
The Meaning Of The Blues
Guess Who I Saw Today?
Quiet Nights
(Author's Note: According to Norman Simmons, this was recorded live at Sugar Hill. The Sugar Hill date was the only one for which Stewart Martin ever recorded with the trio.)

66. With Johnny Keating's Orchestra, for the movie *Hotel*.
Hollywood, 1966, Warner Brothers.
Hotel

67. With Johnny Keating's Orchestra.
London, April 10, 1967, Atlantic.
Flying
I Just Wasn't Made For These Times
Until It's Time For You To Go

68. With Johnny Keating's Orchestra.
London, April 11, 1967, Atlantic.
It's Not Going That Way
For Once In My Life
Don't Talk
Come Live With Me

69. With Johnny Keating's Orchestra.
London, April 12, 1967, Atlantic.
Worlds of Time
The Look Of Love
Got To Get Into My Life
Our Song

70. CARMEN MCRAE (vcl) and HERBIE MANN (fl), other personnel (unknown). New York, October 2, 1967, Atlantic.
Live For Life
Cottage For Sale

71. With Gene DiNovi (arranger and director), John Audino, Jimmy Zito, James Salko (tpt), Francis Howard, Dick Nash, George Roberts (tbn), Henry Sigismonti, Richard Periss (flghn), Ted Nash, Dominick Fera, Gene Cipriano, Justin Gordon, John Lowe (saxes), Norman Simmons (p) Tommy Tedesco (g)), Ray Brown (b), Jack Sperling, Victor Feldman (d), Dale Anderson (perc), Ann Mason (harp), plus strings.
Los Angeles, November 27, 1967, Atlantic.
I'm Always Drunk In San Francisco
I Haven't Got Anything Better To Do
(Benny Carter replaces DiNovi, same session)
My Very Own Person
Boy, Do I Have A Surprise For You

72. With Shorty Rogers (arranger and director), William Hinshaw, David Duke, Henry Sigismonti (horn), George Roberts, Lew McCreary (tbn), Gene Cipriano, Harry Klee (fl), Norman Simmons (p), Howard Roberts, Dennis Budimir (g), Ray Brown (b), Earl Palmer (d), Victor Feldman, Louis Singer (perc), plus strings.
Los Angeles, November 28, 1967, Atlantic.
Elusive Butterfly
When You Get Around To Me
Ask Any Woman

73. With Oliver Nelson (arranger and director), Bob Bryant, Conte Candoli, Al Porcino, Frederick Hill (tpt), Billy Byers, Frank Rosolino, Lou Blackburn, Ernie Tack (tbn), Anthony Ortega, Frank Strozier, William Green, Buddy Collette (saxes), Norman Simmons (p), John Collins (g), Ray Brown (b), Shelly Manne (d).

Los Angeles, November 29, 1967, Atlantic.
Wonder Why
Day By Day
Walking Happy
Loads Of Love

74. With Jimmy Jones (arranger and conductor), Vince DeRosa (flghn), Gene Cipriano (sax), Norman Simmons (p) Francois Vaz, John Collins (g), Joe Comfort (b), Larry Bunker (perc), Lou Raderman (concertmaster), plus strings.
Los Angeles, June 26, 1968, Atlantic.
I Got It Bad And That Ain't Good
Stardust
The Folks Who Live On the Hill
Watch What Happens

75. With Shorty Rogers (arranger and director), Robert Helfer (unknown instrument) Jack Sheldon, Buddy Childers (tpt), Lou McCreary, Dick Nash (b), James Horn (saxes), Norman Simmons (elec-p), Michael Deasy, Tommy Tedesco, Francois Vaz (g), Max Bennett (b), James Gordon (d), Emil Radocchia (perc), David Frisina, Herman Clebanoff, Sam Freed, Nathan Kaproff, Bernard Kundell, Anatole Kaminsky (viol).
Los Angeles, June 27, 1968, Atlantic.
The Sound Of Silence
Gloomy Sunday
Can You Tell?
Don't Go Away
Can You Tell

76. With Shorty Rogers (arranger and director), Robert Helfer (unknown inst), Jack Sheldon, Jimmy Zito (tpt), Lou McCreary, Dick Nash (tbn), John Lowe (saxes), Norman Simmons (p), Michael Deasy (perc), Davis Frisina, Herman Clebanoff, Sam Freed, Nathan Kaproff, Bernard Kundell, Anatole (viol).
Los Angeles, June 28, 1968, Atlantic.

Poor Butterfly
I Sold My Heart To The Junkman
MacArthur Park
My Heart Reminds Me

77. With Norman Simmons (p), Chuck
Domanico (b), Frank Severino (d).
Recorded live at the Hong Kong Bar,
Century Plaza Hotel, Los Angeles,
December 27, 1968, Atlantic.
Openings (unissued)
Miss Otis Regrets
   (Domanico and Severino out)
Never Let Me Go
I Wasn't Dreamin' Last Night
Never Will I Marry
Yesterday
Elusive Butterfly
Away Away Away
No More Blues
On A Clear Day
The Right To Love
If You Never Fall In Love With Me
For Once In My Life
Come Live With Me
Did I Really Leave?
Won't Someone Please Belong To Me
Glad To Be Unhappy
Can You Tell
My Ship
And Spread To All
No More (Domanico and Severino out)
That Reminds Me
Satin Doll
Why Shouldn't I?
   (Carmen in, herself, Simmons out)
I Thought About You
   (Carmen in, Simmons out)
Midnight Sun
The Sound Of Silence
Never Let Me Go
Away Away Away
Got To Get You Into My Life
Trouble Is A Man
And Spread To All

Until It's Time For You To Go
No More Blues
The Right To Love
Poor Butterfly
If You Never Fall In Love With Me
The Folks Who Live On The Hill

78. With Norman Simmons (p), Chuck
Domanico (b), Frank Severino (d).
Recorded live at the Hong Kong Bar,
Century Plaza Hotel, Los Angeles,
December 28, 1968, Atlantic.
Elusive Butterfly
Once In My Life
Won't Someone Please Belong To Me
Alfie
No More Blues
Did I Ever Love?
Walking Happy
Watch What Happens
On A Clear Day
I'm Always Drunk In San Francisco
Never Let Me Go
The Right To Love
No More Blues
And Spread To All
Did I Really Leave?
The Sound Of Silence
Miss Otis Regrets
Satin Doll
Alfie
Elusive Butterfly
Reaching For The Moon
   (Carmen in, Simmons out)
September In The Rain
Sweet Pumpkin
The Right To Love
Won't Someone Please Belong Me?
Hotel
No More Blues
Never Let Me Go
Did I Really Leave?
And Spread To All
MacArthur Park
No More Blues

Until It's Time For You To Go
And Spread To All
Once In My Life

79. With Norman Simmons (p), Chuck Domanico (b), Frank Severino (d). Recorded live at the Century Plaza, Los Angeles, December 27 – 28, 1968, Atlantic.
Elusive Butterfly
Midnight Sun
For Once In My Life
Yesterday
Spread To All
The Right To Love
If You Never Fall In Love With Me
I'm Always Drunk In San Francisco
Introduction
The Sound Of Silence
Away, Away, Away
Did I Ever Love?
On A Clear Day You Can See Forever
Sweet Pumpkin
Introduction
No More Blues
Miss Otis Regrets
Satin Doll
Never Let Me Go
My Ship
Never Will I Marry
September In The Rain
Why Shouldn't I?
   (Carmen McRae in, Simmons out)
I Thought About You
   (Carmen McRae in, Simmons out)

80. With the Norman Simmons Trio. Location unknown, 1969, Hindsight.
He Loves Me
The Sound Of Silence
MacArthur Park
Stardust
Day By Day
I Got It Bad And That Ain't Good
The Right To Love

Alfie
Walking Happy

81. With Richard Tee (p), Eric Gale (g), Chuck Rainey (b), Maurice Marks (d), Warren Smith, Montego Joe (perc). New York, September 8, 1969, Atlantic.
Smilin' Faces (unissued)
The Time To Love Is Anytime

82. With Richard Tee (p), Eric Gale (g), Chuck Rainey (b), Maurice Marks (d), Warren Smith (perc). New York, Atlantic, September 15, 1969.
I Love You More Than You'll Ever Know
Just A Dream Ago

83. With The Dixie Flyers, Mike Utley (organ, elec.p), Jim Dickinson (g, keyboards), Charlie Freeman (g), Tommy McClure (b), Sammy Creason (d, perc), Joe Newman (tpt), Garnett Brown (tbn), George Dorsey (as), King Curtis (as, sop), Pepper Adams (bar), Arif Mardin (arranger and conductor), plus woodwinds, strings, and the vocal group The Sweet Inspirations. Miami, February 16, 1970, Atlantic.
Just A Little Lovin'
Breakfast In Bed
Carry That Weight
I Thought I Knew You Well
I Want You
I Love The Life I Live
What'cha Gonna Do
More Today Than Yesterday
Here, There And Everywhere
Goodbye, Joe
Where Did Our Summer Go?
Something

84. With Al Gafa (g). New York, May 18, 1970, Atlantic.
Didn't We?

85. With Arif Mardin (arranger), unknown accompaniment.
New York, *c.* 1970, Atlantic.
Silent Spring

86. With the Kenny Clarke-Francy Boland Band, Benny Bailey, Art Farmer, Dusko Gojkovic, Idrees Sulieman (tpt), Nat Peck, Ake Persson, Erik van Lier (tbn), Derek Humble, Billy Mitchell, Ronnie Scott, Tony Coe (ts), Sahib Shihab (bar), Francy Boland (p), Jimmy Woode (b), Kenny Clarke (d), Dizzy Gillespie (snare - d on 1).
London, November 3, 1970, Black Lion.
November Girl
Just Give Me Time (1)
Tis Autumn
A Handful Of Soul
Dear Death
I Don't Want Nothin' From Nobody
You're Getting To Be A Habit With Me
My Kinda World

87. With unknown accompaniment.
New York, April 19, 1971, Atlantic.
Behind The Face (unissued)

88. With Benny Carter (arranger, except for Quincy Jones on 1), Cat Anderson, Johnny Audino, Buddy Childers, Gene Coe, Harry "Sweets" Edison, Ray Triscari (tpt), George Bohanon, Nick DiMaio, Joe Howard, Glover Mitchell (tbn), Bill Hinshaw, Alan Robinson, Gale Robinson, Henry Sigismonti, Bob Watt (flghn), Buddy Collette, Bob Cooper, Bill Green, Bill Hood, Marshall Royal, Bud Shank (reeds), John Arnold, Larry Bunker, (vibes, perc), Bob Corwin, Jimmy Jones, Duke Pearson, Jimmy Rowles (p), John Collins, Barney Kessel (g), Ray Brown, Dick McQuary (b), Louie Bellson (d).
Hollywood, November 1971 to March 1972, Temponic.
I'll Never Pass This Way Again
Mr. Love

All That I Can Do Is Think Of You
All The Time
When It's Time To Tell
The Happy Ones
Bobby
Tender Loving Words
When Twilight Comes
A Tribute To Benny Carter (1)

89. With Jimmy Rowles (p) Joe Pass (g), Chuck Domanico (b), Chuck Flores (d).
Recorded live at Donte's, Los Angeles, November 6, 1971, Atlantic.
And That Reminds Me (unissued)
Body And Soul
At Long Last Love
My One And Only Love (unissued)
I'll Remember April
If The Moon Turns Green
    (Carmen in, Rowles out)
Day By Day
Satin Doll
Medley: Easy Living, The Days Of Wine and Roses and It's Impossible
Sunday
A Song For You
I Cried For You
There's No Such Thing As Love
September In The Rain (unissued)
East Of The Sun
Fools Rush In
I Get A Kick Out Of You
But Not For Me
I Only Have Eyes For You
What Are You Doing The Rest Of Your Life?
Three Little Words
They Long To Be Close To You
Behind The Face
The Ballad Of Thelonious Monk
Stardust
It's You For Me
Mr. Ugly (Carmen McRae in, Rowles out)
Reaching For A Star, It's Like Reaching For The Moon
I Thought About You

90. With Dick Shreve (p), Larry Bunker (vibes, perc), Joe Pass (g), Ray Brown (b), Frank Severino (d), plus brass and strings. Los Angeles, February and March, 1973, Groove Merchant.
Hey, John
Imagination
The Right To Love
Where Are The Words?
Inside A Silent Tear
All The Things You Are
Straighten Up And Fly Right
I Fall In Love Too Easily
Nice Work If You Can Get It
It Takes A Whole Lot Of Human Feeling

91. With Zoot Sims (ts), Tom Garvin (p), Bucky Pizzarelli (g), Paul West (b), Jimmy Madison (d) and others.
New York, March 1973, Groove Merchant.
You Are The Sunshine Of My Life
You And I
You're Mine, You
Exactly Like You
It's The Good Life
Masquerade
How Could I Settle For Less?
There Will Come A Time
Livin'

92. CARMEN MCRAE, (p as well as vcl). Recorded live in Tokyo, November 21, 1973, Victor.
As Time Goes By
I Could Have Told You So
More Than You Know
I Can't Escape From You
Try A Little Tenderness
The Last Time For Love
Suppertime
Do You Know Why?
But Not For Me
Please Be Kind

93. With Roger Kellaway (p on 1, arranger and conductor on 5), Dave Grusin (synthesizers, elec-p on 2, arranger, conductor on 6), Frank Collett (keyboards on 3) Dennis Budimir (g), John Gianelli (b), Spider Webb (d on 2), John Guerin (d on 4), Erno Neufeld, Gerri Vinci (viol), Alan Harshman (viola), Ed Lustgarten (cello), Emil Richards (perc), The Morgan Ames Singers, and Byron Olson (arranger, conductor on 7).
Los Angeles, April 1975, Blue Note.
A Letter From Anna Lee (2,3,6)
The Trouble With Hello Is Goodbye (3,4,5)
Faraway Forever (3,4,5)
I Ain't Here (1,4,5)
I Have The Feeling I've
  Been Here Before (4,5)
Who Gave You Permission? (3,4,5)
Like A Lover (2,4,5)
I Never Lied To You (3,4,5)
I Am Music (3,4,5)
You Know Who You Are (1,4,5)

94. With Tom Ranier (p), Harvey Newmark (b), Donald Bailey (d).
Recorded live in Belgrade, November 11, 1975, Jazz Door.
Time After Time
The Folks Who Live On The Hill
Star Eyes
A Song For You
Them There Eyes
The Trouble With Hello Is Goodbye
A Foggy Day
You Are The Sunshine Of My Life
Lost In A Masquerade
T'Ain't Nobody's Business If I Do
Medley: Satin Doll and Mood Indigo

95. With Snooky Young, Bobby Shew, Oscar Brashear, Blue Mitchell (tpt), George Bohanon, Maurice Spears, Grover Mitchell, Ernie Tack (tbn), Jerome Richardson (sop, as), Ernie Watts (ts), Pete Christlieb (fl, ts),

Don Menza (sop, ts), Jack Nimitz (bar),
Joe Sample (p, elec-p), Chuck Berghofer (b),
Harvey Mason (d), Larry Bunker (perc).
Los Angeles, May 3, 1976, Blue Note.
The Man I Love
Would You Believe?
A Child Is Born

96. With Wilton Felder (as and ts on 1)
Joe Sample (p, elec-p), Marshall Otwell
(elec-p), Larry Carlton, Dennis Budimir
(g), Chuck Berghofer (b), Harvey Mason
(d), Victor Feldman (perc).
Los Angeles, May 4, 1976, Blue Note.
All By Myself
Music (1)

97. With Dave Grusin (p, elec-p), Ian
Underwood (synthesizers), Dennis
Budimir, Larry Carlton (g), Chuck
Berghofer (b), Harvey Mason (d).
Los Angeles, May 10, 1976, Blue Note.
Lost Up In Loving You
Only Women Bleed

98. With Buddy Childers, Bobby Shew,
Al Aarons (tpt), Lew McCreary, George
Bohanon, Kenny Shroyer (tbn), Bill
Perkins, Lanny Morgan, Harry Klee,
Abe Most, Bill Green (reeds), Artie Kane
(p), Marshall Otwell (elec-p), Dennis
Budimir (g), Joe Mondragon (b), Harvey
Mason (d).
Los Angeles, May 12, 1976, Blue Note.
Can't Hide Love
I Wish You Well
You're Everything

99. With Dizzy Gillespie (tpt-1), Marshall
Otwell (keyboards), Ed Bennett (b, elec-b),
Joey Baron (perc).
Recorded live in San Francisco, June 15 –
17, 1976, Blue Note.
Introduction
Them There Eyes
Paint Your Pretty Picture

On Green Dolphin Street
A Song For You
On A Clear Day (1)
Miss Otis Regrets (1)
Too Close For Comfort
Old Folks
Time After Time
I'm Always Drunk In San Francisco
Don't Misunderstand (1)
A Beautiful Friendship (1)
Star Eyes
Dindi
Never Let Me Go
T'Ain't Nobody's Business If I Do
Only Women Bleed
No More Blues
The Folks Who Live On The Hill
Closing Song

100. With Marshall Otwell (p), Bernard
Barron (b), Edward Bennett (d).
Recorded live at The Roxy, Los Angeles,
June 28, 1976, Blue Note.
Music
Paint Your Pretty Picture
Them There Eyes
T'Aint Nobody's Business If I Do
You're Everything

101. With Marshall Otwell (p), John
Gianelli (b), Joey Baron (d).
Recorded live at Ronnie Scott's Club,
London, July 8 – 9, 1977, Pye.
Introduction By Ronnie Scott
If You Could See Me Now
Sometimes I'm Happy
I'm Gonna Lock My Heart and
   Throw Away The Key
Baby, Won't You Please Come Home
Poor Butterfly
Evergreen
Sunday
Weaver Of Dreams
Get Out Of Town
With One More Look At You
Miss Brown

102. With With Marshall Otwell (p), Andy
Simpkins (b), Joey Baron (d), The Los
Angeles Philharmonic Orchestra, with
arrangements by Bill Holman.
Recorded live at the Hollywood Bowl,
Hollywood, August 13, 1977, Blue Note.
Star Eyes
The Man I Love
Sunday
With One More Look At You

103. With Virgil Jones, Lew Soloff (tpt,
flghn), Freddie Hubbard (tpt and flghn on
1), Tom Malone, Janice Robinson (tbn, b-
tbn), Hubert Laws (fl and alto fl on 2),
Grover Washington, Jr. (sop on 3), Hank
Crawford (as on 4), Alex Foster (ts), Mario
E. Sprouse (elec-p), Jorge Dalto (p on 5),
Cornell Dupree (elec-g on 6), Buster
Williams (b, piccolo-b, elec b on 7), Chris
Parker (d), Erroll "Crusher" Bennett (perc),
John Blake, Valerie Collymore, Akua
Dixon Turre, Gayle Dixon, Wint Garvey,
Jenny Koo, Garfield Moore, Johnson Ning,
Nina Simon, Tom Suarez, Edith Wint,
Bernard Zeller (strings), and others.
New York, November and December 1978,
Buddah.
I'm Coming Home Again (2)
Burst In With The Dawn (1)
I Need You In My Life (4)
Come In From The Rain (6)
I Won't Last A Day Without You (5)
Won't Cha Stay With Me (2)
Mr. Magic
Everything Must Change (2,3)
Sweet Alibis (7)
The Masquerade Is Over (7)
I'd Rather Leave While I'm In Love
Mr. Magic
New York State Of Mind

104. With Norman Simmons (p), Ray
Brown (b), unidentified (d).
Recorded live at Shelly's Manne Hole,
Los Angeles, *c.* late 1970s, Night Music.

Satin Doll
(Author's Note: Lord says the above incomplete track comes from a private tape recorded by Les McCann and issued on the above named CD with other titles by keyboardist and singer McCann and saxophonists Cannonball Adderley and Stanley Turrentine and singer Roberta Flack.)

105. With Thad Jones and Claude Bolling's
Orchestra.
Recorded live at the Theatre du Casino,
Cannes, January 22, 1979, America.
Body And Soul
This Autumn
Bye Bye Blackbird
A Beautiful Friendship
    (Carmen McRae in, Bolling out)
Them There Eyes (with Joe Williams [vcl],
    Claude Bolling [p], Guy Pedersen [b], Maurice
    Bouchon [d])

106. With George Shearing (p).
New York, June 1980, Concord Jazz.
I Don't Stand A Ghost Of A Chance
You're All I Need
Gentlemen Friend
More Than You Know
Cloudy Morning
Too Late Now
If I Should Lose You
Ghost Of Yesterday
What Is There To Say?
Two For The Road (Shearing, vcl)

107. With With Marshall Otwell (p), Jim
(Jay) Anderson (b), Mark Pulice (d).
Recorded live at Bubba's, Fort Lauderdale,
January 17, 1981, Who's Who.
Black Magic
Last Winter
New York State Of Mind
Underneath The Apple Tree
Thou Swell
Send In The Clowns
I Just Can't Wait To See You

How Long Has This Been Going On?
If I Were A Bell
My Foolish Heart
Secret Love

108. With Marshall Otwell (p), John Collins (g), John Leftwich (b), Donald Bailey (d).
San Francisco, November 1983, Concord.
I'm An Errand Girl For Rhythm
Beautiful Moons Ago
The Frim Fram Sauce
Come In Out Of The Rain
How Does It Feel?
If I Had You
I Can't See For Lookin'
Sweet Lorraine
You're Lookin' At Me
Just You, Just Me
(Author's Note: This was a tribute album to Nat "King" Cole.)

109. With Marshall Otwell (p), John Leftwich (b), Donald Bailey (d), Zoot Sims (ts on 2).
Recorded live at the Blue Note, New York, December 31, 1983, RCA Novus.
Intro
Miss Brown To You
Good Morning, Heartache
I'm Gonna Lock My Heart
   And Throw Away The Key (2)
Fine And Mellow
Them There Eyes
Lover Man (2)
I Cried For You (2)
God Bless The Child (2)
I Hear Music (2)
I'm Pulling Through
   (Carmen McRae in, Otwell out)
Don't Explain
What A Little Moonlight Can Do
Intro
Laughing At Life
You Ain't Gonna Bother Me

Easy Livin'
Yesterdays
My Old Flame (2)
Nice Work If You Can Get It (2)
Billie's Blues
Travelin' Light (2)
Medley: If You Were Mine and
   It's Like Reaching For The Moon
I'm Painting The Town Red
You've Changed
Mean To Me (2)
(Author's Note: This was a two-disc tribute album to Billie Holiday.)

110. With Pat Coil (p), Bob Bowman (b), Mark Pulice (d).
Recorded live at Kan-ihoken Hall, Tokyo, April 15, 1986, Lobster.
That Old Black Magic
I Get Along Without You Very Well
Love Come On Stealthy Fingers
Gettin' Some Fun Out Of Life
Thou Swell
My Old Flame
Yesterdays
Listen Here
If I Were A Bell
But Not For Me
What A Little Moonlight Can Do
That Old Devil Called Love
As Long As I Live
No More Blues
Medley: Love Theme and A Star Is Born
Without One More Look At Me

111. With Clifford Jordan (ts), Eric Gunnison (p), John Collins (g), Scott Colley (b), Mark Pulice (d).
New York, June 23, 1986, Denon.
Tulip Or Turnip
Old Devil Moon
Have You Met Miss Jones?
Love Me Tender
I Hear Music
This Is Always

144

Body And Soul
Prelude To A Kiss
Mean To Me
Any Old Time
It Could Happen To You
I'm Glad There Is You
Billie's Blues

112. CARMEN McRAE and BETTY CARTER (vcl on 1,) Eric Gunnison (p), Jim Hughart (b), Winard Harper (d).
Recorded live at the Great American Music Hall, San Francisco, January 30, 1987, Great American Music Hall; Bet Car/Verve.
What's New (1)
I Hear Music
Stolen Moments (1)
Love Dance
That Old Feeling
But Beautiful
Am I Blue? (1)
Medley: Glad To Be Unhappy (1)
   and Where Or When (1)
Sometimes I'm Happy (1)
Isn't It Romantic? (1)
Sophisticated Lady (1)
It Don't Mean A Thing (1)

113. With Red Holloway (as, ts), Jack McDuff (organ), Philip Upchurch (g), John Clayton (b), Paul Humphrey (d).
Recorded live at Birdland West, Long Beach, December 1987, Concord.
What Can I Say After I Say I'm Sorry?
Fine And Mellow
These Foolish Things Remind Me Of You
Black And Blue (Holloway, Upchurch,
   Humphrey out)
One More Chance
Until The Real Thing Comes Along
   (Upchurch out)
My Handy Man Ain't Handy No More
   (Holloway, Upchurch out)
What Is This Thing Called Love?
   (instrumental)

114. With Charlie Rouse (ts), Larry Willis (p), George Mraz (b), Al Foster (d).
Recorded live at the Great American Music Hall, San Francisco, January 30 and February 1, 1988, RCA Novus.
Straight, No Chaser
In Walked Bud

115. With Clifford Jordan (ts, sop), Eric Gunnison (p).
Recorded live at the Great American Music Hall, San Francisco, April 1988, RCA Novus.
Ruby, My Dear
Well, You Needn't
Blue Monk
I Mean You
Pannonica
Rhythm-a-ning
Ask Me Now
Monk's Dream
Round Midnight (Jordan out)
Ugly Beauty (Jordan out)
Reflections
In Walked Bud
Straight, No Chaser
(Author's Note: This was a tribute album to Thelonious Monk. Carmen McRae contemplated this challenge for a long time, and her manager, Larry Clothier, encouraged her to go ahead.)

116. With the Shirley Horn Trio, Shirley Horn (p), Charles Ables (elec-b), Steve Williams (d).
New York, October 12 – 14, 1990, RCA Novus.
Poor Butterfly
I've Got The World On a String
Misty
Wonder Why
Send In The Clowns
Black Coffee
Tenderly
The Best Is Yet To Come
I Will Say Goodbye

The Lamp Is Low
It's Magic
Dedicated To You
I'll Be Seeing You
Sarah

(Author's Note: This was a tribute album in memory of Sarah Vaughan, Carmen's special friend since the 1940s. The final tune in this album is particularly poignant, and nobody can sing it the way Carmen did. A unique song, it makes this CD highly recommended for any collector of McRae's work.)

117. With Clifford Jordan (ts), Shirley Horn (p), Charles Ables (elec-b), Stephen E. Williams (d).
New York, October 14, 1990, Jazz Heritage.
The Christmas Song.

(Author's Note: Other albums were released, some reissues of Carmen's recordings, some tributes to Carmen by other artists, after her death.

In the 1970s, Carmen may have signed a contract with Universal. She was reported to have done so. She may also have signed with Arista. However, the official discographies do not mention any releases by Carmen on either of these labels. In the 1970s, many jazz artists were without contracts, or they did not record.)

Videography

Jazz Casuals, with Carmen McRae, Rhino label, 1999.

Jo Jo Dancer, Your Life Is Calling, Columbia Pictures, 1986, released as a video by RCA/Columbia Videos, 1987. In this movie, starring comedian Richard Pryor, Carmen McRae plays his grandmother, the madam of a house of prostitution.

Carmen participated in a seven-part series on women in jazz. Three documentaries, each 30-minutes long, were hosted by Carmen McRae, and four were hosted by pianist Marian McPartland. The names of the videos hosted by Carmen McRae are *From Bessie To Billie*, *Scatting*, and *Yesterday and Today*, with live performances of contemporary musicians and archival material. Carmen even demonstrated her ideas by singing a little bit. The videos were written, produced, and directed by Burrill Crohn at the Other End Cafe, New York City, 1981.

Hotel, Warner Brothers Pictures Inc., 1967, released as a video by Warner Home Video, 1967, starring Rod Taylor, Catherine Spaak, Karl Malden, Merle Oberon, Richard Conte, and featuring Carmen McRae as a singer and pianist in a legendary hotel during its last days.

The Square Jungle, Universal International, starring Tony Curtis, 1955, featuring Carmen as a singer.

Carmen also made other videos, including several in Japan, but they aren't commercially available.

Audiography

RADIO INTERVIEWS:
Piano Jazz, with Marian McPartland, on National Public Radio, recorded 1982, released spring, 1985.

PRIVATELY TAPED INTERVIEW:
Carmen McRae interviewed by W. Royal Stokes, at Watergate, Washington, D.C., July 18, 1979.

Other interviews taped for or during radio broadcasts exist, but they were not available for research for this book.

Bibliography

BOOKS

All Music Guide to Jazz, Second Edition (San Francisco: Miller Freeman Books, 1966).

All Music Guide to Jazz, Third Edition, ed. Michael Erlewine (Amazon.com Books, 1998).

Charters, Samuel B. and Leonard Kunstadt, *Jazz: A History of the New York Scene* (Garden City: Doubleday, 1962, reprinted New York: Da Capo Press, 1981). *Prices at Minton's cited in Chapter Two come from this book.*

Dahl, Linda, *Stormy Weather* (New York: Proscenium Publishers, Inc., 1984, first published in paperback by Limelight Editions, 1979).

Davis, Miles, with Quincy Troupe, *Miles: The Autobiography* (New York: Simon & Schuster, 1989).

Feather, Leonard, *The Passion For Jazz* (New York: Horizon Press, 1980, reprinted New York: Da Capo Press, 1980).

Friedwald, Will, "Blew Monk," *Village Voice* (June 19, 1990).

_____, *Jazz Singing* (New York: Charles Scribner's Sons, 1990).

Giddins, Gary, "Carmen McRae," *Village Voice* (May 28, 1991).

_____, *Riding on a Blue Note: Jazz and American Pop* (New York: Oxford University Press, 1981).

Gitler, Ira, *Jazz Masters of the 40s* (New York: Macmillan, 1966, reprinted New York: Da Capo Press, 1983).

Gottlieb, Robert, ed., *Reading Jazz* (New York: Pantheon Books, 1966). Excerpts about Minton's come from "Minton's," first copyrighted 1964, by Ralph Ellison, reprinted in this anthology.

Gourse, Leslie, *Louis' Children* (New York: Quill/William Morrow and Co., 1984, reprinted New York: Cooper Square Press, 2001).

Hennessey, Mike, *Klook: The Story of Kenny Clarke* (London: Quartet Books Ltd., 1990, and Pittsburgh: The University of Pittsburgh Press, 1990).

Hentoff, Nat, *Listen To The Stories* (New York: HarperCollins, 1994).

Jones, Max, *Talking Jazz* (New York: W.W. Norton & Co., 1988).

Lees, Gene, *Singers and The Song* (New York: Oxford University Press, 1987).

Placksin, Sally, *American Women in Jazz* (New York: Wideview Books, 1982).

Pleasants, Henry, *The Great American Popular Singers* (New York: Simon & Schuster, 1974).

Shapiro, Nat, and Nat Hentoff, *The Jazz Makers* (New York: Rinehart, 1957, reprinted New York: DaCapo Press, 1979).

Southern, Eileen, *The Music of Black Americans* (New York and London: W.W. Norton & Company, 1971)

Taylor, Arthur, ed., *Notes and Tones, Interviews with Musicians* (New York: Perigee Books, 1977).

PERIODICALS

"Carmen McRae: A Mystery Solved," *HIFI/Stereo Review* (December 1962).

"Carmen McRae-New Singer Challenges Ella, Sarah for Jazz Supremacy," *Ebony* (February 1956).

"Carmen McRae, 74, Legendary Jazz Singer," *Newark, New Jersey Star-Ledger* (November 12, 1994) reprinted from the *Los Angeles Times Wire Service.*

"Carmen Sings Monk," *People Magazine* (July 2, 1990).

Dawbarn, Bob, "Carmen's OK," *Melody Maker* (October 29, 1960).

_____, "Carmen McRae will extend visit," *Melody Maker* (November 29, 1960).

Duff, Morris, "Audience Spellbound When Carmen Sings," *Toronto Daily Star* (September 30, 1959).

_____, "Sex Appeal Is A Must," *Toronto Daily Star* (February 28, 1959).

Feather, Leonard, "Carmen Blanches on Hearing R&B," Blindfold Test, *Down Beat* (May 18, 1955).

_____, "Carmen McRae," Blindfold Test, *Down Beat* (January 2, 1964).

Freda, Ernest, "Carmen McRae: She's On First Name Basis With Style," *Baltimore Evening Sun* (May 23, 1980).

Gardner, Barbara, "On The Threshold," *Down Beat* (September 13, 1962).

Gleason, Ralph J., "Carmen McRae-An Ecstatic Singer," The Rhythm Section column, *New York Post* (April 17, 1966).

_____, "Carmen McRae Joins The Elite," *Journal American,* (May 13, 1961), reprinted from the *Times Mirror Syndicate.*

Gold, Don, "Carmen McRae, Audrey Morris, Mister Kelly's, Chicago," *Saturday Review* (October 31, 1956).

Goodrich, James, "On The Records," *Storyville* (1955).

Harris, Peter, "Nightclubs," *Toronto Daily Star* (May 22, 1968).

Hentoff, Nat, "On Records: McRae Sings Monk," *The Wall Street Journal* (September 26, 1990).

Holden, Stephen, "Carmen McRae is Dead at 74; Jazz Career Spanned 5 Decades," *New York Times* (November 12, 1994).

_____, "Gillespie and McRae Share Bill," *New York Times* (June 30, 1988).

_____, "Miss Carmen McRae," *New York Times* (May 4, 1990).

_____, "Pop: Carmen McRae Doubles With Stanley Turrentine," *New York Times* (July 9, 1981).

Gavin, James, "The Woman We Loved," *Village Voice* (January 3, 1995).

"Jazz Is Back!", *Newsweek* (December 24, 1973).

K.D., "Carmen McRae, Woman Talk," *Down Beat* (1965).

Korall, Burt, "McRae, Maye and Lee," *Saturday Review* (April 29, 1967).

McNamara, Helen, "Carmen McRae: Call Her Unique," *Toronto Telegram* (May 22, 1968).

_____, "Charmin' Carmen Fills The Town" *Toronto Telegram* (March 14, 1967).

"McRae Sings," photo caption in *Billboard Magazine* (July 21, 1979).

Mitchell, Samm, "Carmen McRae," *Down Beat* (December 12, 1968).

"New Cool Singer," *Hue* (January, 1955).

O'Haire, Patricia, "Carmen McRae Remembered as Top Jazz Stylist," *Daily News* (November 1, 1994).

Ruddy, Jon, "See-Hear," *The Telegram*, (Toronto, December 8, 1960).

Siders, Harvey, "Perfectionistic Carmen McRae," *Jazz* (Fall, 1977).

Tolnay, T., "Caught in the Act," *Down Beat* (May 13, 1971).

"Torchy," a review, unsigned, *Down Beat* (July 25, 1956).

Troup, Stuart, "The Casual Precision of Carmen McRae," *Newsday* (March 13, 1987).

_____, "The Invincible Carmen McRae," *Newsday* (May 4, 1990).

Tynan, John A., "Carmen McRae," *Down Beat* (September 10, 1964).

Wilson, John S., "Carmen Salutes Billie Holiday," *New York Times* (December 14, 1979).

_____, "Carmen (McRae) Sings in a Variety of Roles," *New York Times* (March 11, 1975).

_____, "Jazz: Carmen McRae," *New York Times* (September 14, 1979).

Index

Numbers in italics refer to the photographic inserts; the first number is that of the text page preceding the insert, the second that of the page in the insert.